THE UNIVERSAL SELF

THE
UNIVERSAL
SELF

A Study
of Paul Valéry

by

AGNES ETHEL MACKAY

Routledge and Kegan Paul
LONDON

*First published 1961
by Routledge & Kegan Paul Limited
Broadway House, 68–74 Carter Lane
London, E.C.4*

*Printed in Great Britain
by Richard Clay & Company Ltd
Bungay, Suffolk*

© *Agnes Ethel Mackay 1961*

To
my cousin
Marion Melville

Contents

CONTENTS

Preface

NO MODERN POET offers a finer subject for critical research than Paul
Valéry, and no country presents a more favourable background to the
life of intellectual imagination than France. Twenty years spent here,
in war and peace, have shown me that there still exists an unfettered
spiritual life: France recognises that the independent thinker, who dares
to go alone to the furthest limits of his intellectual consciousness, is the
most valuable and rarest possession of any country. Such a thinker was
Valéry, who, while imposing nothing on others, created for himself a
new poetic universe.

In the following study I have attempted to show, through an analysis
of Valéry's thought, that he turned a page in the history of poetic composition. He did this by creating an intellectual Self through a process
of transformations, and he constructed a scale and a system of abstractions of which thought in general was the material and the music. He
wrote poetry, different in kind from anything hitherto produced, which
demonstrates a fresh principle in poetic method.

In an age in which poetry was essentially drawing closer to spontaneous and sometimes formless expression, Valéry turned his mind to
the more difficult problem of obtaining a complete unity between his
intellectual Self and its language, so as to express the life of the mind
through symbolic images in a language as perfectly composed as he
could make it, and thus reinstate poetry as a 'formal art' and at the same
time enlarge the scope of personal experience through a psychological
relationship with all that appears universal. This conception deserves to
be acknowledged as a definite progression in the art of poetry.

Along with his poetics Valéry proposed and developed for his own use a psychology for poets that defines phases or states of intellectual consciousness through which all artists who advance to a certain mental level must inevitably pass; the realisation of such states of consciousness serves to guide the progression of thought towards its own expression and final abstraction.

My aim throughout this study has been to present a general view of Valéry's intellectual attitude, by examining the principles on which he founded the structure of his thought, and to give some idea of his mental life, through research into the methods applied in his *œuvre*. Instead of judging his poems by accepted literary or objective standards, it seems to me to be worth while to examine them as far as possible from the poet's own point of view: from his thought and theories, his sources and his sensibility, his conception of poetry and his conclusions. This reveals the poet's creation of a constructive system which became a habit of mind and the basis of his thought and his art. I have applied to Valéry something of his own method in considering the point of view from which he approached his interior drama—that Intellectual Comedy whose actors are mental images.

I have not followed him closely in the world of men and events, but have been content to give the circumstances of his childhood, his early impressions and enthusiasms, his friendship with certain poets and the significant changes in the environment of his life. He himself always insisted that the events and circumstances which surround a work of art are of secondary interest and are not essential to a critical examination. He even suggested that the history of literature should be less a history of its authors and more a history of the mind in so far as it produces works.

The riches of Valéry's mind provide a thoughtful reader with a universe formed from the dream and act of the metaphysics of poetry: he shows us how language, each time it exerts a certain independence, may enrich our vision with new vistas and horizons. He invites us to consider a science of ideas—and an art of treating them. To the research of greater consciousness he brings the art of mathematical principles and the science of classical prosody or poetics; and in doing this he bridges the supposed gulf between poetry and science.

His 'pure poetry,' he tells us, is the outcome of the effort of an isolated being to create an ideal. The touchstone of its reality is the poet's sensibility. It is better described as an 'absolute' poetry, in the sense of being an exploration into the possibilities of creating an intellectual harmony.

To future poets Valéry proposes a return to classical rules, as a reaction from the wild romanticism of free prose rhythms. But such a return must also effect a progress by creating a synthesis through an intellectual and psychological approach. This approach constitutes a fresh point of view and proposes a vital theme in the abstraction of the Self, of an absolute of consciousness composed with an absolute of language, and this act of composition consists in the simultaneous direction of syntax, harmony and ideas.

All authentic poets look for expressive rhythms, and Valéry went to the source of this research; no poet has more completely explained his own acts and aims, and I have followed him as closely as possible so as to construct, as nearly as I can, a sort of biography of his ideas.

Valéry's renown has fluctuated since his death in 1945. During the last few years, after a period of comparative neglect, there has been a general renewal of interest in his writings and several important publications have appeared. First among these and of chief interest are the twenty-three volumes of Valéry's *Cahiers* (1894—) in facsimile, with a Preface by Louis de Broglie (Paris: Centre National de la Recherche scientifique, 1956–1960). In 1956 the first volume of the collected works, with an Introduction by Jean Hytier and an introductory 'Note chronologique' by the poet's daughter Agathe Rouart-Valéry ('Bibliothèque de la Pléiade,' Paris: Gallimard), made a valuable contribution to existing editions. Another significant recent publication is the *Correspondance Paul Valéry—Gustave Fourment, 1887–1933* with introduction, notes and documents by Professor Octave Nadal (Paris: Gallimard, 1957).

A circumstance which has helped to bring Valéry before the public is the official recognition of his work as object of study by the Sorbonne, where even during his lifetime he was a welcome guest. One result of this is that the drafts of his poems have been given a new importance. Note-books and loose leaves on which lists of words and half-finished lines and phrases are noted have been reproduced in facsimile as material for scholars to work on. The least scrap of writing is sacrosanct. Many of these fragments have been edited in an admirably presented study by Professor Nadal in *La Jeune Parque: États successifs et brouillons inédits* with the 'Manuscrit autographe de 1942' reproduced in facsimile (Paris: Club du Meilleur Livre, 1957). Another work on the same lines is L. J. Austin's examination of drafts and 'brouillons' of 'Le Cimetière marin' which appeared in the *Mercure de France* as early as 1953 (see Bibliography, p. 252).

In the face of such enthusiastic academic pursuit of detail, and of possible and impossible alternative readings, one hopes that the larger issues will not be forgotten. The final judgement on the poems must inevitably be based on the finished work. But to return to the poet, we may truly say of Valéry what he said of Stendhal: 'On n'en finirait plus avec lui. Je ne vois pas de plus grande louange.'

I should add that I have generally made direct translations, but sometimes versions, when quoting what he himself so well expressed; and I have given the general sources of such passages in my notes. In all cases I have used my own translations.

A. E. M.

Paris, 1960

Acknowledgements

MY GRATEFUL THANKS and acknowledgements are due to Professor Henri Mondor for his generous aid in lending me documents and letters when I began this work; and also for his permission to quote from his books: *Les Premiers Temps d'une amitié: André Gide et Paul Valéry* (Monaco: Editions du Rocher, 1947), and *L'Heureuse Rencontre de Valéry et Mallarmé* (Paris and Lausanne: Editions de Clairefontaine, 1947). Indeed any study of Valéry's early life would be difficult without reference to Professor Mondor's works, which include his admirable *Vie de Mallarmé* (Paris: Gallimard, 1941).

My acknowledgements and thanks are due also to the Librairie Gallimard, Paris, for permission to quote passages from the works of Paul Valéry, and in particular for their authorisation to use passages from the *André Gide—Paul Valéry Correspondance, 1890–1942*. This important publication, edited by M. Robert Mallet, contains all the Valéry–Gide letters. I am much indebted to M. Jean Ballard for permission to quote passages from *Paul Valéry vivant* (Paris: Cahiers du Sud, 1946).

I also wish to thank the Duchesse de La Rochefoucauld for a vivid impression of Valéry in a setting which he knew well, and for showing me a facsimile of one of his note-books and also water-colours and drawings which revealed Valéry as a draughtsman. I am very much indebted to Mme. Julien-Cain for the evidence of a perfect witness of the thought and friendship of Valéry. I also wish to thank Mme. Paul Valéry for kindly confirming certain dates, and M. J. P. Monod for the date of *L'Ange*. My warmest thanks are due to Miss Marion Melville for reading my typescript and for her scholarly advice. Among the friends to whom

xiii

ACKNOWLEDGEMENTS

I am indebted I should like to mention M. André Dunoyer de Segonzac whose kind intervention helped me to overcome many difficulties concerned with my work. Finally I should like to acknowledge gratefully the financial assistance of the Trustees of the Bollingen Foundation towards publication.

A. E. M.

I

First Poetic Period

I. CHILDHOOD AT SÈTE

Le port, les navires, les poissons et les parfums,
la nage, ce n'était qu'une manière de prélude.

(P. V.)

'I WAS BORN,' said Paul Valéry, 'in one of the places where I should like to have been born, where my first impressions came from the sea and the activities of a seaport.' This was the port of Sète, built at the foot of a rocky hill barely attached to the mainland by two banks of sand; on one side is the sea, on the other a salt lake. From this pool a number of docks and canals lead to the harbour, and the houses and warehouses stand in modest rows along the quays. The general impression is that of a painting by Canaletto, at once precise and poetic, without the mysterious grandeur of a Claude Lorrain.

Neither of Paul's parents was of strictly French origin, though both were of Mediterranean and Latin race. His father, Barthélémy Valéry, was a Corsican and held an administrative post in the customs-house of Sète. The family were originally the Valérj, and owned a line of trading vessels which later became La Compagnie Fraissinet. In 1861 Barthélémy Valéry married Fanny, the youngest daughter of Giulio de Grassi, who came of an old Genoese family and had started his career in the Austrian Lloyd at Trieste; political misfortunes had brought him to Sète, where he was for a time Italian Consul. Barthélémy and Fanny Valéry had two children: Jules, born in 1863; and Paul, whose full name was Ambroise-Paul Toussaint Jules, born eight

I

years later on October 30, 1871, in a house on the quay facing the wide harbour.[1]

Here Paul spent the first thirteen years of his life. His nursery on the third floor faced the quay, which was narrower then than it is now, so that the masts of the great sailing ships from the New World were quite near the window. His early childhood passed happily in this world of busy life and sunshine. There was always something to watch from the southern windows looking on to the port, and at an early age he began to draw the ships and rigging, intrigued by the decorative ballet of constantly moving masts. This activity perhaps awakened that desire for accuracy and precision in intricate patterns which he kept all his life.

It is always from our early surroundings that we receive those first impressions which form the background of our future thought. A child sees without seeing what he is looking at, and the decisive hour when thought is formed has its origin in spontaneous and primitive impressions whose strength and sweetness are incalculable. The all-powerful sun, the ever changing sea, the port with its Phoenician-prowed tartanes, and its smells of coal, tar, wine and fish soup, formed the background and the prelude to Paul Valéry's intellectual life. During his first years the small fair child, whose eyes held such wonder, gazed and dreamed, unconsciously forming that intimate relationship with the world around him which is the poet's birthright.

Paul was seven years old when for the first time he climbed the steep road leading to school, holding his father's hand. He felt anxious but also curious as to the consequences of this great adventure, 'ready to laugh and not far from tears.' 'I can still remember the first impressions of my school life,' he said fifty years later, 'the particular smell of new exercise books and the polished American cloth of the school satchels, the mystery of the books all new, stiff and almost impenetrable at first in their armour of cardboard and glue; but which were soon to become the albums in which life is recorded in the form of stains, strange figures, notes, marks of reference and sometimes imprecations.'[2] Together with organised lessons, the incidents of class and playground became all important in this school world with its own laws in which there was 'a curious diversity of hierarchies, each

[1] A.R.V. [Agathe Rouart-Valéry], 'Vie de Paul Valéry,' *Paul Valéry vivant* (Paris: *Cahiers du Sud*, 1946), 11–20.

[2] Paul Valéry, 'Discours . . . [au] Collège de Sète' (July 13, 1935), *Variété*, IV (Paris, 1936), 193. By permission of Librairie Gallimard, Paris.

with its own set of values judged by the masters or by the pupils.' And he remembered vividly his tentative sympathies and antipathies in the midst of so many new faces.

Sensitive and intelligent, Valéry was all the more vulnerable to the rough and ready school life. Later he recalled his anxiety about mistakes, the excitement of competition, the perplexity of the unintelligible problem and impenetrable text, and 'all the agitations of sensibility in circumstances of which the childishness did not in the least diminish the force.' But there were other aspects of his character which must have saved him from being unhappy at school: his quick wit, his acute sense of humour, his ready laughter and that lovable quality so well described by the French word *gentillesse*. Though reserved he was friendly, and evidently was liked by his schoolfellows.

Even the penalities of school life played their part in the development of this thoughtful child, as he noted many years later in his account of remembered emotions. To be put in the corner while the other boys were playing gave him 'an immediate notion of duration,'[1] while the enforced contemplation of the irregularities in the white-washed wall offered opportunities for dreaming. The recollection of such moments may well have been the origin of Monsieur Teste's dying word: 'I have not turned towards the world. I have turned my face to the wall. There is not the least thing on the surface of the wall that I do not know.'

Yet in spite of such disciplinary measures, probably inflicted on account of absent-minded reveries, Paul-Ambroise, as he liked to call himself, seems only to have been thoroughly bored when taken for school walks, parading on the hill 'from cemetery to cemetery.'[2] 'I learnt *rosa* the rose without too much boredom,' he said, 'and I left with regret at the end of my fourth year.'

As there were only four pupils in his class it is difficult to judge his capacities at this early age. He seems to have shared the honour of being first fairly equally with the other boys, that is to say about once in four times; but he confessed that he could never learn a lesson by heart, and found it difficult to concentrate on things which did not rouse his interest. Throughout his life his memory remained selective: he readily forgot events and scenes in general. Yet few writers have so

---

[1] Paul Valéry, 'Discours . . . [au] Collège de Sète' (July 13, 1935), *Variété*, IV (Paris, 1936), 195.
[2] Letter from Paul Valéry, in the Sète Museum.

thoroughly recorded the origins of their art and their intellectual problems.

The life of the port was a continual interest. From the playground the boys could watch the arrivals and departures of French warships, and naturally enough the career of a naval officer seemed to hold immense promise. Alas, such a future required an early proficiency in mathematics, in which at this time Paul was backward.

The truth is that he preferred to dream on the quays, watching the fleet of fishing boats unloading their catch of tunny fish, a picture of epic grandeur, in the strange evening light: 'the sea already very sombre with broken water and splashes of extreme whiteness; and towards the east, a little above the horizon a mirage of towers which were the phantom of Aiguesmortes.'[1]

Thus the truant hours, 'dérobées à l'étude,' dedicated to 'those incontestable deities the sea the sky and the sun,' were of greater importance than the hours spent in school. 'I don't know,' Valéry wrote, 'what book or what author could induce in us those states of fruitful idleness, of contemplation and of communion which I experienced in my first years. Better than the poets, better than the philosophers, certain ways of looking at things, without definite or definable thought, certain states of dwelling on the pure elements of daylight, the vast and simple things, sun, sky and sea, give us the habit of measuring every event, every being and all expression against the greatest visible and most stable things.'[2]

So at an early age certain states of mind and certain habits of contemplation had already laid sure foundations for the symbolic figures of the poet's future thought. When later he was to ask himself how a philosophical thought was born, his imagination at once carried him to the edge of some 'marvellously clear sea' where he found 'all the elements of the most searching questions united in light and space, leisure and rhythm, transparence and depth.'

Although all this happened almost unconsciously, as part of the poet's growth, he had also a conscious love for sunlight and sea. Swimming was his greatest delight and recreation. Always lyrical when speaking of this sport, he cried: 'Mon jeu, mon seul jeu, était le jeu le plus pur: la nage.'[3] From his earliest childhood the sea represented a real and unlimited presence, capable of stirring 'a desire too

---

[1] Paul Valéry, 'Inspirations méditerranéennes' (speech given Nov. 24, 1933) *Variété*, III (Paris: Gallimard, 1936), 251.

[2] *Ibid.*, 256.　　　　　　　　　　　[3] *Ibid.*, 254.

great to be satisfied by anything obtainable,' the longing for an absolute participation in this universal clarity and depth, vastness and measure. This first source of the poet's questioning remained the symbol of life and the background of his thought.

2. MONTPELLIER

Je me trouvais embarrassé de tant de doutes et d'erreurs qu'il me semblait n'avoir fait aucun profit.   (DESCARTES)

The country between Montpellier and Sète is bordered on the north by a range of low rocky hills. The vines which grow in this flat region are mostly muscat, and the vineyards are often enclosed by low stone walls, for stone is plentiful in this wind-swept landscape of Languedoc, across which the *garrigue* endlessly stretches. On this side of the Rhône there are none of the rich variations found in Provence, but the country has a maritime charm of its own. From the marshes where the rose flamingo nests, to the coast with its lost ports, its mirages and sea-reflected light, the effect is a seascape, rather than a landscape; one turns instinctively to the sea, whose murmur can be heard miles inland on those calm days after a storm when the wind dies in an exhausted sigh. This essentially marine atmosphere explains why Valéry found nothing to interest him in the Georgics,[1] for harvest and *vendange* played little part in the scenes of his youth.

The history of Montpellier, ancient capital of the Bas-Languedoc, goes back to the tenth century. Rich in historic associations and essentially aristocratic, the town had been the most frequent meeting place of the États de Provence from 1736 to 1789. The dwelling houses dating from that time are built in a pure French style with majestic stairways, delicate iron work and richly decorated interiors set round wide courts. The outer façades lining the narrow winding streets are severe and even forbidding. The schools of law and medicine still give a studious climate to this now retired town.

In the year 1884 the Valérys moved to Montpellier, which is about forty kilometres from Sète. They lived first in Rue de l'École de Droit

[1] Paul Valéry, 'Inspirations méditerranéennes', *Variété*, III, 254: 'Rien pour moi dans les Géorgiques.'

and later in the narrow winding Rue Urbain V. Here they occupied
the ground floor of an old house with a fine carved door. This old
residential quarter has a peaceful aspect, detached from the life of the
noisy nineteenth-century streets of the lower town.

Coming from the open-air stir and movement of the port of Sète,
the child who loved the sea must at first have found the withdrawn
and shadowed streets of Montpellier strange and rather awe-inspiring,
but not altogether unsympathetic. A new phase of his development
was beginning. Instinctive and open-air impressions were now to be
largely replaced by intellectual and literary interests.

Paul attended the *lycée* at Montpellier. Here he appeared as a pupil
neither good nor bad, but singularly absent-minded; his masters were
surprised when this apparently negligible candidate passed his *bac-
calauréat*. The truth is that he had already begun to be more curious
about his own thoughts than about the subjects taught in class; and
very soon he grew to despise the teaching dealt out to him at school.
'I had masters,' he said later, 'who reigned by terror. They had a
corporal's conception of learning. Stupidity and insensibility seemed to
me to be inscribed in the time-tables. . . . I saw only mediocrity of intelligence and a total absence of imagination even in the best of the
class. I found there the conditions of scholastic success from which a
disastrous state of mind arose: opposition and a systematic antagonism
to the teaching.'[1] We may join to this opinion André Gide's account
of the brutal treatment inflicted on him by the other pupils at the
same school some years earlier, when he stayed with his uncle at
Montpellier.[2]

Since schools were first started there has always been a certain
number of intelligent pupils, not to be confused with the merely
incapable, who resolutely refuse to fit into the conventional scholastic
moulds, whether through an instinctive need to protect themselves
from a meaningless accumulation of facts, or because of their teachers'
inability to interest them in their lessons. But such self-assurance and
such disdain as Paul Valéry possessed at an early age are rare, and in
his case were partly due to the reading of works which deeply interested him quite outside the school curriculum. Perhaps the example
and affection of a much older brother may also have given him a
certain self-confidence.

[1] Cited by A. Berne-Joffroy, 'Valéry Présent,' *Présence de Valéry* (Paris:
Plon, 1944), 67.

[2] André Gide, *Si le grain ne meurt* (Paris: Gallimard, 1924).

I used to think when I was about fifteen, if any one scolded me, 'this is nothing but the association of ideas,' and I exulted in this childish knowledge of the mechanism of my adversary whose authority I scorned—giving myself the agreeable sensation of knowing how to look at him as if I were observing the automatic life of an animal; and who, because encompassed by my observation, was therefore less than myself. Thus I changed him into an accepted phenomenon.[1]

This amusing confession, with its reference to Cartesian automatism, is valuable as showing early signs of the analytical faculty which was to become a controlling characteristic of Valéry's attitude towards life and literature, and which led him to look objectively, not only at the actions of others but also at his own reactions. It also reveals the pride, allied to his intellectual force, which was later expressed in *Monsieur Teste*.

A further confidence confirms this point of view:

When I brooded with a sense of injurious injustice [English in text] over some annoyance, or some disappointment, I used to look fixedly at a point, and an imaginary voice within me said: '*tableau de genre*, a man with a grievance,' and I saw myself consuming myself like some one offended and upset by some other person or by myself.[2]

It is rare to find a young author dramatising himself to such disciplinary ends. Here Valéry tells us of the beginnings of that self-discipline which was a necessary exercise for one whose nature it was to think and speak quickly and then to meditate at length on what he had thought and said, who even as a child combined pride and delicacy of sentiment with a reserve and an almost fierce disdain characteristic of the Corsican race.

But if school was uncongenial, the long summer holidays were altogether delightful; Valéry generally spent them with his mother's family at Genoa, a town which all his life he preferred to any other. He never forgot the long summer days there, when he went bathing with his cousins at Nervi. For hours they would dive and swim in the deep water between the rocks, bask half-naked in the hot sunshine, consumed by the sun and the sea. It was time 'ardently wasted which remained a mental resource and ideal.'[3] At other times he was taken to

---

[1] Paul Valéry, 'Propos me concernant', *Présence de Valéry*, 33.
[2] *Ibid.*, 16: 'Homme songeant avec rancœur'.
[3] Paul Valéry, letter to Valery Larbaud (1928), *Lettres à quelques-uns* (Paris: Gallimard, 1952), 174.

Paris or to London.[1] On his first visit to England at an early age he was terrified by the horrors of Madame Tussaud's. These journeys compensated for the restricted life of a provincial town and stimulated his curiosity as to things in general.

About the time of the move to Montpellier, Valéry began to be interested in architecture and poetry. At the age of twelve he read Victor Hugo's *Orientales*, and two years later *Notre-Dame de Paris* plunged him into a Gothic ecstasy, after which Viollet-le-Duc's *Architecture* became his favourite book. He pored over it for hours 'studying the rules of line and colour' and made drawings which often had architectural motifs; architecture became his favourite art and he began to fill exercise books with his own notes and even his own theories.

In 1887 Barthélémy Valéry died, and Jules Valéry became head of the family. He was Paul's senior by eight years and had started on what was to be a distinguished legal career. For centuries the lawyers of Montpellier had been famous for their subtle arguments, and they held an honoured position in the social life of the town.

On leaving school Paul rather reluctantly decided to follow in his brother's footsteps, but law held no interest for him. His real passion was for poetry and the questioning of his own thoughts. As early as 1887 he was reading and writing poems. After his first enthusiasm for Hugo, Théophile Gautier the Parnassians and Baudelaire were in turn admired. In a confident autobiography, made at the request of Pierre Louÿs in 1890, entitled briefly 'MOI,' he states that he had discovered Mallarmé for himself without the help of any guide and that, 'provincial among provincials,' he 'discovered and cherished some of the secret poems on which Mallarmé's solitary glory rests.' These were evidently the poems which appeared in *Parnasse contemporain* and included: 'Les Fenêtres,' 'Le Sonneur,' 'A Celle qui est tranquille,' 'Vere novo,' 'L'Azur,' 'Les Fleurs,' 'Soupir,' 'Brise marine,' 'A un pauvre,' 'Epilogue,' and 'Tristesse d'été.'[2]

Valéry also seems to have been familiar with the *Album de vers et de prose*, a little book of sixteen pages which was published simultaneously in Brussels and in Paris in 1887. This contained the 'Poèmes en prose,' and the poem 'Sainte' with four sonnets: 'Le Vierge, le vivace . . .,' 'Victorieusement fui . . .,' 'Mes Bouquins refermés . . .'

---

[1] During holiday visits to London, Paul Valéry stayed with his maternal aunt, Jeanne, who married, at Trieste, Angelo de Rhin. They lived in London.

[2] For further details consult Henri Mondor, *L'Heureuse Rencontre de Valéry et Mallarmé* (Paris–Lausanne: Clairefontaine, 1947).

and 'Quand l'ombre menace. . . .' If we add to these the splendid 'Toast funèbre' to which Valéry referred in 1890, we realise that his early enthusiasm for Mallarmé was founded on a thorough knowledge of his lyrical works, and that while still very young Valéry had known the joy of discovering for himself a master mind who seemed to speak for him alone.

It was in July 1889, some months before he had begun his military service, and therefore prior to his first meeting with Pierre Louÿs (spelt at that time Louis), that Paul first read Edgar Allan Poe, as translated and commented on by Baudelaire.

In the Preface to this translation of Poe's *Nouvelles Histoires extra-ordinaires*[1] the idea of 'pure poetry' is given a special significance for the first time. Here Valéry discovered this doctrine which he was later to adapt to his own theories. Even at this early stage in his development, in a growing desire for order and method, he found in Poe's idea of a poetic system the response to the ideal abstractions already suggested to him by Mallarmé's works. Throughout this Preface, Poe's ideas of method and analysis are insisted on, doctrines which were to play a vital part in Valéry's Intellectual Comedy. These ideas had also been the source from which Mallarmé had nourished his genius; they were to inspire Valéry with a fresh conception of Formal Art.

At certain times of transition, some phrases, or even single words, appear to express new values so well that they change the whole conception of the art with which they are concerned. Such was the term 'return to nature' in the Romantic period.[2] Similarly the formula 'pure poetry' flashed as a meteor through the sky of poetic conceptions leaving a trail of glory. In the general movement of the time it acted as a liberating force suggesting a new freedom from cramping conventions. It passed through intermittent, and often contradictory, phases, such as the *volonté de perfection* found in the strict definitions of the Parnassians, and the freedom of *vers libre*, which in turn prepared the way for the *surréalisme* in the work of Paul Éluard and André Breton, where nothing is allowed to intrude between the poet and his dreams.

[1] See Charles Baudelaire, *Œuvres complètes* (7 vols.; Paris, 1868–70), VI.

[2] In painting we find parallel developments. After the analysis of light by the Impressionists, the Cubists, inspired in their researches by the dictum of Cézanne 'Tout est dans le cube,' analysed and regrouped forms and volumes, overthrowing the conventional aspect of things to express new conceptions leading to the abstract.

From the first it was Poe's idea of method that Valéry particularly admired. As for poetry, he placed Mallarmé above all other poets. He seems to have had certain reservations in his early appreciation of Baudelaire, for in speaking of the time when he first read those poets he said of himself:

> We must imagine a young man considerably interested in poetry and especially sensitive to inventions of form and to the diversity of possible solutions in a single line of verse, and having in consequence little opinion of Lamartine and Musset; having also read fairly thoroughly some of the Parnassians, and finding in Baudelaire the rather disconcerting mixture of extraordinary magic beyond all analysis, with some detestable parts, vulgar expressions and bad lines. I insist on this imperfection that I found in Baudelaire, mingled with great harmonic powers, for this impression seemed as if expressly made to create in me the need, or rather the necessity, of Mallarmé.[1]

From an article sent to Karl Boès, editor of the *Courrier libre*, in July 1889, some months before Valéry began his military service, we know that he had also read Huysmans' *A Rebours*. This article, which was not published, was called 'Quelques Notes sur la technique littéraire.' In a brief declaration of his preferences, he places Mallarmé, Verlaine, Huysmans and Poe above all other writers, admiring Poe as 'a mathematician . . . who showed clearly the mechanism of poetic creation. . . .' This precocious essay opens with the statement 'Literature is the art of playing with the souls of others,' an amusing indication of Valéry's already apparent mistrust of literature. It is also of value as a contemporary record of his state of mind at the age of eighteen, showing how definitely his own point of view and his literary tastes were established before he knew Louÿs or Gide.

As far as we know, his first poem to be published was 'Élévation de la lune,' which was signed and dated '23 juillet '89,' and appeared on the first of October in the *Courrier libre*. In a covering letter to the editor, the youthful poet again expressed his admiration for Poe's theories, and his preference for Mallarmé above all others, and ended by stating that he liked a short and concentrated poem—'a brief evocation closed by a sonorous and full line.' The sonnet has something of the tenderness and subdued melancholy of Mallarmé's early poems, and complies with its author's conception as to its ending. Valéry did not reprint it when he published his early poems as *Vers anciens*, dismissing it as a mere childish exercise.

[1] Valéry, 'Propos me concernant,' *Présence de Valéry*, 33.

ÉLÉVATION DE LA LUNE

L'ombre venait, les fleurs s'ouvraient, rêvait mon âme
Et le vent endormi taisait son hurlement
La nuit tombait, la nuit douce comme une femme
Subtile et violette épiscopalement.

Les étoiles semblaient des cierges funéraires
Comme dans une église allumés dans les soirs
Et semant des parfums, les lys thuriféraires
Balançaient doucement leurs frêles encensoirs.

Une prière en moi montait, ainsi qu'une onde
Et dans l'immensité bleuissante et profonde
Les astres recueillis baissaient leurs chastes yeux;

Alors, Elle apparut! Hostie immense et blonde
Puis elle étincela, se détachant du monde
Car d'invisibles doigts l'élevaient vers les cieux!

On November 15, 1889, six weeks after the publication of this sonnet, Valéry began his military service with the 122nd Régiment d'Infanterie garrisoned at Montpellier. Eager, patriotic and filled with the spirit of sacrifice, but used to following his own line of thought, he must have found the gray monotonous months of military discipline and life in barracks a severe trial. He was however allowed to spend his Sundays at home, and so continued to write poetry. His military service lasted for one year.

3. FRIENDSHIP WITH PIERRE LOUŸS

*"Cette rencontre a eu la plus grande influence sur
ma vie littéraire."*   (P. V.)

May 1890 was a significant date in Valéry's intellectual life, for it marked his first meeting with Pierre Louÿs, to which they both attached immense importance. It took place at the festival of the sixth centenary of the University of Montpellier, in which the students who were doing their military service were allowed to take part. 'The town,' said Valéry, 'was nothing but flags, and the strangest "gowns" circulated freely. Never were so many doctors of all sorts so joyously intermingled. One would have said it was a carnival of human attainments: the ignorant looked on.'

The rejoicings ended with a banquet at Palavas-les-Flots. While fraternising before dinner with a group of blond Swiss students, Valéry found himself beside a young man 'who was neither blond nor Swiss.' Destiny had taken the features of this sympathetic neighbour. A few words were exchanged. The stranger Pierre Louÿs was a student delegate from Paris. An illustrated book which Valéry carried led them to speak about art, and they were soon enjoying an animated conversation in which the 'sacred names' of their favourite poets were exchanged. They became friends immediately, comparing their gods and heroes, in an all too short conversation. Called by their Swiss companions they soon lost each other in the twelve hundred guests who attended the banquet. Valéry returned at dawn to Montpellier to dress himself in the yellow-collared tunic of every day. In turning out his pockets before folding his 'full dress' he found a visiting card on which was written 'Pierre Louis.'

Some days later Valéry received an important-looking letter of some twenty pages which contained 'the whole gospel of a young intellectual of 1890.'[1] To this he immediately replied, and a correspondence started in which the two young men exchanged poems and opinions. Their first letters explained their intellectual preoccupations, their conceptions of poetry and their literary ideals. Louÿs spoke of Verlaine, Vigny, Sully-Prudhomme; to which Valéry replied with Poe, Huysmans and 'that impeccable and secret artist' Mallarmé. This correspondence with Pierre Louÿs was a definite factor in Valéry's development and helped him to establish even more surely his own point of view.

The same enthusiasm was shown for each other's poems, Valéry finding 'a strange and magic charm' in his friend's verses. 'Vous êtes un fier décadent,' he declared, explaining that by 'decadent' he meant 'an ultra-sensitive artist protected by a learned language from the insults of the vulgar . . . above all living for beauty and attentive to all its manifestations, always associated with some original and vibrating side of life.'[2] The slightly artificial style of Valéry's early letters alone betrays his provincialism. Louÿs replied in a more natural manner: 'You are I think nearer to Flaubert and Poe than to Ghil and Mallarmé.'

In his letters Louÿs spoke of his visits to Mallarmé at the Rue de

[1] Cited by Berne-Joffroy, *Présence de Valéry*, 72.
[2] Paul Valéry, letter to P. Louÿs (22 juin 1890), *Lettres à quelques-uns*, 12.

Rome, and carefully reported all the master's words of encouragement; he also told of the other guests he met there. Valéry read this
news with eager curiosity longing to meet and converse with these
poets whose work he already knew. 'Tell me about Paris,' he begged.
'How lucky you are to know Mallarmé, Verlaine and that curious
Merrill. It is a pity that you don't like Barrès. Though decadent he is
really one of the most symptomatic of this age and one of the most
subtle.' Louÿs replied that he did not run after those rather over-
whelming relationships, and confessed that he preferred to pass whole
days copying Mallarmé's published but rare works at the Bibliothèque
Nationale. Of this Valéry thoroughly approved and lamented that he
himself had spent two years looking in vain for *Hérodiade* and quite
despaired of ever reading it—'Quel ennui la province!'

Louÿs' response was immediate. On the first two pages of a long
letter he recopied thirty lines of *Hérodiade* beginning 'Oui c'est pour
moi, pour moi que je fleuris déserte,' and ending on the line 'Hérodiade
au clair regard de diamant.'[1] These were the first pages of the copies of
Hérodiade which Louÿs, and later André Gide, sent to Valéry as they
were published and which he received with joy:

> I set off towards the sea a certain distance away, clasping the precious
> copies which I had just received, and neither the sun in all its force, the
> shining road, nor the azure sky, nor the incense of the burning plants was
> anything to me, so deeply was my whole being possessed by those mar-
> vellous verses.[2]

But such moments were too often followed by anxious self-questioning, doubts as to his own merit as a poet and even of his own faith in
poetry. Beneath the enthusiasm of Valéry's letters to Louÿs during
1890, there is a gradual divergence between his love of poetry and his
growing contempt for the effusive outpourings which too often posed,
and passed, as poetry. A critical faculty, which tended towards
scepticism, was gradually bringing him to dismiss scornfully as
'literature' the greater part of contemporary writing.

Thus in August of 1890 he wrote to Louÿs: 'Literature begins to
bore me. I mean by literature the concoctions of the rhymesters
(*quorum pars parva sum*), and all those who babble incoherently about
style, rhythm, art, etc., etc.' And again a few months later at the end of
his military service (November 1890) he spoke despondently about the

---

[1] Mondor, *L'Heureuse Rencontre*, 39.
[2] Letter to Louÿs cited by Mondor in *ibid.*, 58.

choice between a dull safe career, on the one hand, and on the other, the fate of being condemned to spend his time writing mediocre verses.

Such moments of growth are generally filled with hesitations and enthusiasms, and for Valéry there was no exception to this rule. He felt deeply the need for order in the chaos of hopes and refusals which beset his mind. A desire to reduce theory to clear schemes of intellectual activity had begun to rival the joys of writing poetry. At this time, when the choice of a career had to be made, it became imperative for him to examine his whole conception of the art of poetic expression. He already considered that so-called 'inspiration' and 'poetic finds' were not enough to satisfy either his idea of poetry, or his desire for some 'super-effort' which could be the fruit only of training and self-examination.

Nor could the career of law fulfil this need. He wanted to create his own mental laws, not to study established legal procedure. His whole mind must be brought into action, must be made worthy of, and one with, all that might be expressed, and to achieve this, false classifications, and barriers which were limitations, must be swept away: a clearer outlook was necessary. His need for mental effort was such that if poetry was to satisfy him it must do something different, and go further, than any poetry hitherto produced. His love of architecture awoke his desire for purity of form, and now a new interest in mathematics was to lead him to the idea of method which had been suggested by reading Edgar Poe. 'The truth is I believe I am *several* people,' he wrote to Louÿs, feeling that sensibility was too often opposed to the dictates of intellect and reason.

During this time the encouragement Valéry received from his new friend and correspondent was of infinite value. Pierre Louÿs, a poet with high ideals as to the artist's vocation, combined taste and learning with considerable social charm. He was above all a devoted friend and played an important part in introducing Valéry to men who were to become his lifelong associates, of whom the most important were Mallarmé and Gide. Louÿs had a genius for bringing together the right people, and a ready appreciation of the talents of his contemporaries. He had been at school with André Gide at the École Alsacienne, and it was he who introduced Gide to Heredia, and to Mallarmé, and who took him to visit Verlaine at the Hôpital Broussais.[1]

[1] André Gide, *Journal* (le 18 janvier 1890) (Paris: Gallimard, 1940), 13. And Pierre Louÿs, *Vers et prose* (Paris, 1910).

From the first Louÿs appreciated Valéry's genius, and did everything in his power to encourage him, divining in the poet of the early
sonnets one of the finest intellects of the time. Louÿs was an excellent
critic. Two years after their first meeting he wrote to Valéry:

> I think you have the quality which is above all necessary in embarking in
> writing. You are yourself. I would recognise among a hundred others an
> anonymous piece written by you. By what characteristics? First by the
> purity. Your verses are astonishingly pure in ideas, images and sonority.
> They are also delicate slender and fragile. . . . They have a sad and youth-
> ful grace, restrained gestures, and silence. There, that is what I like in
> your work.

In the summer of 1890 Valéry had sent his first sonnets to Louÿs,
who proposed to show them to Mallarmé, and to this Valéry consented.

> Last night I brought [Mallarmé] your sonnet [Louÿs reported]. He read it
> slowly, re-read it, considered, and said in a low voice 'Ah, c'est très bien'
> and as I made him speak about it he added: 'He is a poet, there is not a
> shadow of doubt.' And then as if speaking to himself: 'great musical
> subtlety,' and turning towards me 'Have you others by him?' I had only
> that one, and I think I was right, for you must send them to him yourself.
> . . . He will certainly reply and will perhaps add some intelligent advice
> which he knows how to give. . . .

Valéry at once followed this advice and sent two poems, 'Le Jeune
Prêtre' and 'La Suave Agonie,' with the following letter:[1]

> October 1890
> Cher Maître,
>   A young man buried in the depth of the provinces, who has been
> able to divine and love the secret splendour of your works, through frag-
> ments discovered by chance in reviews, dares to introduce himself to you.
> He believes that art can no longer be anything but a closed city where
> beauty reigns alone. . . . To make himself known in a few words, he must
> state that he prefers short poems, concentrated for a final climax, where
> the rhythms are like marmorean steps of an altar crowned in the last line!
> Not that he can boast of having realised this ideal. But the truth is that he is
> steeped in the profound doctrines of the great Edgar Allan Poe—perhaps
> the most subtle artist of this century.
>   This name alone will suffice to show you the nature of his poetics. So
> he stops to leave room for the verses he wishes to submit to you, hoping

---

[1] Mondor, *L'Heureuse Rencontre*, 39.

for some advice written by the same hand as that which, in *Hérodiade*, dazzles him and fills him with despair.

PAUL VALÉRY

3 rue Urbain V
  Montpellier

The two poems sent with this letter were published in *La Conque* on June 1, 1891 (and were reprinted by Professor Henri Mondor in *L'Heureuse Rencontre*[1]). Here is 'Le Jeune Prêtre,' which was dedicated to Pierre Louÿs and dated July 14, 1890:

> Sous les calmes cyprès d'un jardin clérical
> Va le jeune homme noir, aux yeux lents et magiques.
> Lassé de l'exégèse et les chants liturgiques
> Il savoure le bleu repos dominical.
>
> L'air est plein de parfums et de cloches sonnantes!
> Mais le séminariste évoque dans son cœur
> Oublieux du latin murmuré dans le chœur
> Un rêve de bataille et d'armes frissonnantes . . .
>
> Et, se dressent ses mains faites pour l'ostensoir
> Cherchant un glaive lourd; car il lui semble voir
> Au couchant ruisseler le sang doré des anges! . . .
>
> Là-haut! il veut nageant dans le ciel clair et vert
> Parmi les séraphins bardés de feux étranges
> Au son du cor, choquer du fer contre l'enfer.

This sonnet might have been written by almost any of the established poets who were Valéry's elders at this time; its accomplishment is striking. The second poem 'La Suave Agonie' suggests a definitely literary origin.

'I have just written to Mallarmé—*quelle lettre difficultueuse*,' sighed Valéry, in thanking Louÿs for his introduction. He complained that his own poetry was far from his ideal, while he waited anxiously for the master's reply. He had not long to wait; four days later Mallarmé wrote.

My dear Poet,
      The gift of subtle analogy with the adequate music, which is everything, you certainly possess. I have said so to our friend Monsieur Louÿs: and I say it again before your two short and rich poems. As for advice, solitude alone can give that, and I envy you having it, remembering my youthful days in the provinces somewhere down in your direction, which I shall never recapture.[2]

[1] Mondor, *L'Heureuse Rencontre*, 40.   [2] *Ibid.*, 42.

This letter delighted Valéry. Almost by the same post Louÿs wrote, 'Mallarmé is charming. . . . I should like to see you in Paris and at his house. . . . He is a silent man who speaks low, with a slow voice, but with so much expression that superlatives coming from him have an unknown grandeur . . . he is sincere . . . he never speaks ill of any one . . . and then he is the most intelligent man I know. . . .'

Valéry's reply to Louÿs deserves to be considered for its discernment:

> The few lines he sent me are charming. An unusual thing in such circumstances. . . . What he says to me contains a subtle core. He refuses to give me the advice I asked for, in referring me, as a magician would bestow a talisman, to solitude, the good and unique inspiration . . . and has made me meditate deeply . . . showing me the whole secret of that strange and sumptuous œuvre.

He ends his letter by saying that he has stored Mallarmé's note in a drawer, beneath the precious copies of *Hérodiade*, 'like a family relic which one likes to think protects the children of the house.'

The encouragement and interest shown by Mallarmé were to have far-reaching effect, not only as an intellectual stimulus, but also as the beginning of a lifelong friendship. As for poetry, here was a master who fulfilled his disciple's ideal of an intellectual effort pushed to the furthest extreme, in that 'invisible web of distant interrelations and of magical assonances, which are necessary to rouse in the soul of the reader the light and pure flight of dreams.' Thus Mallarmé, whose motifs were ideas suggested and enriched by sensual symbols, had stated that problem in poetics which Valéry in his later development was to solve.

4. VALÉRY AND ANDRÉ GIDE

Je m'inquiète de ne savoir qui je serai. (GIDE)

The year 1890 was drawing to its close. A time of new friendships and new problems, it still held for Paul Valéry the first meeting with another future friend. This was André Gide, whose uncle Charles Gide was professor in the Faculty of Law at Montpellier, where some years before, André had lived with his uncle and gone to school.

Later he had met Louÿs at the École Alsacienne in Paris, and a close friendship had resulted from their mutual love of poetry.[1] On Louÿs' suggestion Gide now paid his first visit to Rue Urbain V.

Gide has recorded his first meeting with Valéry and described the room at the end of the small enclosed garden in which it took place. Here old cuttings from illustrated journals decorated the walls, dominated by the motto 'Méfie-toi sans cesse,' and on and around the work-table books and manuscripts lay in heaps. Two armchairs invited conversation. Paul-Ambroise, as he signed his name at this time, was slim and fair, animated in manner and gesture, his eyes shining with enthusiasm or suddenly thoughtful, the blue eyes of a Cisalpine Gaul, eyes of an angel, Degas said years later. Valéry's general bearing was unobtrusive and his clothes plain: a contrast to Gide, whose insistence on an artistic effect was discreetly evident, if we may judge from contemporary photographs.

From their first words of greeting they became friends. Gide had brought some of the latest poetry from Paris, including poems by Rimbaud, and he read them aloud in a slow and measured voice, while his host listened with eager attention in an atmosphere of benzoin-scented cigarette smoke.[2] To Valéry's enthusiasm for the Huysmans of A Rebours and for Mallarmé, Gide replied with his admiration for Baudelaire, Flaubert, Shakespeare and Schopenhauer, showing a wide knowledge and sensitive appreciation.[3]

This was the first of many happy hours spent in each other's company. Valéry delighted to show his new friend all that pleased him most; and Gide found everything sympathetic, from the study where Paul-Ambroise spent his time dreaming and working, while the damp walls of the overgrown garden echoed the solemn evening bells, to the ancient cathedral, the old houses, the winding and forsaken streets. One evening they walked together down to the Botanical Gardens, the Jardin des Plantes which was Valéry's favourite walk, and which inspired many of his poems. It was a clear winter night, the bare trees and the mysterious tomb of 'Narcissa' lost nothing of their charm in the moonlight, in that 'dark garden where water dreams alone.'

---

[1] Pierre Louÿs, Les Débuts d'André Gide (Paris: Editions du Sagittaire, 1931), passim.

[2] Ibid.

[3] Henri Mondor, Les Premiers Temps d'une amitié (Monaco: Editions du Rocher, 1947), 12. For a description of Montpellier see also André Gide, Si le grain ne meurt, passim.

Another day they strolled together on the sunlit terrace of the Peyrou between the sea and the hills.

After their first meeting, while Gide was still at Montpellier, Valéry wrote to Pierre Louÿs, 'I am absolutely in ecstasy and rapture over your friend Gide. What a fine and rare mind and what enthusiasm for beautiful rhymes and pure ideas.' Again on December 21, in the course of a long letter, he tells how they walked together in the moonlight 'conversing about that inner life of the artist which for certain people like myself is so difficult to grasp and control, and to carry through successfully.' He continues, 'I explained to him my subjective theory of those indispensable ethics which are at the origin of all solid work. . . . Gide told me of his laborious days, and yours, and I am quite amazed. I who rarely spend two hours at my work-table and alas! gather verses as if they fell from the trees or from the subtle stars, but do not know how to control them or how to spur them on with golden and precious rhymes, nor how to add beauty to the tabernacle of the sonnet. . . .'

In the correspondence which followed Gide's return to Paris, Valéry showed complete confidence in his own judgement when speaking of other poets, but as far as his own work was concerned he was full of anxious doubts and fears. His first letters expressed admiration for the things they had discussed together.

> I have excited in myself the desire to feel to the very marrow the magic of things [he wrote on January 19, 1891]. I have read great passages in Schopenhauer, and I have gone deeply into that aspect of Baudelaire which I have made my own, my familiar, that of certain passages of ecstasy. Then I have read, again and always, the solitary Poe and a little of Mallarmé! All of which is not 'literature', it is very far from Flaubert and it is very great.[1]

Yet in spite of this ardour, his tone changes when he goes on to speak of his own work which he had shown to Gide, and which now lay neglected on his table. 'Verse is so difficult,' he sighed, 'that page of flesh that one must tear from oneself, not howling like Musset, but secretly and unheard.'

In his first letter Gide had spoken of his 'childish fears' of doing anything that might displease his new friend, and he outlined the form that their correspondence should take. In his second letter he spoke of

---

[1] Paul Valéry, letter to André Gide, in *Correspondance André Gide–Paul Valéry*, ed. by Robert Mallet (Paris, 1955), 44. By permission of Librairie Gallimard.

his admiration for Symbolism and for Mallarmé in particular, the result of reading an article in *La Plume*, and he proposed Maeterlinck as dramatist of the new movement and himself as its novelist. 'Tell me what you already know of Mallarmé and I will copy new passages,' he promised, and ended a long friendly letter with 'the wish for a gesture of discreet tenderness.'[1]

In his reply Valéry ignored the news of schools and movements, and eagerly accepted the offer of copies of Mallarmé's poems. 'Thank you for your offers of Mallarmé: it is a corner of heaven that opens. I know his *Après-midi d'un Faune* which they are going to play in Paris, and a few other poems. . . . Of Hérodiade I know the fragment in *A Rebours* and one other copied by Louÿs.'[2]

'Above all,' the letter ends, 'show me your early verses which I imagine are as delicate, as subtle and profound as I have found you to be.' This mutual sympathy and understanding appear all through the early correspondence. It was a time of fresh enthusiasms, in which both felt the stirrings of infinite possibilities for the future of their art. Gide had just written his *Cahiers d'André Walter*, which he published anonymously at his own expense a year later, and of which Valéry wrote, 'I have never felt my own intimate existence and the painful youth of an intellectual so well as in your André Walter. . . .' And he congratulates Gide on being so far from 'the sycophantism and the crafty cleverness of Barrès.'

For Valéry this was the period of 'Le Bois amical,' written while Gide was staying at Montpellier and dedicated to him. Valéry, who had been impressed by Gide's art in reading aloud, read it to him in a low-toned voice, aiming at pronouncing each word with great precision. Except when reading, his speech was rapid and indistinct. Modestly described by its author as being 'very vague in technical quality' and as a 'very indifferent suggestion of friendship,' this lyric has a rare quality, and is the first poem in which the symbolism of the future Self was, perhaps all unconsciously, expressed.

Many young intellectuals are poets for a brief moment; such was the case of André Gide. 'Mallarmé has written all the poetry I would have dreamt of writing,' he confessed, knowing that he had not the power to realise such dreams for himself. His prose *Traité du Narcisse* mainly reflected Mallarmé's ideas. Essentially a prose writer, Gide had

---

[1] Paul Valéry, letter to André Gide, in *Correspondance André Gide–Paul Valéry*, 47.

[2] Paul Valéry to André Gide, *Correspondance Gide–Valéry*, 49.

one very definite theme, and although he perfected his means of expression, he never really extended his personal adventure to any universal or spiritual interpretation beyond the quest for happiness treated in his *Nourritures terrestres*. His preoccupations were such that they tended to narrow rather than to expand his universe, for the necessity of justifying the ways of Gide to man was by its nature limiting. Yet even here there is greatness. Any man who dares to stand alone, is almost always impressive. He who ventures to express his own truth, and who looks for what he considers as spiritual freedom, is worthy of admiration.

In his youth, Gide's inner life was one of spiritual conflict between the puritanical discipline of his upbringing and the growing force of his erotic desires and preferences. Diffident, in spite of an attitude of self-assurance, he expressed in the early pages of his *Journal* an underlying anxiety caused by the conflict of his spiritual and material desires. The necessity of dramatising his moral defeat was later revealed in passages dealing with his marriage. This need of self-justification became his central theme and dominated his fiction. There is ample evidence in his *Journal* that he considered his vocation as a writer with the utmost seriousness. 'My head is encumbered with my work,' he wrote in 1890. 'It is an intolerable anxiety of mind.'[1] This artistic integrity, this constant desire for strength and distinction in his workmanship makes him one of the most sympathetic and influential writers of his time.

Gide's tact and his ready generosity made him a good friend. Both Valéry and Louÿs were greatly drawn to him, the more so because all three, in spite of their different literary preferences, were unanimous in their admiration and spontaneous appreciation of Mallarmé. This showed their intuitive judgement in literary matters, and remained as a bond of friendship despite their different points of view in other things. Inevitably, as each of them developed his own ideas and carved out his own destiny, intellectual and temperamental differences became more pronounced.

Louÿs, until his too early death in 1925, was the generous friend and critic on whom, especially during the period of writing *La Jeune Parque*, Valéry depended. Valéry and Gide remained lifelong friends, though their intercourse was necessarily modified by circumstances. Undoubtedly Valéry became more reserved, and Gide seems to have felt a certain strain in their relations, which however remained unbroken. Many years later (1907) Gide confessed in his *Journal*:

[1] Gide, *Journal* (1890), 15.

'Valéry will never know all the friendship I need to listen, without protesting, to his conversation, I come out of it shattered. . . .'[1] And again, 'Valéry's conversation puts this frightful alternative before me: either I must find what he says absurd, or else find what I *do* absurd. If he suppressed in reality all that in conversation he proposes to suppress, I would no longer have any reason to exist.' Yet despite all contradictions, Gide thought, and often said, that Valéry was always right; and he declared that no one understood friendship so charmingly, referring to Valéry after his death as a saint.

Two years before these entries in Gide's *Journal*, Valéry had given *his* mature reflections on Gide, in a letter to Léautaud (1905):

> Gide and I feel the things of the spirit differently. We understand and know each other admirably. Unfortunately he thinks that I disparage him, while I am sure that he stimulates me. I have noticed that I don't see him as the rest of his friends do. I see Gide rather as I see myself—that is to say he appears to me as worthy of justice—this abject word that has no sense except when applied egotistically. Please understand me. When I like someone I treat him as I treat myself, that is to say very meticulously and with intimate severity. I become intolerable—but the other person (the subject of my intolerance) does not know how much and how frankly I identify myself with him in speech and thought. This frankness has been my most cherished ideal. I said all this to Gide thirteen or fourteen years ago. . . . There is between us something which is neither literature nor mutual or complementary tastes, nor anything that can be expressed by regular calculation, but something that is of a vital kind, of the faculty of following each other's thought, of adapting ourselves instantaneously and of understanding one another with pleasure.[2]

Perhaps the essential difference between the point of view of Gide and that of Valéry, when they were young, was that Gide wished to encourage and cultivate his sensibility and his sentiments, and nourished his art exclusively on his feelings. But Valéry from an early age mistrusted sentiments, rather in the same way as the Greek philosophers mistrusted the evidence of the senses. 'How much I hate to write about my sentiments,' he noted, 'or to record what others enjoy putting on paper. And this is in agreement with my sensibility which has always had a sacred horror of itself. Otherwise I might have been a novelist. . . . But my sensibility is my inferiority, my most cruel and detestable gift, for I don't know how to use it.' Very soon he

---

[1] Gide, *Journal* (1907), 237.
[2] Paul Valéry, letter to Léautaud (mai 1905), *Lettres à quelques-uns*, 67.

decided that the expression of all natural sentiments was vulgar and useless in print. He thought it indecent or hypocritical to preach of virtue, justice or humanity, or to speak of love. To write on such themes seemed to him to show a lack of modesty, and to do so was to take an unfair advantage. 'Comment peut-on ne pas se cacher pour sentir?' he asked.

As early as 1891 he had begun to consider most forms of literature as impure, and he was becoming more and more sceptical about easy effects; already he mistrusted literary works which did not give him the impression of mental effort pushed to the extreme. It followed that novels and drama, because they were inventions depending on circumstances, bored him extremely. His need of precision was such that he suffered from 'the coarseness of approximation in description of men and things.' Indeed, he had always disliked *describing* things he had felt or seen. What he wanted to do was 'to use his pen for the future of his thought.' Though this formula dated from a few years later, Valéry had, at the time of his first meeting with Louÿs and Gide, already decided to develop his capacity of analysis and thought.

In December 1890 Valéry had summed up his religious creed in a letter to Pierre Louÿs:

> As for belief, it is the grossest hypothesis to believe that God exists objectively. For, like Satan, he exists, but within ourselves. And the cult we owe him is the respect we owe ourselves, and by this we must understand the effort to improve our proficiency in directing our abilities. In short: 'God' is our particular ideal. 'Satan' is that which tends to turn us from it. . . .[1]

Many will agree that this could not have been better expressed.

5. GROWTH OF A POET

Je me plaisais surtout aux mathématiques, à cause de la certitude et de l'évidence de leurs raisons. (DESCARTES)

Freed from his military service in November 1890, Valéry returned to the study of law. But he had little interest in this subject and he felt bored and uncertain as to the future. 'Boredom makes me sulky,' he

[1] Paul Valéry, letter to P. Louÿs, *Lettres à quelques-uns*, 41.

confided in a letter to Louÿs, 'for with liberty the old worries come back.' He was, he said, 'repelled by the cold stink of the rebarbative Code, the gray lecture rooms where juridical eloquence flows sadly like a glacial tap in a *morgue*—on me.'[1]

This was a period of rapid intellectual development, for although Paul-Ambroise appeared to his friends to be entirely preoccupied with poetry, he was nevertheless gifted with an intellectual curiosity and a love of precision which led him to mathematical speculations in which he soon became deeply interested. From the first, the theories and the method especially excited his imagination. He now made a new approach to the study of geometry, finding in it analogies between poetry and mathematics: in a letter to Gide of this period, he suggests that prosody might be considered as an algebra, that is to say 'the science of variations of rhythm fixed according to certain values given to the signs of which it is composed.' So too, from this point of view, 'the line [in verse] is an equation, rightly stated when its solution is an equality, that is to say a symmetry.'

Such ideas were to bear fruit, and were to influence the whole trend of his future thought. From this time he seems to have visualised geometry as a most exact art in which the geometrician, equally with the poet, is obliged to create the instruments of his thought. This conception of mathematical science as an art gave him his first idea of the possibilities of 'constant' symbols which would convey universal truths. He was, of course, still feeling his way, and flashes of intuitive perception were followed by moods of despair.

It would be a mistake to conclude that at Montpellier Valéry was isolated from intellectual companions. Among his schoolfellows Gustave Fourment was perhaps the most intimate. Fourment, who was interested in philosophy and poetry, kept throughout his life a deep affection for Valéry. Four years before Louÿs and Gide appeared on the scene, Gustave Fourment shared Valéry's intellectual preoccupations, and encouraged him to read widely. There is no doubt that the scholarly interests and lucid criticisms of this friend, who became a Professor of Philosophy, were of great value to Valéry at this time and during the years of study in Paris. The letters which they wrote to each other between 1887 and 1933 contain interesting information on their early researches.[2]

[1] Paul Valéry, letter to P. Louÿs (19 novembre 1890), *Lettres à quelques-uns*, 34.
[2] *Correspondance Paul Valéry–Gustave Fourment*, Introduction by Octave Nadal (Paris: Gallimard, 1957).

It was Valéry's friend and neighbour Pierre Féline, living on the first floor of the same house, who initiated the poet in the science of mathematics. The evidence of this contemporary is of great value, for he tells us that at the age of twenty (1891) Valéry was deeply interested in the 'theory of functions,' and also, and all important, the theories of 'groups of transformations.'[1] Such theories were to become part of his mental equipment and undoubtedly suggested a new line of approach to his own problem of language. Thus many years later he wrote, 'The properties of the "ensembles" are more worthy of the intellect than that which they transform.' We shall see that it was in fact the adaptation of mathematical principles to language that enabled him to develop his power of abstraction, which he cultivated so systematically that it became both a means and an end, a problem and the power of solving it.

It was not only mathematics which roused Valéry's interest; music also was becoming of equal significance with architecture as a perfect art founded on exact principles. The contemporary master of musical method was Wagner, and Valéry's interest in him may have been wakened by Mallarmé's essay, which begins thus: 'Richard Wagner treats with singular defiance the poets, whose function he usurps with the most frank and splendid bravura.'[2] A musician, who wrote his own libretti, and so thoroughly used the music to illuminate the poem, could not pass unnoticed by poets. Baudelaire had been the first to examine this question and he had prepared the way for the Symbolists' ultimatum of their intention to take back from music what rightly belonged to their own art. The Parnassians had adopted to some extent the manner in which Wagner developed a musical emotion in his listeners. Thus musicians and poets had been brought very close to each other.

Valéry was no musician, at least as far as execution went; he never got further than picking out notes on the piano with one finger. But the theory and the principle of construction in musical composition interested him intensely, and music moved him deeply. He would listen for hours while Pierre Féline played Wagner on the piano. In fact such music almost made him despair of ever doing anything that he thought worth while in his own art. 'I am up to the eyes in

[1] Pierre Féline, 'A Montpellier,' *Paul Valéry Vivant*, 42. By permission of M. Jean Ballard.
[2] Stéphane Mallarmé, 'Richard Wagner: Rêverie d'un poète,' *Œuvres Complètes* ('Bibliothèque de la Pléiade') (Paris: Gallimard, 1946), 541.

Lohengrin,' he wrote to Gide in the spring of 1891. 'I don't know a note of music, but I listen and dream while one of my friends at the piano plays to me in the evening the Prelude or the Duo or the mystic March of the second act. This music will lead me to write no more—for it is coming to that. Already too many difficulties hold me up.'[1]

In the summer of 1891 Valéry passed the examinations of his second year in the three years' course of his legal studies. He was now planning a visit to Paris for the autumn. His letters reflect his unsettled state of mind. Science bored him, and the mystical forest had led him nowhere.

> I have visited ships and cathedrals [he complained], I have read the most marvellous works, of Rimbaud and Mallarmé, I have, alas! analysed their means and have always met the most beautiful illusions as to their genesis and birth. Where shall I find a newer magic; a secret of living and creating which would surprise me? You will smile here, in thinking of my poor efforts. If you only knew how truly I detest them! My great poems of the future are looking for their form and it is sheer madness.[2]

We may detect the shadow of Rimbaud in this passage: discontent mingled with disgust of one's own efforts, on finding one's moods discerned and dominated by the genius of another, who has, in explaining himself, made one feel that one's own interpretation is inadequate.

But Valéry was not content to dwell on such reactions, and in the same letter he firmly established his own position and his individual point of view:

> You see in passive, as in active art [by which he meant his own or that of others] I have only found motives for anger and disgust. To begin with, all those who study 'man' in himself, make me sick. Only the church has an art. It alone gives a little comfort, and detaches us from the world. I would say and shout: we are all children beside the liturgists and the theologians—since the greatest of us—Wagner and Mallarmé—bow before them and imitate them.[2]

This significant passage reflects Valéry's attitude towards literature and emphasises his feeling for form, and the ritual of formal art. Nothing was satisfying that was not perfectly expressed, and each new perfection could exist only in its own complete expression. It was not surprising therefore that he took such delight in the High Mass, and he

---

[1] Paul Valéry, Letter to Gide (27 mars 1891), *Correspondance Gide–Valéry*, 72. By permission Librairie Gallimard.
[2] *Ibid.* (septembre 1891), 125.

often returned to his idea that it was the purest form of drama. 'I am solemnly disconcerted,' he wrote, 'to find that all drama is impossible after the Mass'; and he considered that this ritual had everything that one looks for in drama: exoticism, speculation and the beauty of pure and solemn language, the gestures, the organ music and the emotion which increases at each moment while the mystery lasts, 'the flesh tortured and abolished by the unique Power of Thought.' Was it not 'the supreme marvel of art'? From such reflections his doctrine of 'formal art' was gradually to develop, through long and arduous study.

In the meantime it was full summer, and there at Palavas within walking distance was 'lointaine et fameuse la mer!'[1] 'I am frantic,' he cried, 'such a breeze blows from the sea my hair is damp with it, I breathe it with ecstasy!' Swimming was his greatest joy. His whole being trembled with delight as he approached the sea to dive into the great transparent waves, to throw himself into its mass and movement. This sport seemed to him to be comparable with love, as an action in which his whole body became entirely signs and forces. In the sea he became 'the man he would like to be': his body became the direct instrument of his mind and the author of all his ideas. Often and joyously, in his essays and letters, he described the delight of such moments.

At home in his room, he spent many hours surrounded by his favourite books, which crowded together on his work-table. There was Plato's *Symposium* at ease between a treatise on heraldry and plates of 'perspectives'; a Book of Hours, then Virgil full of marvels; Rossetti's works and life, which Valéry 'dawdled through and dreamt over.' Exercise books full of notes concerning architecture and ornament lay always under his hand, together with sheets of geometrical figures. But beloved above all these were his great marine volumes 'crushing, dominating, rolling' everything in the waves of their immense pages 'embossed with red, antique, dressed in sombre calf crackling with gold'—such as admirals wear—and with astonishing illustrations where 'the light-sailed frigate, the "flute" [Dutch cargo boat], the hooker, the galleass and the xebeck, are all at anchor under the gaiety of flags and the protection of their batteries of cannon.' Stimulated by the beauty of things of the sea Valéry gave himself freely to its adventurous and triumphant spirit. 'You must re-read the admirable 'Bateau ivre,' to be able to understand what I feel,' he wrote

[1] Paul Valéry, Letter to Gide (mai 1891), *Correspondance Gide–Valéry*, 87.

to Gide in August. 'Its poetry is astonishing, authentic and a little mad —like the compass. . . .'

Valéry had first read Rimbaud in 1890. In December of that year he had sent a note to Gide, then staying at Montpellier, to ask him for 'Les Chercheuses de poux.' Evidently he had been impressed by the 'original and unknown radiations' of Rimbaud's lyrical genius and fresh images. Although the methods of the two poets differed so completely, there was a similarity in their aims, in so far as the poet of *Une Saison en enfer* and the poet of the Pure Self both abandoned everything for the research of an absolute of consciousness. Both looked for spiritual freedom; both felt the urgent necessity of transcending the usual sphere of thought; and both renewed poetry. There is a certain affinity between Rimbaud's latest poems such as 'Chanson de la plus haute tour,' and the delicate lyrics in *Charmes*, even if Valéry never quite equalled the passionate force of 'O saisons ô châteaux!'

In the letter of Madame Teste are statements reminiscent of passages in *Une Saison en enfer*, but the resemblance goes no further. Yet there can be no doubt that Valéry was excited by Rimbaud's lyrical splendour, while the idea of Rimbaud's revolt and escape passed like a shadow, troubling as a sigh, over the clear pool in which Narcissus gazed. Yet, characteristically, Valéry's sensibility to the methods of other poets had the effect of a defensive reaction against the *means* of their art, and this was one of the initial factors which protected his idea of 'pure poetry.'

Nothing could have been more different than the methods of these two poets. Rimbaud sang with fervent and revolutionary force, with a magic power of imagery, which expresses the astonishments and strivings of his impatience to feel, to know. He drove himself to furious sensual experience, to end by breaking the wings of his passionate and full-throated song, finally gathering up the rich harmony in the later lyrics—after which he had nothing more to say. Valéry's outlook was quite different. The school of Verlaine was not for one who desperately sought discipline and measure for the greater glory of self-knowledge; who could find food for his intellectual curiosity, and a possible future for his own expression, only in the high altitudes of the 'symbolic calculus' proposed by Mallarmé's poems.

Nevertheless on a wet Sunday, feeling imprisoned by the severity of the old town, Valéry, looking out from his window on the enclosed garden still trembling and fresh after a shower of rain, and listening to the deep-toned bells of the neighbouring cathedral, felt strangely restless and dissatisfied with himself and the restrained world around him, and may well have thought of Rimbaud's

oisive jeunesse
à tout asservie,
par délicatesse
J'ai perdu ma vie.

But Valéry was too actively intelligent to waste time in regret. A void always suggested to him some sort of bridge. Now he turned to his work-table to write to Gide: 'I have few illusions about things,' he said, explaining that he had set himself the task of reducing all theories to schemas and forcing himself to make such schemas enter into the practice of his life. He ends a long letter with an amusing self-portrait.

Many people would define me as not at all sentimental, not even philosophic but a little fellow who abstracts the quintessence of aesthetics. I pass for being gentle; I am violent, absent-minded. I appear light-hearted and happy, I am really boredom and despair personified. But I smile ineluctably, I never say to intruders what I really think, but what I suppose will please or rile them, according to the circumstances. I never speak of 'my soul' in verse or in any other literature.[1]

This was a period of wide though desultory reading. Valéry mentions in his letters 'De Quincey's *Confessions of an Opium Eater* and always and above all Poe—*un opium vertigineux et comme mathématique;*' he was also reading Flaubert's *Éducation sentimentale*. And then naturally enough he fell in love. Discussing his attitude towards this sentiment he said later, 'In my youth I placed love so high and so low that I found nothing strong enough or sufficiently tender in the most renowned books on this theme.' Meanwhile he analysed his new state of mind in his letters to Gide:

It is a new friend who speaks, the other spirit is as if dead. Slowly I had assembled my being. The substance of my thoughts was devoutly chosen from among the chaos of things. I had formed myself, incompletely but harmoniously, feeble but measured. And now unknown days have come. A glance has made me so stupid that I no longer exist: I have lost my clear vision of the world, I am an exile from myself. Ah! do you know what a skirt is—even from outside, especially from outside—all simple desires of the flesh. But the dress and the eye alone. The idealist is in agony. The world—does it exist?[2]

[1] Paul Valéry, Letter to Gide (septembre 1891), *Correspondance Gide–Valéry*, 125.   [2] *Ibid.* (4 juillet 1891), 107.

In replying to this letter Gide was gently ironical on the subject of pure minds, and, while advancing his own theories, gave sympathetic advice:

> Nothing in this world should be disdained except what is untrue; and we should not say that something belongs to art and something else does not. All things belong to universal art—or rather art is in us and we project it on all things and even on banal and ravishing love.[1]

Ten days after his first letter Valéry wrote again to Gide:

> If you only knew! How much I am suffering and how much my trans-figured stupidity appears admirable to me. What is most remarkable in these new ideas is that the whole Drama was, and is, mine. I allowed my-self to look on love. . . . The pure spirit, the familiar of my meditations has been put to flight, wounded.[2]

This intellectual and abstract love that Valéry so well described is well known to poets and sometimes rules their whole life. By its nature it remains unsatisfied; thus the poet becomes the high priest of an idol which he has himself created and which he has neither the desire nor the strength to abolish. But, as in Valéry's case, for all its imaginative and ideal nature, such a sentiment is capable of becoming a most painful obsession. For the mind suffers more than the body; the longing, despair and constant preoccupation are as actual as sensual desires. Later perhaps one may laugh at the force of the absurd, but at the time it is no laughing matter.

On September 11, 1891, Valéry confided to Gide:

> The existence of my body is the least beautiful of my dreams, therefore silence. But a woman goes by, already some years past youth, and who does not know me. While I barely know her name. Probably she is not beauti-ful. Yet her image remains with me. I feel her beside my desk. What hypotheses have I not woven for her. Have I neglected one single possi-bility of distress and tenderness? I have not even written. The letter is in my drawer.[3]

And again he asks himself what he is looking for in love . . .

> It is myself, this self that steals away and eludes my greedy grasp, it is this man who breaks loose at every trepidation of the spirit, through every wound, raising perhaps or defying the whole being and the sorrowful

[1] Gide, letter to Valéry (9 juillet 1891), *Correspondance Gide–Valéry*, 107.
[2] *Ibid.* (juillet 1891), 110.
[3] *Ibid.* (1 septembre 1891), 127.

spectator who is present. I would also look, and have looked here, for a revelation of the exterior mystery, an occult correspondence, a harmony of wills. . . .[1]

The object of so much eloquence was a young woman of Catalonian birth about ten years older than Valéry, met by chance, to whom he had scarcely spoken. On one occasion at some local fête she is said to have offered the poet—of whose sentiments she was unaware—a glass of champagne. This is beautifully symbolic, and why should it not be true—'Every man has a past, it is a matter of imagination,' declared Valéry's Faust when dictating his memoirs.

6. 'NARCISSE PARLE'

Gardez ce ton rare.   (MALLARMÉ)

During the spring and summer of 1891 Valéry was still writing poetry. 'Hélène,' 'a large fresco which should evoke antiquity,' and 'La Fileuse,' are both of this period, but the most characteristic poem among his early works, and which played a part in his evolution, was 'Narcisse parle.'

The theme had been suggested in the first place by the tomb of Narcissa in the Botanical Gardens at Montpellier. Here in a secluded corner under an arch of rock there is a marble slab that bears three words, 'Narcissae Placandis Manibus.' According to local tradition this was thought to be the tomb of the step-daughter of the English poet Edward Young (1684–1765), author of the *Night Thoughts on Death*.[2] Narcissa, the daughter of Young's second wife, died at Montpellier, it was said. As she was a Protestant she could not be buried in the cemetery, and Young was supposed to have dug her grave in this lonely spot at midnight by moonlight. This is confirmed by the evidence of Blake's drawing of the poet burying Narcissa, illustrating in the second 'Night Thought' the lines

> With pious sacrilege a grave I stole
> In midnight darkness whispered my last sigh.

[1] Gide, letter to Valéry (juillet 1891), *Correspondance Gide–Valéry*, 113.
[2] Professor Mondor says that Narcissa's real name was Eliza, and that her tomb is in the Protestant cemetery at Lyon (near the Hôtel-Dieu).

Valéry came often with his friends to this romantic tomb. The name 'Narcissa' fascinated him, and had suggested the classical myth of Narcissus, a theme that became for him almost a sort of poetic auto-biography. His first 'Narcisse,' an irregular sonnet, written before his first meeting with Louÿs, was the origin of the successive poems.

In November of 1890, Pierre Louÿs, at the moment of creating his first number of *La Conque*, begged Valéry to send him a poem of forty lines. In answer to this appeal Valéry wrote, in two days, the poem 'Narcisse parle,'[1] a development of the first sonnet. He would have preferred to have had more time to work on this theme. He considered that the poem he had wished to write should have been carefully and slowly created. He was almost appalled by the facility with which this hurried version was written, fearing that anything done so rapidly could not be of much value.

The first number of *La Conque* did not appear till the following spring, a delay typical of new publications despite the urgency of their editors. 'Narcisse parle' was signed 'M. Doris' and was highly praised in *Le Journal des débats*, rather to the disgust of Valéry who was dissatisfied with the poem. A letter to Gide reflected his feelings: 'I wrote it in two days—or six hours work—on request as you know, and I regret it.' A little later, after publication, he confirmed this view:

> Narcissus has spoken in the wilderness. When I saw it printed I had such horror of it that I closed the pages at once. To be so far from one's ideal. And it is bad. It isn't even readable. But then what written page will ever be at the height of the few notes that are the motif of the *Graal*. *Hérodiade* alone in French poetry can be read without too much disgust and embarrassment. And even it isn't sufficiently 'diamond'. You see I am difficult. . . .[2]

Valéry knew that he was still far from doing what he wanted, and, irritated by the poems he had written, he hated to be judged and placed on the strength of work which fell short of his ideal of what was 'concentrated, crystalline and total.' Under the circumstances it was not surprising that he despised easy glory, or that he began to shun publicity. It seemed more urgent to retire within himself to meditate on the future of his thought. So we find him telling Gide that there is nothing further from his mind than the idea of publishing a small book of verse.

[1] In Paul Valéry, *Album de vers anciens*, in *Poésies* (Paris: Gallimard, 1933), 33.
[2] Paul Valéry, letter to Gide (27 mars 1891), *Correspondance Gide–Valéry*, 74.

Yet in spite of his discontent with 'Narcisse,' Valéry thought it worth while to send it to Mallarmé, not so much on account of its own merits, but as a pretext for approaching one from whom he longed for sympathy and advice. From his first contact with Mallarmé's work there is never the least doubt as to the exceptional importance that it had assumed for Valéry, whose enthusiasm was such that most other poetry appeared to him to be reduced to 'clumsy attempts and happy fragments followed by insignificant or prosaic passages.' He had noticed that Mallarmé's poems were easy to memorise; though he had always found it difficult to learn by heart, these condensed lines fixed themselves in his memory without any effort. His enthusiasm was such as to make the younger poet despair of his own efforts. The master had set a standard of perfection impossible to surpass. Valéry's pride forebade anything facile, and since the poetry of most of his contemporaries appeared to him as unworthy of serious consideration, was it not almost a betrayal of his integrity to write useless verse?

Preoccupied by these problems, he found it a relief and almost a necessity to ask Mallarmé for advice, and wrote the following letter in April 1891.

Cher Maître,

For the second time I come to beg for your advice, and to know whether a few aesthetic reveries accumulated during this winter in a distant province are not rash and illusory. A poem published in *La Conque* under the title 'Narcisse parle' gives some indications of these, but the practice, as often happens, makes game of the theory, and leaves me at a standstill and perplexed.

Poetry appears to me as a delicate and beautiful explanation of the world, contained in strange and continual music. While the art of metaphysics sees the Universe constructed of pure and absolute ideas, painting sees it in colours, the art of poetry will be to consider it dressed in syllables, organised in phrases. Considered in its nude and magic splendour, the word is raised to the elemental power of a note, a colour, of the keystone of an arch. The line is revealed as a chord allowing for the introduction of two 'modes'; where the mysterious and sacred epithet, mirror of subterranean suggestions, is like an accompaniment played very softly.

A quite particular devotion to Edgar Poe leads me then to give 'analogy' as the poet's kingdom. He testifies to the mysterious echo of things, and their secret harmony, real, and certain as a mathematical ratio to all artistic minds, that is to say, and rightly so, to all violent idealists.

Thus the supreme conception of a high symphony asserts itself, unifying the world around us with the world which haunts us, constructed according

33

to rigorous architectonics, fixing simplified types on a background of gold and azure and liberating the poet from the ponderous help of commonplace philosophies, from false tenderness, and from lifeless descriptions.

The *Après-Midi d'un faune* alone in France realises this aesthetic ideal, and the extraordinary perfection which it insists upon clearly indicates the future disappearance of the exasperated sham poets who are, as it were, mechanically annihilated by their own mediocrity. And here ends this confession which you may think artless and childish, alas! but which I had to make to justify myself in my own eyes.

I think this, I have written that, where is the truth? . . . One believes in one's art as one believes in an eternally crucified, one exalts and denies it, in the pale and blood-stained hours, one seeks a word of comfort, a luminous gesture towards the future, and it is this that I dare to ask of you, cher Maître. . . .[1]

This letter, which ends with a symbolic image of the isolation of true poets, is remarkable both as a statement of poetic faith and as a confession of doubt. It also foretells the 'rigorous architectonics' on which Valéry's poems of the future were to be built.

Mallarmé must have been touched and perhaps surprised to find anyone who so closely followed his principles and shared his ideals, while remaining intellectually independent. Here is his reply:

Yes, my dear poet, in order to conceive literature and give it a reason for existing we must reach up to that 'high symphony' which perhaps no one will achieve; but which has haunted even the most unaware, and its principal features whether simple or subtle mark all written works. Music, strictly speaking, which we should pillage and which we should plagiarise, if our own is mute or insufficient, suggests such a poem.

Your 'Narcisse parle' charms me and I have said so to Pierre Louÿs. Keep this rare tone.[2]

In March of this year (1891) Valéry's first significant essay in prose appeared in *L'Ermitage*. The ideas recorded in his letter to Mallarmé were here carefully developed. The essay was called 'Paradoxe sur l'architecture.' It was dedicated to 'Claude Moreau' and 'Bernard Durval,' pseudonyms of Pierre Louÿs and André Gide—and ended with a sort of irregular sonnet to Orpheus, printed as prose, and later published in sonnet form in the third number of *La Conque* (May 1891).

In this poetic yet severe essay, Valéry spoke for the first time of the superiority of music and architecture as formal arts which are the most

[1] Paul Valéry, letter to Mallarmé (18 avril 1891), *Lettres à quelques-uns*, 46.
[2] Cited by Mondor, *L'Heureuse Rencontre*, 86.

apt to express the essence of things as opposed to their mere appearance. He starts by tracing the decadence in modern architecture from the time when it had veritable musical qualities: when 'the basilica was the antiphone of stone, and the high naves expressed eternal prayer.' In the Orphic centuries the spirit breathed on the stone, and music and architecture were intermingled in man's highest creation. Valéry saw in the works of Beethoven and Wagner a possible inspiration for future architects, for he thought the ideal architect should also be a musician, and should be for a long time a recluse in the pure solitude of his dream. Poe's attempt to construct 'formal' poetry, and the value of such theories, are discussed and praised. Valéry was already searching for principles on which to establish a theoretical base for a universal art.

André Gide was the first to realise the value of this essay, and he wrote with generous praise: 'I hope for all sorts of beautiful things from you. . . . I find the irregular sonnet irreproachable and splendid.' He transcribed the last part of the essay, writing it out in its alexandrines, and particularly noticing the line 'Il chante, assis au bord du ciel splendide, Orphée.'

As the poem is difficult to find in the original form, it seems relevant to quote it here, so that readers may compare it with the later version in *Vers anciens*.

> Il évoque en un bois thessalien, Orphée
> Sous les myrtes; et le soir antique descend.
> Le bois sacré s'emplit lentement de lumières
> Et le dieu tient la lyre entre ses doigts d'argent.
> Le Dieu chante, et selon le rythme tout-puissant,
> S'élèvent au soleil les fabuleuses pierres,
> Et l'on voit grandir vers l'azur incandescent
> Les hauts murs d'or harmonieux du sanctuaire.
> Il chante assis au bord du ciel splendide, Orphée!
> Son œuvre se revêt d'un vespéral trophée,
> Et sa lyre divine enchante les porphyres,
> Car le temple érigé par ce musicien
> Unit la sûreté des rythmes anciens
> A l'âme immense du grand hymne sur la lyre! . . .[1]

This version is, I think, finer than that of the *Vers anciens*, where the influence of Heredia's *Trophées* is evident in its Parnassian finish.

[1] First printed in *La Conque* (1 mai 1891). Gide copied out the passage on Orphée. See *Correspondance Gide–Valéry*, 75.

Here there is a wide horizon which is peculiarly Valérian; and the idea of the movement and transformation of the world of solid rock by the magic of song is expressed for the first time, to be used again in *Amphion*.

7. FIRST VISIT TO MALLARMÉ

Un pèlerinage radieux. (MONDOR)

The long-projected visit to Paris took place late in September (1891), when Paul accompanied his mother there for the *concours d'agrégation de droit* of his elder brother. This explains why he had fixed a date for his arrival when neither Gide or Louÿs were in town; and rather disconsolately he waited for their return. He felt confused and insignificant in the vast bustle and movement of Paris, and reflected that 'the crowd rules here.' His first visit was to Huysmans, but whether he went to see the various sights recommended by Gide is not recorded.

However, reassuring letters foretold the return of his friends, Gide recommending him to call on Camille Mauclair. This visit had the effect of rousing Paul's jealousy. Sitting in 'the squalid refuge' of a café, he wrote addressing Gide as 'prostituée sans fard' and accused him of writing 'such words and so appreciated'—to others. Gide was quite unperturbed and even amused: 'sache que je t'aime assez pour que tu me laisses aimer un peu les autres,' he replied, and assured Paul of his deep affection.

Meanwhile Pierre Louÿs was back in Paris, and his first gesture was to write to Mallarmé asking for permission to bring Valéry to the Rue de Rome. This was promptly granted and Mallarmé himself welcomed them on the doorstep.

In brief phrases Valéry noted his first impressions.[1] Mallarmé appeared to his guest as a short little man of the *bourgeois* class, of about fifty, who looked tired. Geneviève, the poet's daughter, had a classical face, strange and charming; she and Mme Mallarmé sat under the lamp working on embroidery, rose-coloured against the brown shadow of the small room; while the poet sat in a rocking-chair his pipe in his hand. At first, Valéry noted, there seemed to be almost a provincial

---

[1] Recorded by Mondor, *L'Heureuse Rencontre*, 101.

calm. Then Mallarmé spoke of Villiers; of René Ghil, of rhythm being inseparable from 'idea'; of *vers libre* and the colour of vowels. He saw *A* vermilion, *U* blue-green, as Valéry also saw it, and *O* black. We remember that Arthur Rimbaud saw *A* black, *U* green, *O* blue. Punctuation in poetry, said Mallarmé, seemed henceforth superfluous, and gently mocked those who uselessly prolonged its usage. The alexandrine, he considered, should be kept for important passages. He complained that his life was abjectly tied down by teaching at a moment when people expected him to produce more poetry.

So the gentle voice flowed on in unpremeditated phrases. That the themes were evidently chosen at random may well have been caused by Valéry's intervention, since in his summing-up of the evening he says, 'I made the conversation turn on all subjects.',[1] Later he was to realise that it was considered indiscreet to interrupt while in a modulated voice the Master followed his own line of thought.

> It was better to listen than to speak [Mauclair reported], to be attentive than to dispute . . . for experience had proved to the regular visitors that their participation was negligible and that the precious monologue, scarcely commented on, accepted with reverence, was what infallibly assured a brilliant evening.[2]

Yet Mallarmé never preached. He seemed more preoccupied in following his own meditations than in dazzling the young men who listened respectfully. He evidently found it amusing to try out his ideas and watch the result on the faces of his disciples. Valéry was to become one of the happy few who went there regularly, and his discreet analogies and comments must certainly have been approved by Mallarmé.

Before leaving Paris—'la ville du cauchemar'—Valéry again visited Huysmans, who entertained him with descriptions of Montesquiou, on whom Des Esseintes was modelled.

Valéry returned to Montpellier on October 25 to follow the course of his third year of Licence en Droit. It was with a certain relief that he found himself again in his little study where the provincial silence seemed to close round him. On a mild wet morning he watched the rain dripping from the last autumn leaves in the enclosed garden, and recalled the past weeks with their deceptions, triumphs, conversations and new contacts. 'So far I can only feel,' he wrote to Gide, and

---

[1] Recorded by Mondor, *L'Heureuse Rencontre*, 102.
[2] Camille Mauclair, *Mallarmé chez lui* (Paris: Grasset, 1935).

evoked the Luxembourg gardens and 'our shadows better than its statues.' Now the rain, and the friendly letters on his desk, were in tune with his mood of wishing to be modern

> shiveringly modern so as to feel more isolated, more snug, more deliciously inside one's own shell along with three or four kindred spirits despising history, dogmas and even mathematics! Loving only lucid sleep, a crystal, a flower, and above all the drop of water which drips from a leaf and the unseen belfries that one hears ringing the hours. . . .

Bored by law, and disdainful of all he had written, he was shocked when Gide addressed him in a dedication as 'poet': 'Please do not call me a poet, either great or small,' he protested. 'I am not a poet. Nor have I any title. Must I repeat to you what I have already said to Louÿs:—that I am no poet but a bored gentleman who is put off by all normal beauty, cubic or affirmative. I jeer at phrases and their rhythm, and all that too-foreseen mechanism which does not amuse me. *L'expression seule me conquiert*.' [1]

He was, however, still writing poetry, and continued throughout the winter to work on his Narcisse theme. Yet as the year drew to its close he became more and more despondent. His letters to Louÿs and to Gide reflect his disgust with life in general and with law in particular.

Early in the new year, February 2, 1892, he gave a lecture on Villiers de L'Isle-Adam. This had been arranged under the auspices of the Société Languedocienne by their president Vacher de Lapouge, who was at that time librarian at the faculty of law. Lapouge had started a course of anthropology which Valéry had joined; under Lapouge's direction, he had assisted in the Hamletesque occupation of measuring skulls.[2]

In his lecture Valéry showed a wide knowledge of Villiers and his contemporaries. He sketched the part played by Gautier, Banville, Flaubert and Hugo in that inventive epoch. He praised Baudelaire's translation of Poe, and commented on Wagner's achievement in renewing in his lyrical dramas the ancient aesthetic truths. One wonders whether Mallarmé's fine text on Villiers was known to the lecturer. Every aspect of Villiers was considered: his style, his powerful phrasing and his use of learned words. The phrase of Maître Jacques in

[1] Paul Valéry, letters to Gide (octobre–novembre 1891), *Correspondance Gide–Valéry*, 132, 138.
[2] Berne–Joffroy, *Présence de Valéry*, 68.

'Axel' served as a conclusion. 'Sublimate yourself, rise, gather up, grow, become your own flower.'[1]

In an amusing letter to his elder brother then in Paris, Paul described his impressions of this his first lecture:

> At last this lecture is over. Just imagine, I was still writing at half-past seven. I went off with it unfinished. I arrive. The hall is full. The Bonnets, the Gides, Tebars, Auriol Barral are all there. I begin: tremolo for five minutes then my delivery gains assurance, my voice booms—they tell me that it was a success. Lapouge's skull radiated with joy.
>
> I was, I still am, exhausted. Impossible to sleep, my back aches. The best of it is that towards the end I was obliged to improvise completely. I related the death of Villiers. I dwelt on each syllable while searching for words—funereal silences prolonged my reticence in the mind of the spectators—effect of emotion! Some of them were thrilled.
>
> Ladies were there in great numbers—one went to sleep! . . . Compliments and congratulations followed. . . . On the stairs I might have been at a memorial service having to shake all the passing hands.[2]

Throughout the spring and summer months of 1892, Valéry reported to Gide the progress of his various occupations. In March he begged for news of Mallarmé and complained that neither Louÿs nor Gide wrote to him often enough. The study of law depressed him for he could not give himself entirely to either reading or writing. However he was deep in Poe's *Eureka*, and Rimbaud's *Illuminations*. He had also read *King Lear*, which he found 'a bit better than the famous Maeterlinck, the pure triumph of all literature.'

Narcissus, he reported, had written another letter that was hidden away in a drawer. A month later he declared that he was tired of *cette histoire* and that being in love had made him spoil a poem:

> The Medusa has disappeared for the time being . . . at her future return I fear a certain fatal interview . . . which will take place at some Charity gathering or suchlike. I am quite capable of fainting or some physical stupidity, a thing that has just missed happening several times simply on meeting her in streets—that now terrify me. . . .[3]

[1] Mondor, *Premier Temps d'une amitié*. In February 1890, Mallarmé lectured on the same subject at 40 Rue Villejust. See Mondor, *Figaro littéraire*, 25 juin, 1955.

[2] Paul Valéry, letter to Jules Valéry (probably Feb. 3 or 4, 1892), in *Paul Valéry Vivant*, 259. By permission of M. Jean Ballard.

[3] Paul Valéry, letter to Gide (not dated), *Correspondance Gide–Valéry*, 159. By permission Librairie Gallimard.

At this time he was saddened by his mother's failing sight, he curtailed his walks so as to remain at hand, and he spoke of accompanying her to Paris at some future date. In May he sent a manuscript of ten poems to Pierre Louÿs; about the same time he also gave Gide another copy of the same poems which eventually became part of the *Vers Anciens*. Though he felt throughout the months prior to his examination that he was obliged to be nothing but a stupid student, he could not altogether suppress the thoughts that crowded his mind on reading in his leisure moments the works of Poe. 'I have imagined a strange theory of mathematics,' he wrote to Gide, and went on to speak of his uncertainty about the future: 'perhaps I shall go to Italy . . . or perhaps Paris to look for a job of scratching on official paper—*vivre selon l'absurde*.' He was not altogether pleased when he heard in June that Louÿs had shown Mallarmé the ten poems. Gide had also been present, and Valéry wondered why neither of his friends had told him 'textuellement le précieux et pur éreintement dû par le Maître.' Louÿs had said nothing and Gide had only spoken vaguely. Probably they had agreed not to worry him before his law examinations, for it was only at the end of July that Gide reported Mallarmé to have said: 'I am astonished, that with his talent and the knowledge of verse he sometimes shows, that he leaves here and there lines which seem to me facile.' The day after his 'finals' Valéry replied, 'Mallarmé's remark astonishes me a bit—above all because it is isolated. What he says is true but I would have liked a criticism that went nearer the bone.'[1]

A period of repose, and time to clarify many problems, seemed now essential. This last criticism, coming from Mallarmé, had the effect of increasing Valéry's disgust at the idea of writing occasional verse. He was convinced that sooner or later he must take some drastic step—but how to do so, or in what such action would consist, he had not yet decided. Added to this there was the other problem of earning his living, which was more or less to thwart him all his life.

[1] Paul Valéry, letter to Gide (juillet 1892), *Correspondance Gide–Valéry*, 167, 168.

8. THE CRISIS AT GENOA

Un homme qui renonce au monde se met dans la
condition de le comprendre

(P. V. ON MALLARMÉ)

Valéry was now twenty-one; he had passed his finals in law and was sure that he did not want to make a career in that profession, nor did he wish to become a professional writer. What he really wanted was to develop in his own way, and this required time. He has given us some indications as to his state of mind. He believed in thought, and he suffered from 'being and not being'; sometimes he felt that he had infinite powers, which, however, when faced by problems, tended to evaporate, and this 'weakness of his actual strength' often led him to despair.

> I was sombre, frivolous, easy-going in appearance [he recorded], fundamentally tough, extreme in scorn, absolute in admiration, easy to impress and impossible to convince. However, I had faith in some of my ideas, and because they suited me, and appeared clear to me, I considered them invincible. I kept these shades of thought like secrets of state. I was ashamed of their strangeness, I feared that after all they might be absurd. For when considered by themselves they were worthless, but at the same time they were powerful because they gave me confidence. Thus jealously guarding this mystery of my weakness, I came to have a sort of strength.[1]

He did not wish to write verses, or to read, but to work out his own intellectual problems. Neither poets nor philosophers elucidated any of the difficulties that tormented him. He felt that philosophy never communicated any real power, and that it was useless to speculate on abstractions which had not first been defined. On the other hand mystics had brought no comfort to his inquiring mind. He had studied them sufficiently to discover that 'one finds in Mysticism just what one brings to it.' As for religion, it was the dramatic perfection of its ceremony that he venerated.

A letter to Gide, written from Genoa on September 5 of this year, gives some idea of the nature and climate of Valéry's thought. Speaking of the need of mental discipline he wrote: 'At each moment millions of electric reactions, sad and pure, sublimate one and sum one up to a

---

[1] Paul Valéry, 'Au sujet d'*Eureka*,' *Variété*, I (Paris: Gallimard, 1924), 115.

geometrical point, void and solitary, where one is, absolutely and as if for ever, one's only and single confidant. I am now master of certain aesthetics—supreme—naturally!' he adds ironically. And then cautiously: 'I will say no more of this for fear of *mille erreurs écrites*.'[1]

The source of these new ideas was Poe's *Eureka*, in Baudelaire's translation. Perhaps also Rimbaud's insistence on the poet as 'seer' may have been encouraging, but hardly more. Poe alone had formulated certain problems, and had declared that the artist's intuition could lead to the most subtle conclusions which hitherto had been demonstrated only by mathematics. It remained, said Poe, for a more profound analysis than the world had yet seen to investigate fully the highest possibilities of poetic consciousness, and he had suggested that 'abstract poetry' might even be constructed on mathematical foundations. This was to be Valéry's starting point.

Here was food for thought, temptingly presented, and acceptable to a young poet who wished to make the fullest use of all his potential powers. It appeared not only worth while but even urgent to attempt to raise one's consciousness to the highest possible abstraction by applying the exact principles of mathematics to thought, which in its nature was unstable; to govern intuitive awareness, and to construct oneself through a disciplined system of thought. This was the field of investigation that Poe's cosmogony proposed. Henceforth poetry was to be replaced by this research.

In his 'Philosophy of Composition' (translated by Baudelaire under the title of 'La Genèse d'un poème'), Poe had treated the art of literature as a psychological problem to be approached through strict analysis and in which the effects were deliberately produced by logical and mechanical means. The problem for him was largely a question of the contacts created between the author and his readers. Valéry, interested in the theory rather than its concrete uses, carried the whole question much further. Given that a thoughtful reader can grasp an image, Valéry's ultimate problem was to deal with the transposition of pure thought into a possible sequence of comprehensible figures, and to unite such figures into a significant whole. However the time was not yet ripe for this. At the moment he was set on applying 'system' to his personal difficulties, and to self-development. It was therefore no exaggeration when he said: 'two or three statements of Edgar Poe's gave me the capital sensation which woke the being of desire, the demon which possessed me.' If, as Baudelaire had done, he

<hr>

[1] Paul Valéry, letter to Gide, *Correspondance Gide–Valéry*, 171.

in turn read into Poe's aesthetic doctrine all that he wished to develop in himself, it was because he had found there the germ of contemporary and modern thought,[1] as well as a possible way of dealing with his own dilemma.

Disappointed with his early poems, Valéry felt that he had not dominated his art, but that was only a part of his problem. His most profound need was for a new intellectual basis which would give him fresh power and, in doing so, would necessarily create its own expression through its own exigencies.

Most young poets have known something of this necessity which gives new significance to words. For words can express only the sensation or thought which lies behind them, and if poetry is to be other than occasional verse, there must be some singular urgency, some waking of intellectual sensibility combined with the continuity of an intuitive necessity. Passages, in which Valéry speaks of Mallarmé, throw light on this truth, and on Valéry's point of view.

> He imperiously obliged the reader to accept a whole system of thought applied to poetry—controlled, worked on and endlessly revised—as an essentially infinite study of which the works produced, or possible to produce, could only be fragments, experiments and preparatory studies.

Again speaking of Mallarmé:

> A man who measures himself against himself and remakes himself according to his lights, seems to me to be a superior achievement that moves me more than any other. The first effort of humanity is that of changing their disorder into order, and chance into power. That is the true marvel. I like a man to be hard on his own genius. If he does not know how to turn against himself, his 'genius' in my eyes, is nothing more than virtuosity, natural but unequal and unstable.[2]

Those who have too rashly dismissed Valéry as a nihilist might do well to consider this stimulating point of view.

To create order from disorder, how could this be achieved? Again it was Poe who, through his conception of psychological and intellectual system in poetry, pointed the way in linking up the idea of art with that of intellectual and psychological methods. To study the

---

[1] Many years later Valéry remarked that Poe's generalised relativity was a forerunner of Einstein's relativity, for a formal symmetry of which Poe speaks is the essential characteristic of the presentation of Einstein's universe. See Valéry, 'Eureka', Variété, I, 122.

[2] Valéry, 'Je disais à Stéphane Mallarmé,' Variété, III, 22.

43

consciousness of oneself, for oneself, and thus through the power of organised thought to create a new self in a second consciousness, was to become Valéry's major preoccupation. This gradually led him to the conception of a universal transformation of all human activities in the domain of thought and art. If in the process the means became an end in themselves, this would be quite in accordance with his culture. For it seemed to him that to know how to create, in itself a true act of creation, was infinitely more important than to create what he described as *fables*, to which category all second-hand or inherited beliefs, all fiction and almost all poetry were scornfully assigned. In fact, these considerations led him to make a deliberate break with poetry. That this rupture should have been the result of an enthusiastic admiration for another poet's doctrines, furnishes a curious paradox.

Valéry had been at Genoa during the summer, and then went to Paris, probably with the idea of looking for some employment. While he was in Paris the most painful incident in the last phase of his imaginative and all-absorbing passion for 'la Catalane' took place, if we may rely on a letter to Pierre Louÿs, written some time later, in which Valéry said:

> I begin by reminding you that the whole of my intellectual life is dominated by the climax of November 1892. Having just returned to Paris to settle there, I was victim of a coincidence which was the strongest of all those that had reduced me to absurdity during the years 1891 and 1892, and finally drove me to flight. This was a dangerous moment. I imposed on myself a sort of severity—a rigorous discipline to save myself from the jaws of stupidity which takes the form of very successful experiments on the inevitability of the improbable.[1]

Strangely enough neither the climax nor its immediate cause were mentioned in Valéry's letters to Gide. Yet he wrote from Genoa at the end of October, and again on November 9, explaining that he was waiting there for a German doctor to examine his mother's eyes; and he remarked that he had seen fine things without being particularly impressed by them. It was only later that he spoke of the resolutions which he felt obliged to impose on himself: 'I was obliged to take very serious action against idols in general . . . and one in particular which obsessed me making life almost unbearable. . . . This crisis made me oppose my sensibility in so far as it encroached on the liberty of my

[1] Paul Valéry, letter to P. Louÿs, cited by Mondor, *Les Premiers Temps d'une amitié*, 157. For further details of Valéry's love affair, see letters to Gide quoted by Mondor, *ibid*.

mind.'[1] Though this was written years later it rings true, and we know from *La Jeune Parque* and many prose sources the importance that Valéry attached to this crisis. If at the time he did not confide in his friends it was because henceforth the new-born 'Self' became, as he had said, his 'only and single confidant.'[2]

It was during a night of storm that raged over the town of Genoa that Valéry, sitting on his bed in a small room from the window of which only the sky was visible, took his final decision to renounce all idols except that of the intellect. These storms on the Mediterranean coast, which often last throughout a night, have a dramatic intensity impossible to ignore. The whole sky is charged with the passion of a terrible battle, as if the gods were at war, and man, who trembles and watches, feels as if he were the object of this fierce struggle. It might well appear that the force of Intelligence warred against the force of Voluptuousness for the mind of a being whose inquiries reached towards the truths of their universe. This time Intelligence won.

Henceforth all those intimate desires, all the torments that threatened to overwhelm Valéry's inner life, were to be abolished. All ideas of a facile literary career were also to be abandoned. Now as he looked back on the spiritual conflict that had lasted throughout 1891 until 1892, his being seemed suddenly to be illuminated, his mind realised its pure aims. His life was to be subjected to rigid laws through whose discipline he would arm himself against a sensibility which had threatened to usurp his intellectual powers. His existence was to be focused on systematic meditation and interior research, consecrated to abstract problems.

This mental *coup d'état*, in which Valéry's intelligence projected the scheme of its future activities, is not to be confused with conversions in the order of faith. A similar crisis had played its part in Descartes' development and makes a striking analogy with Valéry's experience. Descartes throughout a night of visions and questioning had prayed for 'a method which would safely lead his reason towards belief and fundamental confidence in himself'—a prayer which might well have been repeated by Valéry who commented on it thus: 'I know nothing more truly poetic, than this extraordinary modulation which leads a mind to survey in the space of a few hours the unknown degrees of all

[1] Valéry, 'Propos me concernant,' *Présence de Valéry*, 12. Berne–Joffroy, 'Valéry présent,' *Présence de Valéry*, dates the crisis August 1892.

[2] See Octave Nadal, 'Paul Valéry et l'événement de 1892,' *Mercure de France* (avril 1955), 614–26, for further discussion.

its nervous and spiritual force.'[1] Such words are exactly applicable to his own experience. And like Descartes, he was to develop his consciousness for the ends of knowledge. Intellect was to be his only idol, and Monsieur Teste was to be created as its high priest.

This same autumn Valéry moved to Paris with the idea of definitely settling there.

9. EARLY POEMS

De la musique avant toute chose   (VERLAINE)

Although the *Album de vers anciens* was not published until 1920, it contained most of the early poems written before 1892, the year of Valéry's intellectual crisis. Many of them, however, had been rigorously revised before appearing in the first collected edition.[2] In the editor's note to this slim volume, Valéry said that almost all the poems had been printed between 1890 and 1893 in the following reviews: *La Conque, Le Centaure, La Syrinx, L'Ermitage* and *La Plume*; and that two unfinished poems and the prose 'L'Amateur de poèmes' had not been previously printed. The two poems referred to as being unfinished in 1899 are 'Profusion du soir: Poème abandonné' and 'Anne.' In editing this collection of his early verses Valéry said of them, 'these poems had led their author to a sincere and lasting aversion to poetry.' There were in all sixteen poems and 'L'Amateur de poèmes' in the first edition. In later issues (1932–42) there are twenty poems and 'L'Amateur'; the four pieces added are: 'Orphée,' 'Même Féerie,' 'César,' 'Les Vaines Danseuses.' Valéry sent a copy of the 1920 edition to Marcel Proust with an inscription 'Du côté de chez Mallarmé etc.'; it was found after Proust's death with most of the pages still uncut.

A manuscript copy, a sketch for the future '*Album*,' was given to Gide in 1892. This was written in an exercise book, and decorated by Valéry. On the cover he had printed 'P. A. VALÉRY. SES VERS.' 'There are,' says Professor Mondor, 'ten poems in this precious cahier':[3]

---

[1] Paul Valéry, 'Une Vue de Descartes,' *Les Pages immortelles de Descartes choisies et expliquées par P. V.* (Paris: Corréa, 1941), 18.

[2] Paul Valéry, *Album de vers anciens* (Paris: Cahiers des Amis des livres, 1920).

[3] Mondor, *Les Premiers Temps d'une amitié*, 94.

'Arion' (not printed in published editions), 'Les Vaines Danseuses,' 'Épisode,' 'Le Bois amical,' 'Intermède' (not in published edition), 'Hélène,' 'Orphée,' 'La Fileuse,' 'Ballet' (never published), and 'Baignée.' Those which were published underwent considerable changes and some were almost entirely rewritten. In May 1892 a manuscript copy of poems, presumably the same as those sent to Gide, was given to Pierre Louÿs. Unfortunately this has been lost. It must have been this collection that Louÿs showed to Mallarmé (July 1892) and that Valéry called 'an unsatisfactory collection, studies that do not exist as a harmonious whole.'

In those early poems Valéry was still feeling his way, using all that he had absorbed from Parnassian technique; his mature conception of poetry had not yet been formulated. Although in his 'Paradoxe sur l'architecture' he had postulated a formal and pure art of poetry, as in architecture and music, the Intellectual Comedy still waited for its poet. Valéry had to devote many years to meditation on the possibilities of method, so as to constrain poetry and poetic sensibility to become the means of expressing intellectual thought; that is to say, he had not yet taken the position which was to give him a new approach to his art—through the conscious transformation of the Self, by which he became a creative poet.

Nevertheless the germ of his future poetry appears in his early work, though as yet scarcely free from the poetic conventions of the time. The influence of the Parnassians, particularly Heredia, and also that of Mallarmé, is apparent in both the vocabulary and the form of the early poems. Tears are 'vain,' azur 'mortal,' and weeping 'eternal.' Other images, used with great subtlety in Mallarmé's very personal orchestration, when repeated lose much of their charm. But we must not too severely reproach Valéry for his 'silken swans,' 'august trophies' and 'fatal diamonds.' All young poets have known similar temptations, which their maturity condemns. And together with such mannerisms there are irresistible harmonies in Valéry's early verses, often combined with a deliberately intellectual symbolism, which foretell the future poetry of *Charmes*.

What is of consequence here is that, behind the literary images and echoes, there is the constant presence of sea and sky, that wide horizon before which the poet shows lucid observation, and with which he so evidently communicates. This is the essential, the poet's birthright which differentiates him from other men, and it is this that gives his early poems vigorous life. His Venus rises from the sea's immensity to run on the wide shore; his heroes stand against the vast sky; his windows open on the twilit seaport in the changing shadows of sunset.[1]

'La Fileuse,' the first poem in *L'Album de vers anciens*, appeared in *La Conque* in 1891 in a slightly different form from that of the manuscript copy sent to Gide; and in the first published edition of 1920, two tercets and one line are entirely transformed. As printed in the subsequent editions of *Vers Anciens*, the poem consists of eight verses in terza rima, and one single line after the last verse.

> Assise, la fileuse au bleu de la croisée
> Où le jardin mélodieux se dodeline;
> Le rouet ancien qui ronfle l'a grisée.

This is the first verse of this richly harmonised little poem that echoes the hum of the spinning wheel in delicately spun sound and sense. Throughout the verses the vowels and their attendant consonants are as carefully adjusted as the threads in a tapestry or as notes in a piece of music. The poem is almost overladen with assonance and alliteration, present in every line. The musical scheme is constructed on the harmonic values and interplay of *r*'s and *l*'s, accompanied by *f*'s and *d*'s—the *r*'s and the open vowels *ou, o* and *oi* for the *rouet* (the wheel), the *l*'s, *f*'s and the closed vowels *u*'s, *a*'s and *ai* for the *laine*.

The poet's virtuosity is already remarkable. Gide had reported that Heredia had read the poem to Regnier and had particularly praised the line 'Dédiant magnifique, au vieux rouet, sa rose,' but had criticised the epithet 'le salut vain' as nasal and flat, and suggested 'le salut clair' or 'bleu' as an alternative.[2] But though Valéry gave much thought to the work of revision, he did not change this line, 'Courbe le salut vain de sa grâce étoilée.' Certainly the elder Parnassians must have approved of the objective effect of the decisive image 'tout le ciel vert se meurt. Le dernier arbre brûle,' and also the chords of the last line, 'Au bleu de la croisée où tu filais la laine,' in which the image exists in its musical expression, with nothing superimposed.

The sonnet 'Hélène,' in spite of its virtuosity, is too obviously a literary exercise in the manner of Heredia to excite enthusiasm. The two first lines however suggest a wide horizon:

> Azur! C'est moi . . . Je viens des grottes de la mort
> Entendre l'onde se rompre aux degrés sonores.

---

[1] See, 'Profusion du soir,' *Vers anciens*, in *Poésies* (Paris: Gallimard, 1933), 45.
[2] André Gide, letter to Paul Valéry (Paris, 15 novembre 1891), *Correspondance Gide–Valéry*, 136. By permission Librairie Gallimard.

Echoes of Rimbaud and others follow and we understand Valéry's dissatisfaction with much of this early work, for he had a valuable gift of self-criticism. 'You know that I am a fourth-rate poet and paved with good intentions,' he wrote to Gide.

The sonnet 'Orphée' is much changed from the version I have quoted, only the ninth and the final line being retained. After the literary inspiration of the first sonnets, 'La Naissance de Vénus' gives a welcome breath of sea air:

> Le frais gravier, qu'arrose et fuit sa course agile,
> Croule, creuse rumeur de soif, et le facile
> Sable a bu les baisers de ses bonds puérils.

A real girl runs along the shore and the freshness of observation gives this sonnet its vitality. The baroque 'Féerie' which follows is indeed fairyland with its 'tissu d'argent,' 'cygnes soyeux,' 'échos de cristal' and 'diamant fatal.' Even if we are reminded of the paste and scissors of pantomime scenery, we must at least admit that the verses are contained in their own delicate music, and the last verse is compelling:

> La chair confuse des molles roses commence
> A frémir, si d'un cri le diamant fatal
> Fêle d'un fil de jour toute la fable immense.

In spite of some good lines there seems little of new interest in the sonnets which follow. 'Baignée' embarrasses us by its echo of Mallarmé's idiom, and 'Au bois dormant' and 'César' are little more than period pieces, and might have been included in Heredia's *Trophées.* One image however is memorable:

> Heureux là-bas sur l'onde, et bercé du hasard,
> Un pêcheur indolent qui flotte et chante. . . .

It is not until we turn the page to 'Le Bois amical' that we seem to hear Valéry's authentic voice. This is the first subjective piece, if we take the poems in the order in which they appear in the *Album.* There is a perfect balance of sound and sense in its lyrical simplicity. Written for André Gide, it might also be considered as the earliest of the poems symbolising the pure Self—in the 'cher compagnon de silence,' and its poetic sensibility places it with the lyrics of Charmes.

> Et là-haut, dans la lumière immense,
> Nous nous sommes trouvés en pleurant
> O mon cher compagnon de silence!

49

Even if Valéry had written nothing else, future generations would have admired him for this poem.

In 'Les Vaines Danseuses' the sonnet form is discarded for rhymed couplets. The line 'Comme un pâle trésor d'éternelle rosée'[1] relentlessly reminds us of Mallarmé's early poems, and 'Mélodieuses fuir dans le bois éclairci' seems a transposed echo of the music of Mallarmé's 'Victorieusement fui le suicide beau,' setting aside the completely different content. This poem is too evidently an exercise and explains the dissatisfaction which the poet expresses in 'Un Feu distinct,' a poem that states his intellectual position, and has an autobiographical interest. We feel its sincerity, and it seems to indicate that, after the first ardour of musical creation, if poetry is deliberate it must all the same be nourished from authentic forces within the poet's mind. This necessity is expressed in the following lines from the first verse:

> Un feu distinct m'habite, et je vois froidement
> La violente vie illuminée entière . . .
> Je ne puis plus aimer seulement qu'en dormant
> Ses actes gracieux mélangés de lumière.

The last lines of the poem are characteristic:

> Comme à la vide conque un murmure de mer,
> Le doute,—sur le bord d'une extrême merveille,
> Si je suis, si je fus, si je dors ou je veille?

The theme of Narcissus forms a link between the early and later poems, Valéry constantly returned to it as admirably suited to symbolise the motif of the Self on which almost all his poetry of the second period was based. The first mention of the Narcissus poem is in a letter to Pierre Louÿs, September 1890, some months before Valéry had met Gide. 'I was still working yesterday,' he wrote, 'on a very difficult sonnet called "Narcisse parle." I have abandoned it in despair of ever putting all that I wanted into it.' This irregular sonnet, as we have seen, was the origin of all the successive Narcissus poems. Only the first four lines were used in the 'Narcisse parle' of the *Vers anciens*. The version sent to Mallarmé was that which Valéry later regarded as 'the first state of the poem.' Nothing better illustrates the amount of thought and care that Valéry gave to his poetry than the different drafts of the Narcissus poems, culminating in the 'Fragments du

---

[1] 'L'antique rosée' in versions prior to 1942.

Narcisse' in *Charmes*, to which we shall return. One of the chief interests in these early texts is that they are the first symbolic expression of the idea of knowledge of consciousness which dominates the later poems. Here it is still overcharged with musical effects, but shows that Valéry at the age of twenty was already turning towards that intellectual centralisation which he demonstrated a few years later in his 'Méthode de Léonard de Vince.'

'Épisode' is a musical fragment describing a nymph bathing, and may well have been suggested by a *chose vue*; the first image was repeated in *La Jeune Parque*, where 'Un soir favorisé de colombes sublimes' became 'Ressusciter un soir favori des colombes.'[1]

The short lyric 'Vue' evidently belongs to a slightly later date: words are used with greater precision, the reader is joyfully reminded of bathing on the Mediterranean coast. Both 'Valvins' and 'Été' are also of a later date. Valéry did not become familiar with 'La fluide yole à jamais littéraire,' which Mallarmé sailed on the Seine at Valvins, till sometime after his move to Paris in 1892. We know from André Fontainas that the first version of 'Été' was not finished till 1896, Valéry having arrived one morning, in Paris, to ask his help, or rather his moral support, in filling up the blank spaces.[2] The six additional verses in the edition of 1942 do not add much to this sea-poem, which opens with the warm block of sea air:

> Été, roche d'air pur, et toi ruche
> O mer!

Both 'Vue' and 'Été' were published in *Le Centaure* in 1896.

'Profusion du soir: Poème abandonné,' a sea-piece evoking a port in the evening light, is the sort of poem that a critic might describe as promising. It is Valéry's farewell to his youthful poetry, to the 'passé précieux' of his happy life on the port of Sète:

> Adieu, Adieu! . . . Vers vous, ô mes belles images,
> Mes bras tendent toujours l'insatiable port! . . .
> Et ce grand port n'est plus qu'un noir débarcadère.

In 'Anne' there is a vaguely Baudelairian atmosphere. But the poem is sensual without Baudelaire's redeeming passion; and the last line seems to echo Rimbaud. The same motif of a sleeping girl is treated in

---

[1] Paul Valéry, *La Jeune Parque*, in *Poésies* (1933) line 186.
[2] André Fontainas, 'Jeunesse de Valéry,' *Paul Valéry vivant*, 71. By permission of M. Jean Ballard.

a more abstract manner in 'La Dormeuse' of *Charmes*, where it has a symbolic sense.

The last poem in *Vers anciens* is 'Air de Sémiramis.' It was included in the first edition of *Charmes*, that is in the collection of lyrics belonging to the second poetic period, but its air of grand opera seems to place it about 1892, when Valéry was much under the influence of Wagner. Doubtless it was revised, for certain lines, such as those on sleep, seem to belong to a later date:

> Je réponds! Je surgis de ma profonde absence!
> Mon cœur m'arrache aux morts que frôlait mon sommeil.

Here too there are autobiographical glimpses of Valéry's problems: as the warrior queen wakes at dawn, so the poet wakes to the idea of poetry:

> Existe! Sois enfin toi-même! dit l'aurore.

Nourished by a lyrical force, which saves the 26 verses from monotony, the constant use of exclamations seems to suggest an operatic libretto:

> Ose l'abîme! Passe un dernier pont de roses!
> Je t'approche, péril! Orgueil plus irrité!
> Ces fourmis sont à moi! Ces villes sont mes choses,
> Ces chemins sont les traits de mon autorité! . . .

After the rather Hugoesque grandeur of such musical waves, it is almost with relief that we enter the calm port of 'L'Amateur de poèmes,' a prose tête-à-tête with the poet. Here in five paragraphs, he reveals his method of thought. In the third of these he tells us one of the essential secrets of his future poetics.

> A poem is a duration, reader, throughout which I breathe a law which has been prepared; I give my breath and the organ of my voice; or only their power which becomes reconciled with silence.

Of language and metre he says:

> I abandon myself to the adorable habit of reading, and living where words lead me. . . . I feel each word in all its force, through having waited indefinitely for it . . .

The whole page is a manifesto of the rights of intellect on poetry.

We may sum up the *Vers anciens* as a whole by calling them contemporary, that is to say similar in execution to the works of Valéry's contemporaries, whom in fact he often surpasses in their own characteristic virtues. This explains the immediate success of his early work with the poets and authors whose acknowledged ideals he fulfilled. It also shows why he soon became displeased with much that was considered adequate and admirable by his fellow poets, whose poetic ideals left his analytical and intellectual powers dissatisfied and in fact not fully employed. As a final judgement on *L'Album de vers anciens* we may borrow a phrase used by its author many years later in discussing modern verse, and say that it lacks real and intimate tears.

II

Valéry and Mallarmé

I. POETRY IN PARIS

Une ville où la vie verbale est plus puissante, plus diverse, plus active et capricieuse qu'en toute autre. (P. V.)

INTO THE WORLD of literary Paris with its agitations and competition, its enthusiasms and denials, Valéry was now to enter. Standing aloof from the complex mobility of opinion, he was content to observe, while beneath a discreet and smiling manner he cultivated the secret virtue of attentive thought.

On his arrival in the autumn of 1892 he stayed first at a *pension de famille* in the Rue Gay-Lussac, and moved later to the Hôtel de l'Elysée in the Rue de Beaune, where Chateaubriand had at one time lived. The little room in Rue Gay-Lussac has often been described. It had something of the severity of a monk's cell and was certainly emblematic of Valéry's state of mind. The walls were hung with white sheets, and the only decoration was a photograph of the skeleton by Ligier-Richier. The most imposing piece of furniture was a blackboard on which mathematical problems were to be worked out.

This was the beginning of a period of asceticism which found expression in *L'Introduction à la méthode de Léonard de Vince* and in *Monsieur Teste*. To understand Valéry's development we must realise the importance of his decision to give up all idea of a literary career and to renounce all worldly ambition in spite of his early success. Writing to Gide a year later (July 1893), he said that it would

54

be an error to suppose that he was looking for a new type of literature within the renouncements and limitations which he professed. His enthusiasm for mathematics was of considerable consequence and he now devoted much of his time to the study of mathematical and scientific methods. This was not with any idea of becoming a mathematician or scientist, for he had no special aptitude for invention in those sciences and confessed that at school a page of algebra or geometry absolutely paralysed his brain. What he wanted to do, he said, 'was to take from the well-made language of mathematics certain "syntactics" [syntactic forms]' which would be useful in constructing a precise inner language through which he hoped to systematise his thought in order to increase his self-knowledge and intellectual power. In this state of mind he set himself to study the methods of such scientists as Newton, Laplace and Kelvin, whose names had been revealed to him in Poe's *Eureka,* and now, starting from Poe's concepts, he turned to organise his own intimate universe.

'When I began to frequent Mallarmé,' he said many years later, 'literature no longer meant much to me. Reading and writing bored me—and I confess that I still feel something of this boredom. The consciousness of my *Self* for itself, and the anxiety to define clearly my own existence hardly ever left me.'[1] This is his statement of the problem on which, at the age of twenty-two, he had decided to concentrate his intellectual life. It is a problem he never abandoned, to which he refers in all his works from *Monsieur Teste* to *Mon Faust,* and which is also the theme of *La Jeune Parque.*

Nothing would have pleased Valéry better than to devote the whole of his time to such research; but there were material considerations to be dealt with. He felt a moral obligation to earn his living. His rare works published during this period were almost always commissioned, which helped towards this end, while with considerable anxiety he looked round in Paris for some regular employment. This accounts for the various missions which he undertook. Thus in 1894 he went to London and returned there in 1896 to work for a time in the editorial department in the office of the chartered company of Cecil Rhodes.[2]

During the visit of 1894, he met William Henley—of impressive appearance and reassuring bursts of laughter. Commissioned by Henley, Valéry wrote, while staying in a small room in Russell Square,

[1] Paul Valéry, 'Dernière Visite à Mallarmé,' *Variété,* II (Paris: Gallimard, 1929), 203.
[2] Frédéric Lefèvre, *Entretiens avec Paul Valéry* (Paris: Flammarion, 1926), 12.

'Une Conquête méthodique,' which appeared in the *New Review* in 1895 and was intended to form a philosophical conclusion to a series of articles showing the commercial penetration of German goods into England. In this essay, as in all his future prose, Valéry based his arguments on one of his own problems, that of method, to which I shall return later.

It was Marcel Schwob who gave Valéry an introduction to George Meredith, saying, 'Unfortunately his cooking is English, but he has good French wine.' Dining with Meredith at Flint Cottage, 'below the green billard-table of Boxhill,' Valéry was impressed by his host's devotion to France. Among other subjects they discussed Napoleon, Meredith declaring that the gods turned Napoleon against himself in despair of ever finishing him off by their own energies.[1] In a letter to Schwob, Valéry regrets that he did not know Meredith better; if only the physical disadvantages of an ear-trumpet and a drawling voice had not made their intercourse so difficult. In this letter he refers to Schwob's novel *Monelle*, which he reviewed in his rubric on 'Methods' in the *Mercure de France* (1897), and the letter ends with a graceful acknowledgement of Schwob's 'sincere and lucid encouragement.'

Yet despite these various occupations, and his own almost esoteric researches, Valéry had time to observe the climate of literary Paris, of which he gave a delicately ironical picture in describing a journey there. 'Every one of the Parisian population,' he tells us, 'wishes to be unique and to do what no one has ever done or will ever do.' Each one lives for nothing but to have and to keep the illusion of being the only one, 'for superiority is only a solitude at the actual limit of the species.' So each founds his existence on the non-existence of the others from whom he must 'extort their consent not to exist.' As Valéry speeds towards Paris spiritual events pass rapidly before his mind; disgust and even despair are mingled in his brain as he contemplates with 'terrible curiosity the imaginary drama of the immense activity that one calls "intellectual." ' And he adds, 'Nothing attracts me but clarity! Alas, I hardly ever find it.'[2]

These conclusions, however, did not prevent him from frequenting literary circles and enjoying the company of literary men, among whom he made numerous friends. Chief of these was J. K. Huysmans, with whose work Valéry had been long familiar, and for whom he always kept a sincere admiration. Huysmans owed to Mallarmé much

[1] Frédéric Lefèvre, *Entretiens avec Paul Valéry*, 17.
[2] Paul Valéry, 'Lettre à un ami,' *Monsieur Teste* (Paris: Gallimard, 1929), 73.

of the material of *A Rebours*, a work that Valéry had considered as his Bible. This opinion was not shared by Pierre Louÿs, who said of Huysmans, 'he talks of sacred things in the tone of a journalist. . . . We need something better, higher, more intense.'

This was the period between *Là-Bas* and *La Cathédrale*, and Huysmans, now aged about forty, had not yet turned to the consolations of religion. Valéry describes him as having a large round skull bristling with short grey hair, an immense brow above a strangely twisted snub nose, shaggy eyebrows arched demoniacally, and a disillusioned mouth 'from one corner of which, under a thick moustache, came bitter or comic statements, hasty and atrocious judgements, extreme disgusts.' He welcomed all that was worst in humanity, with a thirst for the excessive. But he was clean-handed and as generous as a man almost poverty-stricken could be. As for his style, 'it lived on his nerves. His language was always unexpected, pushed to the extreme, overcrowded with perverted adjectives living beyond their means.'

It was perhaps the singularities of Huysmans' art that made him a powerful influence for many of the younger generation; but, as Valéry points out, he also had the merit of reflecting the contemporary reactions to religion and the anxious spirit of the time. Although there could scarcely have been a greater contrast to Valéry's habit of positive thought than this unbelievably credulous author, it did not prevent them from enjoying each other's company. Valéry recorded that he would call about five o'clock at the office of the Sûreté Générale in Rue des Saussaies, where Huysmans worked, and together they would stroll to his flat in Rue de Sèvres, discussing 'all sorts of questions from God and the devil to art and women.'[1]

Another poet whom Valéry frequented was José-Marie de Heredia, 'à la voix farouche et vibrante', author of *Les Trophées*—classical sonnets which had been collected in a single volume in 1891, and had placed him as the leader of the Parnassians. At the time of Valéry's arrival in Paris, Heredia was an important social figure. He welcomed to his Saturdays, in his large and sunlit rooms in the Rue Balzac, not only established writers but all those who needed help, and particularly the younger poets, to whom he was always ready to give the formula for making a good poem, if only they would listen to him. To these gatherings came Pierre Louÿs and André Gide, and now Paul Valéry, listening attentively to the generous encouragement of his host who

[1] Paul Valéry, 'Souvenir de J. K. Huysmans,' *Variété*, I (Paris: Gallimard, 1924), 235.

thought it was a pity that so young a poet should have given up writing verse. Doubtless Heredia felt this all the more since Valéry knew so many of the *Trophées* by heart, and also, astonishingly, all the technical secrets of their perfect structure.

At this time Heredia, together with Catulle Mendès, François Coppée and Léon Dierx, still carried on the Parnassian movement, of which Théophile Gautier, *un romantique à demi-corrigé*, had been the initiator, with his *Émaux et Camées*, as early as 1852. Another powerful factor in the creation of the movement had been the poems of Leconte de Lisle. He had perhaps been influenced by the Hugo of *Les Orientales*. His *Poèmes antiques*, evoking classical themes, had added new poetic material and had even created a fresh aspect of Hellenism. A new light, the burning sunlight of the Midi, had appeared in his poems. If his scenes lacked fantasy, if, as Valéry said, the unicorn and the 'simorg' were missing from his bestiary,[1] we may nevertheless admire the direct observation in his 'éléphants rugueux, voyageurs lents et rudes' and also 'le songe intérieur qu'ils n'achèvent jamais' of his dreamy-eyed oxen.

'No one will make better verses than we do,' Leconte de Lisle had boasted to his disciple Heredia. And this acceptance of perfect verse without any new technical ideas was both the strength and the limitation of the Parnassians. There was something static and artificial in the pseudo-classical sculpture of their verse which led to the pose of art for art's sake. Yet the movement had been an efficacious and natural enough revolt against the loose and formless alexandrines and the general sentimental decrepitude into which the late Romantics had fallen. It was, said Remy de Gourmont,[2] almost a 'movement de pudeur' against the 'pseudo Musset et George Sand' atmosphere in which theatre audiences and others languished. There is no doubt that the Parnassian objectivity and return to classical subjects had been signs of healthy regeneration in the life of poetry. But the Parnassians were now on the decline. Leconte de Lisle was no longer their leader; his disdainful criticism of Symbolism had degenerated into grunts and groans, and he was to die in 1893.

Rimbaud, who had died in 1891, was for the moment curiously neglected. Those, who were to discover much later how deeply they had been influenced by him when they were young, were apparently

---

[1] Paul Valéry, letter to P. Louÿs, *Lettres à quelques-uns* (Paris: Gallimard, 1952), 33.
[2] Remy de Gourmont, *Promenades littéraires* (Paris, 1913), 53.

indifferent to his death. *Les Illuminations*, which had first appeared in *La Vogue* (numbers 5 to 9) in 1886, was now published as a brochure, but during the first few weeks after its appearance, it was bought by only one reader—Paul Bourget.[1]

It was towards Verlaine and Mallarmé, the first as leader of the *Décadents*, the second as the creator of *Symbolisme*, that the younger generation of poets *à l'oreille très fine* now turned.

Valéry has described how, during his first years in Paris, he used to see almost daily near the Luxembourg gardens, two very different figures, each going at mid-day to lunch: Henri Poincaré,[2] in long coat and top hat, absorbed in some calculation vaguely punctuated by movements of his umbrella on the wall; and Verlaine going in the other direction. 'Je m'amusais de ces passages au méridien d'astres si dissemblables,' he recorded, and the idea occurred to him of approaching Verlaine, who certainly would not have stood on ceremony. However, an intuitive and obscure resistance kept him from talking to the strange city-faun, a lamentable figure whose eyes blazed beneath bristling eyebrows, who passed by leaning on the arm of some Bacchante, gesturing with his stick, in the midst of a motley group scuffling along in wooden shoes to a neighbouring café.[3]

Verlaine had been the first to react against the frozen perfection of the Parnassians. Together he and Arthur Rimbaud had brought fresh intimacy and freedom into lyrical verse. Less of a visionary than Rimbaud, Verlaine was penetratingly concerned with life and human misery. His sensibility ruled his life and his poetry. He prepared the way for Guillaume Apollinaire, Éluard and many others. Religious and satanic, he mingled in an intimate symbolism an innocent perversity and a poetic Catholicism, expressed in delicately confidential undertones,

> Car nous voulons la nuance encore
> . . . Pas la couleur, rien que la nuance
> Et tout le reste est littérature.[4]

[1] Reported by Gustave Kahn from the publisher Stock. See also Henri Mondor, *Vie de Mallarmé* (Paris: Gallimard, 1941), 691, note 2.

[2] Valéry did not know Henri Poincaré personally (Poincaré died in 1912). He often consulted his works, and spent two hours with Raymond Poincaré—Henri's cousin—talking about him in April 1930. 'Notes chronologiques' in Paul Valéry, *Œuvres complètes* (Paris: Gallimard, 1956).

[3] Valéry, 'Passage de Verlaine,' *Variété*, II, 174.

[4] Paul Verlaine, *Fêtes galantes* (Paris, 1891).

This was a point of view that had certainly been ignored by the honourable company of Parnassian goldsmiths. Thus Verlaine and his followers in their return to free lyricism were labelled—for what labels are worth—the Décadents.

Although in one sense Verlaine's verse was decadent, its ease and musical perfection renewed the grace and freshness of song that French poetry had somehow lost or overlooked since the days of Ronsard's lyrical splendour. Verlaine had also shown a new intimacy with poetry, henceforth to be considered as the human companion, rather than the goddess, of the poet's heart; a mistress to be addressed informally in whispered regrets and sighs. This nineteenth-century poet echoed the religious sentiments of François Villon.

A more direct ancestor was of course Baudelaire, who is of immense weight in the assessment of all subsequent poets: *Les Fleurs du mal* had disclosed a new world of poetry wide enough to be cultivated by separate groups according to their own disposition and needs. Mallarmé on the one hand and Verlaine on the other were the direct heirs to this modern conception of poetic thought. But the sensitiveness to human misery, which had been foresung by Baudelaire, was accompanied in Verlaine's work by a quite personal tone and freedom in verse forms. He in his turn had opened a road on which many others were going further, and *vers libre* had already become acknowledged as a manner of poetic expression.

Technically as well as spiritually a new freedom was inevitably developing. If this did not amount to a revolution, poets such as Tristan Corbière, whose tone so many others have echoed, had nevertheless come out into the street in their shirt-sleeves and proclaimed their own laws. The first person to write in the unaccentuated and vaguely rhythmic free lines known as *vers libre* seems to have been a Polish lady, Marie Krysinka, living in Montmartre. However Jules Laforgue has more solid claims as leader of this mode, while Gustave Kahn, the translator of Walt Whitman's *Leaves of Grass*, was certainly the theoretician if not the originator of the movement.

'Each poet in his corner plays his own flute,' said Mallarmé in 1891; and this had been true of Jules Laforgue (1860–87), one of the first to publish *vers libre* in his *Moralités légendaires*. This Baudelairian *pierrot*, poet of sad suburban Sundays and the halting plaint of untuned pianos, used admirably the rhythm of everyday speech to express a state of disillusioned sensibility and the mood of the *crépuscule célibataire* which was later to become almost universal. Laforgue became, in his own phrase, 'la plus noble conquête,' not of a mistress—as he had hoped—but of a young American poet who adroitly used many of his most original images and phrases, which have indeed a general appeal, audacious or 'Simple et sans foi comme un bonjour.'

Thus in the last decade of the nineteenth century French poetry had two main currents: the Decadents who used *vers libre*, conversational rhythm and simple lyrical or broken metres to express their intimate sentiments in a gesture towards simplicity, not unlike that of the early Romantics;[1] and the Symbolists led by Mallarmé's intellectual and strictly musical poetry, which aimed at nothing less than 'l'explication orphique de la terre' as 'le jeu littéraire par excellence.' Different as were the methods, the masters who developed them were striving to express, each in his own way, the highest spiritual freedom of which humanity is capable.

As early as 1864 Mallarmé, then aged twenty-two, had stated that he intended 'to paint not *things* but the effect they produced,' and he added as an example of what he meant that it was not enough just to name precious stones as did the Parnassians; one should evoke their brilliance by suggestion. Expression was to be non-descriptive and non-rhetorical. He had been the first to speak of the 'symbol,' seeing in it 'a living and decorative synthesis without critical commentary.' Four points were of importance: *not* to use lyrical or romantic anecdote; to refuse to write vaguely or to 'write down' to one's public; to reject the closed art of the Parnassians; and to protest against the platitudes of the 'petits naturalistes.'

The appearance in 1872 of *L'Après-midi d'un faune* had shaken the foundations of the modern Parnassus, awaking enthusiasm in the minds of many younger men who henceforth upheld Mallarmé against all attacks. In 1886 Jean Moréas had made a statement which appeared in *Le Figaro*. Although it provoked a keen discussion, it seems to us now to have been merely writing round what Mallarmé had already said. In 1888 a weekly called *Le Symboliste* appeared under the direction of Moréas, Gustave Kahn and Paul Adam, but it survived for only four weeks. It was not until Kahn in 1889 edited *La Vogue*—a title which Mallarmé greatly disliked—that Symbolism found its special press in which the position of Symbolists and Decadents was established.[2]

Many good points were made in *La Vogue*. Supporters as well as

---

[1] Cf. the English poets Lady Winchilsea and William Wordsworth.
[2] Gustave Kahn, *Symbolistes et Décadents* (Paris, 1902), 5.

enemies were numerous and in its pages furious battles raged round the gonfalon of Symbolism. Meanwhile, aloof and preoccupied, Mallarmé pursued his own dream of a synthetic, transformed and contemplative poetry, on the path which Novalis had said 'went to the interior,' where one could hope to discover *l'univers des essences*. Here Mallarmé had created a new use of allusion, ellipsis, and metaphor and image, a technique in which synthesis and unity, analysis and music, were essential.

The achievement of the Symbolists, and of Mallarmé in particular, was to have introduced their readers to a universe of language, an aspect of the written word which was neither rhetorical nor the common system of using words as signs for acts and ideas.[1] It was the music of a creative magic (*magikos*), in part intuitive, in part intellectual, which had to embody both the symbol and that which was symbolised; becoming in itself a symbol of the poetic substance, of the poet's very being. It was a poetry for poets yet universal in its application.

All poets use words in a way different from ordinary usage, just as musicians distinguish sound from noise, but Mallarmé went further than any poet before him. He had a genius for the orchestration of language, and he created such harmonious verbal music that, except for Paul Valéry, he had no important successors. He was too difficult a master to follow. The school of *vers libre* of Laforgue, Corbière and the liturgic Péguy was by its very facility to become the universally popular model.

Mallarmé's experiments in technical research were highly abstract; when interviewed on this subject in 1891, he said:

> As poetry consists in creating, the poet must take from the human mind these states, which are flashes of such absolute purity that, when well expressed and brought to light, they constitute the treasures of humanity. In this there is *symbol*, in this there is *creation* and the word poetry has here its real sense: it is in fact the only human creation possible. . . .[2]

Again in his definition of Symbolism, which admirably sums up his art, he wrote:

> of what use is the marvel of transposing a fact of nature almost into its vibrating disappearance by a play of words, if from it there does not

[1] Paul Valéry, Préface, *Anthologie des poètes de la Nouvelle Revue Française* (Paris: Gallimard, 1936).
[2] Jules Huret, interview with Mallarmé, *Écho de Paris* (1891). See also, Mondor, *Vie de Mallarmé*, 598–9.

emanate, unhindered by any close or concrete memories, the pure concept.

I say: a flower! and out of oblivion into which my voice relegates any contour, musically arises, as distinct from all known chalices, the suave and veritable idea—absent from all bouquets. . . .

After explaining that the poet's use of words should be altogether different from their current usage (an idea to which Valéry often returned) Mallarmé continues:

> The verse which from several vocables reconstructs an aphorism new, foreign to the language, and as it were incantatory, completes this detachment from ordinary speech . . . and gives you the surprise of never having heard any such fragment before, while your memory of the thing named is bathed in a new atmosphere.[1]

This declaration and definition are the expression of a moment of perfection in French poetry: images replace description and musical quality is insisted on as a poetic necessity. In this verbal aestheticism words appear to be recreated, grouped to give a new significance, to suggest rather than record, to reach almost into the domain of music without losing anything of their seriousness, adding to the intellectual content by their force and purity. Never before had words been used in quite the same abstract patterns as suggested by Mallarmé's poems, and as realised in those of Valéry. The poet who could continue in the master's footsteps would require an intellectual sensibility of unusual depth combined with the qualities that Mallarmé suggested when he noted, at Avignon in 1886, that his ideal would be:

> A strange little book, very mysterious, rather in the manner of the early Fathers, very distilled and concise—especially in the parts which might lend themselves to enthusiasm.
>
> In other parts Descartes' ample and long period. Then in general: something of La Bruyère and of Fénelon with a flavour of Baudelaire.
>
> Finally something of the 'Self' and something of mathematical language.[2]

Is this not almost a Valérian formula?

I have touched on Mallarmé's theories and the substance of his poetical creation to show on what foundations Valéry was to build. For in this all too brief summary of the master's general aims, we find

[1] Stéphane Mallarmé, *Œuvres Complètes* ('Bibliothèque de la Pléiade') (Paris: Gallimard, 1945), 857 (my translation).
[2] *Ibid.*, 851.

the background of much of the disciple's future research. The closer we look at the two poets, the more clearly may we discern the similitudes as well as the differences in their aesthetic outlook. But all such developments take place gradually; each poet creates his own world; he does something different with the materials offered; and sometimes, as did Valéry, he goes on where his master left off. Therefore classifications, definitions and conclusions must not be too rigid.

At certain times special tendencies seem to be in the air. At the epoch we are dealing with, thanks to Baudelaire, and to Poe seen through Baudelaire's translations, and through their joint influence on the Symbolists, the term 'scientific poetry' had rather surprisingly appeared in the literary world. A positive attitude was one of the characteristics of a generation who had seen the renewal of science and the application of new techniques in general, and who in their turn questioned the conventional traditions in all the arts. Bold experiments were being tried. For instance, René Ghil had invented 'La poésie scientifique,' a curious theory of verbal music which he was the only one to follow. He had in fact reduced ideas from Mallarmé and Rimbaud *ad absurdum*. He is, however, of interest to those who are curious about methods.[1]

In the spring of 1891, a journalist, Jules Huret, had published in the *Écho de Paris* an inquiry into the state of literature, for which he had interviewed most of the best-known writers. Mallarmé's reply, from which I have quoted, had been much talked about. Astonished to find the poets and authors more ready to tear each other to pieces than to discuss any purely literary theme, Huret ironically classified them as: blessed and blessing, acid and staccato, boxers and bunglers, vague and bored, ironic and boasting, and theorisers. Mallarmé was among the theorists, Barrès among the ironic, Anatole France among the acid. Moréas, Huysmans and Zola were in the category of boxers. As a result of this edifying classification, fierce battles raged between Psychologues and Naturalistes, Symbolistes and Parnassiens—battles in which happily only ink was spilt.

Both Verlaine and Mallarmé were now at the zenith of their fame, and took part in the social side of literary life, each according to his measure. Mallarmé, despite his dislike of ceremony when applied to literature, had nevertheless consented to inaugurate meetings, and to

---

[1] René Ghil, *Les Dates et les œuvres: Symbolisme et poésie scientifique*. Cf. Valéry, 'Questions de poésie' (1923), *Variété*, III (Paris: Gallimard, 1936), 42: 'Rien de plus trompeur que les méthodes dites scientifiques.'

preside at literary banquets such as those of *La Plume*—obligations which he gracefully fulfilled. Verlaine also accepted similar invitations. It is recorded that at a banquet at which he took the chair, while in an atmosphere of general gaiety the guests laughed loudly to see their chairman 'as drunk as a lord', Mallarmé, who was present, turned away from so sad a sight with tears in his eyes. The two poets were on the best of terms. One Tuesday evening Moréas coming to the Rue de Rome to offer his *Pèlerin passionné* to Mallarmé, found Verlaine there decidedly tipsy. Was he reading a poem to his host—'Je ris, je pleure, et c'est comme un appel aux armes'—the tears running down his short nose, his eyes lit by a lurid flame, his voice muffled and urgent? Mallarmé was kind and attentive. Each was wrapt in his own dream yet was poignantly aware of the integrity—as well as the difference—of the other.

Grouped round Mallarmé were the younger poets in sympathy with his ideas. Among them were André Fontainas, poet and translator of English poets; Camille Mauclair; Albert Mockel, the Belgian poet; René Ghil; Francis Vielé-Griffin, enemy of the alexandrine, original in form and matter; André Lebey, who became Valéry's friend. Mallarmé's statement on Symbolism had definitely placed him as *le cher Maître* of many ardent young men who sent him their books, begged for his advice and came every Tuesday to listen to his soliloquies— inspired monologues, in which he raised poetry to a transcendent activity.

Not only youthful poets came to the Rue de Rome to attend the famous Tuesdays. Most of the literary world and also many painters had been there. Among the latter came Gauguin, with his general air of an old sea-dog in his blue seaman's jersey, his clothes stained with paint. Another fairly frequent visitor was the reserved Odilon Redon, gentle and mysterious, who found a constant refuge in his dreams, disdaining in a secret glory everything but his own researches, for whom faces were flowers in the light. Whistler too had been there, brilliant but careful not to venture beyond his depth. It was largely due to Mallarmé that the portrait of 'Whistler's Mother' was bought for Paris, and the poet's sympathy for painters was untiring. I need not comment here on his well-known friendship with Edouard Manet and Berthe Morisot.

Painting was undergoing changes somewhat parallel to the contemporary evolution of poetry. In both arts, values had been challenged, and technical experiments were being made. Such names as

Cézanne, Monet and Renoir help to bring this fruitful epoch before us. Indeed Manet had much in common with Mallarmé's ideals, and Degas was as certainly an inspiration to Valéry.

If painting held a high place in intellectual circles, music was of even greater significance. Any account of literary life in Paris at the end of the nineteenth century would be incomplete without the mention of music; for in this art the same transformation as in poetry and painting was taking place. Broken melodies were replacing accepted and carefully constructed harmonies. Cadence was less strongly marked. Dissonance had opened a way to new impressions. Debussy, followed by many others, was renewing the life of music by infusing impressionist technique into classical methods. Such innovations were to music what *vers libre* was to poetry, and doubtless people of conservative taste may have felt, in listening to some of the more daring composers, that noise sometimes threatened to usurp the part of sound, just as prose was apt to intrude into free verse.

Music was in fact one of the dominant interests in the cultivated Parisian world. Wagner with his immense artistic energy had transferred poetic aspirations into his music, and seemed to the poets of his time to be orienting such art towards a pure destiny. His work had been both a challenge and a rich source of ideas to the Symbolist poets. Mallarmé's declaration that the Symbolists aimed at taking back from music what musicians had borrowed from poetry[1] was therefore no idle boast, for rhythm and sonority in language, sense dependent on sound, had always been the domain of poets.

'We were nourished on music,' Valéry confessed, 'and our heads filled with literature; we dreamt only of extracting from language almost the same effects which purely sonorous causes produced on our nervous systems.'[2] It was not surprising that the younger generation of poets, in close relationship with Mallarmé, should free their poetry from almost all the 'impure' elements which music could not express: descriptions, moralising, all teaching and preaching were avoided.

The Lamoureux orchestral concerts, held weekly at the Cirque d'Été, from late autumn to early spring, attracted an enthusiastic audience. 'The young men crowded in the gallery, for which they paid

---

[1] Valéry, *Variété*, I, 97. See also Mallarmé, 'Musique et lettres,' *Œuvres complètes*, 1600.

[2] Paul Valéry, 'Avant-propos' for *La Connaissance de la déesse* of Lucien Fabre *Variété*, I.

two francs, formed a block of attentive silence;[1] no one wished or dared to stir,' while in the crowded house, on a bench of the *promenoir*, Mallarmé listened to Beethoven or Wagner, and may have felt at the end of the performance a sort of divine jealousy of those masters of harmony.

Thus the epoch in which Valéry came to Paris was remarkable for an almost religious feeling for beauty. This was partly excited by a spirit of opposition to the current ideas of Taine and Renan, and partly as a protest against the extreme realism of Zola. It followed that young intellectuals, such as Louÿs and Gide, Gustave Kahn and many others, should see in art the only issue and the only atmosphere for a possible culture of expression. The artist's work, the emotion communicated by works of art, seemed the sole means of redemption, and, as Valéry said, 'gave the force of faith without exacting any beliefs.'[2] Of all the arts music may well have appeared the most suitable to produce this sentiment of strength and certitude.

This tendency towards 'purity' in art, towards beauty always more conscious of its origin, always more independent of all 'subject' and all effect of eloquence, while aspiring to a revelation, led to an almost inhuman state; for such art can proceed only by exceptional perceptions which appear as marvels. It is easy to see how such an atmosphere was favourable to Valéry's desire to enlarge the scope of his intellectual activities.

2. FRIENDSHIP AND THEORY

Le Monde est fait pour aboutir à un beau livre.
(MALLARMÉ)

It was at Mallarmé's Tuesday evenings in the Rue de Rome that Valéry felt most at home. Very soon he became the most remarkable member of the group of young men who came there, which included at this time Camille Mauclair, Dujardin, Fontainas, Mockel, Pierre Louÿs and André Gide. Valéry was seen by Mauclair as brown-haired

---

[1] Paul Valéry, 'Au concert Lamoureux en 1893,' *Pièces sur l'art* (Paris: Gallimard, 1934), 68.
[2] *Ibid.*, 65.

and timid, with fine prominent eyes such as mystics have, a strong meridional accent and a slight lisp.[1]

Mallarmé would stand leaning against the white porcelain stove. He spoke in a pleasant unaffected voice, and his whole bearing expressed a mixture of gentleness and pride. He knew how to hold the attention of his guests by the quiet authority and magic of his words. In cold weather he folded a Scottish plaid over his shoulders. The pictures on the walls, by Manet, Redon and Berthe Morisot, with a small statue by Rodin, enhanced the friendly atmosphere.

A conversation on Poe's *Eureka* had awakened immediate sympathy between Mallarmé and his new disciple, who also became a fairly frequent visitor during the summer months at the little house at Valvins, where they sailed on the river in Mallarmé's boat, or rambled in the fields along the banks of the Seine. From the first, Mallarmé represented for the younger poet the figure of pure art, beside whom other writers seemed never to have known 'the unique god of poetry' but to have given themselves up to idolatry. Other poetry 'seemed like arithmetic to which Mallarmé's poems appeared as algebra.'[2] This statement shows the high place that Valéry assigned to such work. It had already become evident to his analytical mind that research of a drastic order would be necessary if poetry was to be carried further into an abstract world of its own; but in a letter to Gide, Valéry denied that his studies at this time were in any way directed towards poetry. It was, he said, consciousness and greater knowledge of Self which entirely occupied his thought.

Mallarmé's interest in metaphysical questions was completely focused on their bearing on poetry, in which he saw the whole salvation of man.[3] All the arts converged to the same unique end, that of man's expression: 'Le Monde est fait pour aboutir à un beau livre.' The real destiny of the universe was to be finally expressed by poets. In following his own line he did nothing less than deify the written word, and his life was concentrated round the task of putting his dream into words. But dream it must remain. Mallarmé's emotional response consists in unfolding a sequence of suggestive images arising from an association, born of sound and sense, in which the central theme is symbolised, and from which, though it rarely emerges, radiates its in-

[1] Camille Mauclair, *Mallarmé chez lui* (Paris: Grasset, 1935).

[2] Paul Valéry, 'Visite à Mallarmé,' *Variété*, II, 205.

[3] See Henri Mondor, *Eugène Lefébure* (Paris: Gallimard, 1951), 348, and L. Austin, 'Mallarmé et le rêve du livre,' *Mercure de France*, I (1953), 81–108.

tense, and as it were rarified being. The images are not linked together by explanatory passages, but are generally condensed to form plastic groups, and are often composed in classical periods. The expression of such poetry is therefore elliptical, always composed in an elaborate orchestration, but never degenerating into facile music—it is much too fiercely poetic for that. Valéry summed up Mallarmé's art by saying that it consisted in making

> admirable transformations of his conceptions into words. He placed the 'word' not at the beginning but at the end of all things. No one had ever confessed with such precision, such constant and heroic assurance, the eminent dignity of poetry, beyond which he saw nothing but hazard. . . .

Literature was therefore the supreme aim of his life.[1]

But Valéry's preoccupations during his first years in Paris were different. His endeavour to establish a new statement of psychological and intellectual values led him to study scientific methods, which in turn brought him to the consideration of possible systems of language and even of thought. Yet there can be no doubt that Mallarmé's methods, in tending to organise the whole domain of letters through the general consideration of form, in the rather special use and *place* of words and figures of speech, must have helped Valéry in his idea of a system of analysis, and in the research which for a long time made him abandon poetry. Perceiving that Mallarmé had actually arrived at a conception of art as abstract as the high conceptions of certain sciences, Valéry found the idea of applying scientific methods to thought through the medium of language more than ever valid as a means of investigation into the workings of his own mind. It is interesting to notice that, although he had given up writing verse, his inquiries were directed towards the drama of the analogy of thought and word; and he endlessly stated for himself the subtle problems of what he called 'verbal mechanics.'

The outcome of this study was that both poetry and prose took the form of a sort of calculation. In this application of the conception of 'problem' or 'operation' to what was found or given, the initial idea was treated as a basis for future structure or progression of thought. This method might have degenerated into an amusing, though sterile, intellectual game, had it not been constantly referred to progressive states of mind tending always to the statement of a greater consciousness.

[1] Paul Valéry, 'Stéphane Mallarmé,' *Variété*, II, 190.

Valéry's transformations were therefore of a different order to those which he attributed to Mallarmé. For though he followed his master closely enough in the use he made of the example of musicians, who work by a kind of calculation to develop and transform a musical theme, he also used the idea of mathematical transposition in his doctrine of mental progression from one phase to another towards the ultimate expression of the Pure Self. Both poets transpose, both search for the absolute of expression. For Mallarmé the important factor is the *Word*: the unique, imperishable and ultimate statement of some aspect of life; and this expression gives to man an effective grandeur, a reason for being. For being who or what? asks Valéry. What is this conscious Self, at once solitary and universal, of which all intellectual life partakes, and how far is it truly aware of its own being? These questions suggest a unity of theme and a possible fusion of reason and imagination so as to express a consciousness at once unique and total, a Self that could have its being only in an ultimate state. Only the pure Self could give a perfect expression of itself in poetry in which form and content would necessarily be in unison. Therefore the method is all important, since only through method may the mind construct.

This thought was curiously allied, yet at the same time opposed, to Valéry's admiration for Mallarmé, who gave such importance to the written word; for now such a point of view appeared almost trivial to one whose constant preoccupation was to acquire greater self-knowledge, and whose concern was to give exact form not to art but to his very existence. Such were the ideas and problems that were turning Valéry more and more from literature, whence they had originated.

'I could not tolerate that the state of poetry should be opposed to the complete and sustained action of the intellect,' Valéry confessed. 'I felt myself detached from the desire to write verse, and I deliberately broke with that poetry, which nevertheless had given me the impression of treasures of mysterious value.'[1] The existence of this contrast between the exercise of literature and the austerity of strictly abstract thought involved for Valéry a delicate case of conscience in his relations with Mallarmé, to whom he hoped to confess his doubts. But with characteristic tact the younger man hesitated to declare that he had ceased to believe in what was of vital importance to his beloved master. To suggest to such a poet that, after all, poetry was not of the first im-

[1] Paul Valéry, 'Mémoires d'un poème,' *Variété*, V (Paris: Gallimard, 1945), 103, 108.

portance in the intellectual world, would have been difficult, if not impossible.

Nevertheless one cannot doubt that Mallarmé would have understood Valéry's point of view, and he might well have answered it by arguing that, since thought (unless auditive or visual) cannot be completely detached from language and must in fact express itself in some figure or symbol, words may be purified to express it. This would have been in accordance with Mallarmé's own conception, of which I have spoken. Might he not even have suggested that an abstract poetry, such as Valéry was in fact to create, would be the answer to this very problem?

However, Valéry never raised this vital question, and perhaps his reluctance to do so may partly be accounted for by his desire to perfect a 'manner of thought' which because of its complications would need full development before it was ripe for discussion.[1] For it is strange how an abstract conception eludes definition when concerned with thought, through which the thinker is to approach nearer to himself. Undoubtedly there is a delicate point in time when all outside comment relative to what one is thinking would be deadly.

'I did not wish to *say* but to *do*,' murmured Valéry. And so time passed, and the propitious moment for such confidences never came. After Mallarmé's death in 1898 the question lost all immediate interest.

3. 'UN COUP DE DÉS'

Tel qu'en lui-même enfin l'éternité le change.

(MALLARMÉ)

Although Valéry had abandoned poetry in his pursuit of a new line of thought, his appreciation of Mallarmé's works was always ardently enthusiastic. No other critic has understood so well the hidden significance of the more difficult poems. One of the most remarkable appreciations offered by one poet to another is to be found in Valéry's essay on *Un Coup de dés jamais n'abolira le hasard*.[2]

[1] Cf. Valéry, letter to Mallarmé (15 janvier 1894), *Lettres à quelques-uns*, 49: 'Ainsi, dans une entreprise, que l'on raisonne ce qu'il n'y faudra pas raisonner et le point délicat du temps où (sic) toute pensée relative à ce qu'on est en train de faire, sera funeste.'

[2] Paul Valéry, 'Le Coup de dés,' *Variété*, II, 198.

Before discussing what Valéry wrote about this poem, we may note a few details of its construction. It is to be read across the double page, and the spaces represent silences, between one image and another, necessary for the versification. The large print in capitals indicates the extreme *fortissimo* of music, as in the full clash of the opening chord 'JAMAIS.' Then comes the first phrase of the argument:

QUAND BIEN MÊME LANCÉ DANS DES
CIRCONSTANCES ÉTERNELLES

and after a pause the reply

DU FOND D'UN NAUFRAGE...

Such the opening of a symphony; the words that follow float through space, vast as the wind or short as a sigh, an orchestration of vocables in the harmony of musical thought.

'N'ABOLIRA' opens the second movement. Here the solo instruments, violin or flute, enter *andante con molto*, and the *crescendo* chords that question and deny. Then again come the clash of cymbals and the trombone:

C'ÉTAIT   LE NOMBRE...
issue stellaire

The third movement opens with the cosmic significance of 'LE HASARD' and the whole conception of the odds against which the artist contends:

UNE CONSTELLATION froide d'oubli
d'un compte total en formation.
    veillant
       doutant
          roulant
             brillant et méditant.

It ends at the last point of universal concentration beyond which 'Toute Pensée émet un Coup de Dés.'

This strange poem seems to me to be the first modern expression of that cosmic conception which is the ultimate aim of all intellectual poetry, and which is to some extent found in all great poetry from the

Greeks to our own day. It holds the esoteric sign which poets pass on only to their own kind. Here the thought is high and difficult, but pure and absolute.

The rudimentary argument, which does *not* govern the full significance of the poem, is simple enough. It is that although the poet is master only of his genius and not of circumstances, a throw of dice is possible: he can always try his chance, and that is the only way to work out his destiny and escape, through poetry, from the tragic abyss of hazard.

That Valéry was the first person to see the poem shows how much Mallarmé counted on his friendship and intelligence. It had been printed as Mallarmé wanted it to be, spaced out on wide, often almost blank, pages. Valéry's admiration was unbounded:

> Here in truth infinity spoke, thought and gave birth to temporal forms. Expectation, doubt and concentration were visible things. My sight had to cope with silences which had taken form. I contemplated at my leisure inappreciable moments: the fraction of a second during which an idea blazed up, glittered and vanished; the atom of time, the seed of psychological centuries and of infinite consequences, appeared at last as living beings, all surrounded by their perceptible void. . . . Here were whispers, insinuations, thunders made visible, a whole spiritual tempest developed from page to page to the extreme of thought, to the point of ineffable rupture. Here the miracle was performed; here on every page I know not what radiance from the furthest stars trembled infinitely pure in the same void between different consciousness, where like a new kind of matter, scattered in heaps, in tracts, in systems co-existed The Word.[1]

Awed by such unparalleled concentration, and fascinated by the whole effect, Valéry felt as if a new cluster of stars had appeared in the sky, or as if a new constellation which at last signified something had 'swum into his ken.' It seemed to him as if he were taking part in an event of a universal order, and that in fact the ideal spectacle of the Creation of Language was being shown to him, and he concluded, 'I was a mixture of admiration, resistance, passionate interest, analogous to the state of being born, when confronted by this intellectual discovery.' This is the evidence of an intelligent and sympathetic witness, testimony which cannot be denied or lightly dismissed by those who see only a sort of decadent folly in Mallarmé's masterpiece.

A little later, at Valvins, Mallarmé showed his friend the proof-

[1] Paul Valéry, 'Le Coup de dés,' *Variété*, II, 194-5 *et seq.*

sheets of the edition which Lahure proposed to print (but which was never published). The same evening as the two poets walked together to the station where Valéry took his train, under a starlit sky that enclosed everything in a shining galaxy of other worlds, 'in the midst of the Serpent, the Swan, the Eagle and the Lyre,' it seemed to Valéry as if Mallarmé were 'involved in the very text of the silent universe'—a text

> full of clarity and enigma; as tragic, and as indifferent as one could wish; that speaks and does not speak; that is woven from multiple senses; that embraces order and disorder; that proclaims a God as loudly as it denies one; containing in its inconceivable whole, every epoch of time, each one associated with the remoteness of a heavenly body.[1]. . .

As they continued their walk through the depth of such a night, in silent sympathy, Valéry, meditating on the poem, thought, what a model, what instruction in the sky! 'Where Kant naïvely enough found the Moral Law, Mallarmé undoubtedly saw the imperative of poetry: a science of Poetics.' And seeing so much abstract beauty in the skies, Valéry questioned, 'should not all that self-contained glory, the strange sum of reality and contradictory ideals, should it not suggest to some one the supreme temptation of producing its effect?' 'Mallarmé has tried,' he concluded, 'to raise a page of poetry to the power of the starlit sky.' [2]

In a moving essay Valéry tells us of his last visit to Mallarmé at Valvins, on July 14, 1899. There was nothing to give him any foreboding on his friend's account. The day was golden in summer light, all was calm and happy. Yet, as they discussed the *mise en page* of *Un Coup de dés*, Valéry felt curiously aware of the actual moment, which seemed 'to have an entity in time, and an absolute value, an intrinsic significance of its own.' It appeared to him, as they discussed the poem, as if Mallarmé's destiny was magnificently fulfilled, and that 'the work of this disinterested and generous poet was a complete and perfect whole.'

Later as Mallarmé and Geneviève walked with Valéry through the fields, in the sunlight under a clear sky, their arms full of wild flowers, it seemed as if, in the great light, 'being and non-being were merged in one vast symphony.' 'Is not poetry—like music—the supreme game of transmutation of ideas,' Valéry wondered. Turning towards the gleam-

---

[1] Paul Valéry, 'Le Coup de dés,' *Variété*, II, 196 *et seq.*
[2] *Ibid.*, 199.

ing fields ripening to gold, Mallarmé said, 'Look, this is the first clash of autumn's cymbals on the earth.'

'When autumn came Mallarmé was no more.' Thus ends Valéry's testimony to a friend whom no one could replace, and for whom he had a deep and filial affection.[1]

---

[1] See *Correspondance André Gide–Paul Valéry*, ed. by Robert Mallet (Paris: Gallimard, 1955), 331, for letter to Gide telling of Mallarmé's death.

III

The Intellectual Comedy

1. TOWARDS A METHOD

Hostinato rigore[1]

THE FIRST WORK in which Valéry discussed and developed his ideas on method, in relation to language and thought, was his 'Introduction à la méthode de Léonard de Vince.' It was first published in 1894 in *La Nouvelle Revue*, and reprinted twenty-five years later by the N.R.F., along with the 'Note et Digression'—a lucid commentary on the early attempt to formulate a system.

This essay is not a historical or biographical study—forms of which Valéry disapproved—nor is it really an introduction to Leonardo's life or work, except in so far as it lays down general principles applicable to a creative mind. Valéry insisted that he did not wish to give a specific portrait of the great artist whose name he used, but rather to discuss the details of an intellectual life. In the 'Note et Digression' he said:

> I saw in Leonardo da Vinci the principal personage of that *Intellectual Comedy* which until now has never found its poet, and which in my opinion would be even more precious than the *Human Comedy* or even the *Divine Comedy*. For I felt that this master of his means, this adept in drawing and calculations, had found that central attitude, starting from which the enterprises of knowledge, and the operations of art, are both equally possible.

He did not wish to tell Leonardo's story but 'to take from that brow laden with crowns' only the *Amande mystique*,[2] the central jewel, and

---

[1] 'Steadfast rigour,' motto of Leonardo da Vinci.   [2] *Vesica piscis.*

he adds: 'I could find nothing better than to attribute to the unfortunate Leonardo my personal agitations, transforming the disorder of my mind into the complexity of *his* mind. I changed my difficulties into his supposed power.'[1]

The name of Leonardo da Vinci therefore serves as a symbol or a synonym of intellect, and almost becomes a mathematical constant round which a calculation of combinations could be effected: he is the Universal Man. It is easy to see that this thoughtful artist, who possessed an extraordinary gift of analysis, would appeal to the sensitive mind of the nineteenth-century *homme d'esprit*. All that Valéry tells us of the working of the artist's mind applies equally well to his own intellectual life; and the essay is an attempt to show how the intellect of an artist functions, or in other words, a psychological study of mind in its ideal state and 'an endeavour to show the working of such a mind.'

It is the drama of the mind itself that Valéry wishes to examine—that Intellectual Comedy in which mental images are the actors, images from which all particularities are eliminated so that

> their succession, frequency, periodicity and their diverse powers of association and finally their duration, may be studied in order to find analogies for such images in what is called the material world, and to use scientific analysis in composing them.

Accordingly, this introduction to a possible method is packed with subtle considerations and reflections on the origin and operations of thought; classifications are indicated rather than insisted on, and combinations and associations of art and science are evoked. We shall return to consider these in detail when analysing the system of thought and the poetics; here we need merely notice how Valéry proposed to group the material with which he was to build.

First, it is interesting to note that a new relative classification of the elements of the formation of thought is constantly proposed, though not yet given the terminology which actually fixed it, while precision, analysis and construction are shown to be the triumphs of mind over itself and over the chaotic world by which it is surrounded. Yet Valéry makes no general rules to fit all minds, for his only desire is to carry the terms of his thought and all its imaginable expressions to their furthest limit.

It was in creating his Leonardo that Valéry evolved his conception

[1] Paul Valéry, 'Introduction à la méthode de Léonard de Vince,' *Variété*, I (Paris: Gallimard, 1924), 170 *et seq.*

of an Absolute of Self. Faced with the necessity of inventing a person-age capable of all kinds of great works, he was led to exclude all ex-terior details and to consider the functioning of the mind and the man-ner in which men created their masterpieces, and thus he imagined a theoretical being, a psychological model, round whom to reconstruct the method that he proposed to formulate. If such a method did not solve the problems of mental parthenogenesis, it at least opened the way and cleared the ground for methodic research, bringing into the light of modern thought the eternal problem which, in the words of Blake, is 'To cleanse the face of my spirit by self-examination.' For who but ourselves can reply when we call up a spirit? In order to reach a universal understanding, we must inevitably first know ourselves.

This then is the initial statement of the desire for knowledge of the working of his own consciousness, that *conscience de soi-même* which, Valéry tells us, using the English word, 'is the "consciousness" of Poe.'[1] The knowledge of this consciousness is the intimate concern of the Self, for in classifying and retaining the changing images of the encircling world the intelligence becomes aware of itself. Here there should be no confusion in the reader's mind between consciousness and moral conscience, which is the secondary meaning of the French word *conscience*. Both are from the Latin *conscientia*, the feeling of one-self. Valéry uses the word in its pure sense of knowledge of oneself. Thus when he speaks of *conscience de soi* he means 'self-knowledge,' and when he uses the word *conscience* by itself he means that awareness or understanding which is necessary to and receptive of knowledge. He rarely, if ever, in reference to his work or thought, speaks of that moral conscience which plays such an important part in the works of Gide, Péguy and Claudel.

Self-knowledge comes from an intellectual and conceptual con-science. It leads to awareness of the evolution of its own thought. It is a faculty of creative sensibility which has the property of revealing its own reality combined with the power of mental figuration. Thus the mind realises for itself a state of intellectual vision, an Absolute of Self conceivable without relation to other things. This was the poet's initial definition.

It is interesting to notice how Valéry's conception of an Absolute of Self differs from the religious mysticism of the Yogi who, guided by the sacred texts of the *Bhagavad-Gita*, looks for God through his own

[1] Paul Valéry, letter to Albert Mockel (1917), *Lettres à quelques-uns* (Paris: Gallimard, 1952), 124.

soul and seeks a religious revelation through a negation of all that is material, passing through arduous discipline to a passive beatitude. The primal idea of this cult is to transcend, by passing into the sphere of pure Being, the necessity of re-incarnation of the Soul in the seething material life into which all are born and reborn. Valéry's conception of the Pure Self differs from this in one essential: his desire to extend his own consciousness so as to acquire a greater power of *creation*. His effort to 'construct himself' partakes of the creative intelligence which lies at the centre of all art. What he says of Leonardo applies admirably to himself: that in the domain of knowledge, though his thought is capable of subtlety and depth, 'he never abandons his preoccupation with figurative creations, applications and tangible proofs of his attentive abilities.'[1]

Thus the future poet of the Intellectual Comedy—of which comprehensive term he is the author—set out to unite his conception of the Self with a system of thought as exactly mathematical as possible, and to carry such a system to its furthest conclusions.

Valéry gives us a preliminary sketch of his method, which consists in finding and stimulating combinations of thought, and searching with precision for all their logical and imaginative implications. At a certain point of this awareness, which reduces ordinary thought to the dream of a waking sleeper, all the series of this 'dream,' the cloud of associations, of contrasts and of perceptions, which are grouped round some research, or which float indeterminately, are developed with a perceptible regularity and with the evident continuity of a machine. Then comes the idea of accelerating this process, so as to carry its terms to their limit, that is to the limit of imaginable expression, beyond which all will be changed.

Through some such method the 'inspired' author has been ready to perform his task long before it was achieved, he has been prepared for it and has been thinking of it always. The secret of Leonardo, or of Bonaparte, says Valéry

is in the relationship that they found, that they were forced to find, between things whose laws of continuity escaped other people. It is certain that at

[1] Paul Valéry, 'Léonard et les philosophes,' *Variété*, III (Paris: Gallimard, 1936), 167: 'Cependant, à l'écart de la philosophie ... ont paru quelques existences singulières dont on sait que leur pensée abstraite, quoique très exercée et capable de toutes subtilités et profondeurs, ne perdait jamais le souci de créations figurées, d'applications et de preuves sensibles de sa puissance attentive. Léonard de Vince est le type suprême de ces individus supérieurs.'

the decisive moment they had only to carry out some definite acts. The achievement that impressed the world, the supreme achievement, was finally quite a simple affair like comparing two lengths.[1]

This passage emphasises the importance which Valéry gave to the systematic progression of thought, and to the transmutations which may be effected by means of clearly defined affinities. So too, at a certain level or preparation, even the most subtle thought becomes simple: it is a perfect mental act, the result of conscious development; and this act of the intellect incarnates the real creation. This logical and intuitive method led Valéry to consider all the possible results of a contemplative act and to acquire the faculty of divining more intense and exact states of thought:

> for the sense which leads the mind to foresee its own activities; to imagine as a whole the structure of what has to be imagined in detail, and the effect of the sequence thus calculated—this sense is the condition of all generalisation—and frees the mind from fixed ideas.

Here the reasoning by recurrence, of which Henri Poincaré had shown the philosophical significance, is closely followed. Poincaré had indicated various means of deducing concepts of the relations between things. And Laplace, much earlier, had put forward the proposition that a sufficiently developed intelligence, if acquainted with the positions and motions of all atoms at any instant, could predict all future events.

But though Valéry proposed to adapt scientific methods to his own ends, he was frankly scornful of philosophers, and considered that their business was to contend against the thought of their predecessors. In contrast, the thoughtful artist, the 'universal man,' who begins by simple contemplation like everyone else, is different from the others because he returns to be permeated by what he sees: he relives the exaltation and the emotion, which the least of real things may arouse,[2] so that his experience forms a new relationship between his interior and exterior worlds.

Valéry had the creative sensibility of the artist type of imaginative thinker. We have only to compare him with philosophers or scientists of his time, such as Poincaré or Bergson, to realise how much the poet

---

[1] Paul Valéry, 'Introduction à la méthode,' *Variété*, I, 223. Cf. the methods of modern Synarchists for mathematical classification of mental states.
[2] *Ibid.*, 228 et seq.

in him dominates all his thought and theory. This view is confirmed by an amusing passage where, pursuing the analogy between geometry and language, he comments on the movement that language confers on objects:

> As geometricians can introduce time and speed into their study of forms, and as they can also separate these forms from movement, so language confers movement on objects: a pier runs out, a mountain rises, a statue stands up; and the logic of continuity transports these actions to the limit of their tendencies, to the impossibility of any stop.

To save ourselves from infinite complexity, Valéry tells us that we must have recourse to 'the great gift of orderly forgetfulness,' and, without destroying the notions that we have acquired, establish an abstract conception: that of the order of importance. Thus the innumerable relations between objects and movements have led us to an abstract conception.[1]

In revolt against the preconceived ideas on 'beauty' inherited from the Romantics, which at the time of this essay (1894) had become conventional, Valéry declares that most men have static ideas of the world around them, and that they are too ready to accept what they have been told to admire. In fact they see things so vaguely that they have invented the 'beauty spot,' and so they see what they expect to see, and this blinds them to the living changes of light and life. On the other hand, the universal artist or poet whose vision is analytical, though he starts by having a general impression, gradually sifts things in his mind: some impressions are forgotten, others retained. He links objects, or aspects of things, and arranges his impressions as he wishes. In this way he becomes capable of appreciating strange combinations, for 'he wishes to figure to himself invisible groups of which the parts have been given.'[2] . . . 'He divines the volutions which a bird makes in its flight, or the curve described by a stone thrown in the air.' Here Valéry comes very close to Leonardo and to the artist's world of form and movement: 'quivering insects, movement of trees and wheels, the human smile, the tide,' bring vividly before our minds the artist's means of reconciling art with the development of the whole of his intelligence, which is exactly what Valéry himself proposed to do. For we can only fully imagine another mind through the consciousness of the working of our own.

[1] Paul Valéry, 'Introduction à la méthode,' *Variété*, I, 229 *et seq.*
[2] *Ibid.*, 233 *et seq.*

The problem stated in this thoughtful 'Introduction à la Méthode de Leonard de Vince'[1] was to dominate Valéry's mind through years of study, to be finally resolved and expressed through the medium of his poetry.

2. MONSIEUR TESTE

O poètes, Vous avez toujours été orgueilleux soyez plus, devenez dédaigneux. (MALLARMÉ)

If Leonardo represented the highest type of creative artist, the complete and universal man, Monsieur Teste was specially created as the high priest of the idol of intellect, to suit the needs of his author. Both Leonardo, as seen through the 'Méthode,' and Monsieur Teste, as invented by Valéry, present different aspects of intellectual life, and serve as pretext for meditation on the possibilities of the human mind.[2]

The dramatic personage of Monsieur Teste (Mr. Head) was created to express the self-discipline that followed the crisis of 1892. He demonstrates the 'manner of being' which was implied in Leonardo's method: he is the outward sign of significant thought, the symbolic image of a desired state of mind, the portrait of a Self crystallised from moments of mental vision.

'Why is Monsieur Teste impossible?' demands his creator. 'This question is the very centre of his being. It changes you into Monsieur Teste. For he is nothing else than the demon of possibility,'[3] and this statement brings us to the heart of the matter. Hostile to all that was vague or easy, and therefore impure, Valéry created in Teste a character through whom states of mind could be accurately recorded and who thus became the 'very demon of what it was possible to reach in this direction.' The existence of such a type, Valéry admitted twenty years later, 'could not be prolonged for more than a few brief half-hours,' for he is 'the exceptional creature of an exceptional moment.' It is interesting to note that Valéry frequently spoke of Teste in the same sense as he spoke of the creation of a poem—a duration in which he 'breathes

---

[1] Paul Valéry, 'Introduction à la méthode,' *Variété*, I, 236.

[2] Unless stated to the contrary, the passages quoted in this chapter are all taken from the text of *Monsieur Teste* (3rd edition; Paris: Gallimard, 1929).

[3] *Ibid.*, 16.

a law' which he has already prepared—and also of the poetic universe 'which has been created in a moment of time.'

Valéry remained faithful to Teste all through his life. 'I am being and seeing myself; seeing myself see myself,' murmurs Teste, expressing the central attitude of Valérian thought, echoed again in *La Jeune Parque*: 'Je me voyais me voir, sinueuse et dorais/De regards en regards, mes profondes forêts.'[1]

It was during the summer of 1895 that Valéry wrote *La Soirée avec Monsieur Teste*, in a room where Auguste Comte had passed the first years of his life, in the Rue de la Vieille Intendance, on the slope above the Cathedral at Montpellier. Valéry said that he had passed several years there dreaming and working, and that it was between two journeys to Paris, during an epoch of great intensity of purpose in the pursuit of self-knowledge, that he wrote the *Soirée*. The 'Lettre d'un ami,' 'Lettre de Madame Emilie Teste' and 'Extraits du Log-Book de Monsieur Teste' were added in later editions. *La Soirée avec Monsieur Teste* was first published in *Le Centaure* in 1896, and has since appeared in various editions. For the second English translation Valéry wrote a preface which was reprinted in the third French edition of 1929. In 1946, after the poet's death, a new edition appeared augmented by hitherto unpublished fragments. Valéry had put these later notes and sketches together with the intention of using them in a final edition.

Some critics have seen in Teste a portrait of Mallarmé; others find in him a study of Degas. Certainly Mallarmé must often have been in Valéry's mind as a type of intellectual perfection; and he tells us that his portrait of Teste was partly founded on his idea of Degas, but before they had met. However Teste's real identity is that of the Self and his *raison d'être* is to demonstrate the application of exact laws to the human mind.

Teste is dominated by the Absolute. He observes, 'he manœuvres he does not let himself be manœuvred.' He recognises only two values, two categories 'which are those of consciousness reduced to its acts: the possible and the impossible.' In this strange brain, says Valéry, where philosophy is given little value, and where language is always suspect, there is hardly a thought which is not considered as merely provisional: 'thought whose intense and brief life is spent in observing the mechanism by which the relations of the known are established and organised.' These obscure and transient forces are even used 'to evolve

[1] Paul Valéry, *La Jeune Parque*, lines 35–36, in *Poésies* (Paris: Gallimard, 1933), 72.

relentlessly the properties of a system in which the infinite does not figure.'[1] The idea of knowledge of consciousness dominates, guides and explains most of Teste's attitudes and points of departure, and this is conveyed through the almost mathematical discipline that Valéry imposes on language.

Throughout *La Soirée* the arguments are close but clear; one is almost tempted to call them mathematical. Yet the whole conception proves the truth of Valéry's statement that it is wrong to oppose sensibility to intelligence; for sensibility is shown to be the moving power of intellectual perceptions.

'La bêtise n'est pas mon fort': Stupidity is not my strong point. Thus the narrator introduces himself, and we are prepared for the entrance of Monsieur Teste by this *alter ego* who speaks in the first person and represents a disillusioned and lucid state of mind ready to receive, analyse, and enter into relation with his strange hero. Teste, we are told, lived on modest weekly speculations at the Bourse. He used to take his meals at a small restaurant in the Rue Vivienne. Here he swallowed his food as if it were a purge. From time to time he would allow himself a fine and leisurely meal elsewhere. He is described as a man of about forty who spoke rapidly in a low voice. Everything about him was unobtrusive, his eyes, his hands. His shoulders however were military, and his step surprisingly regular. When he spoke he made no gestures of arm or hand—he had 'killed his puppet.'[2] He did not smile and he never greeted his friends. He had trained his memory to store only that part of his impressions which his imagination alone would be unable to furnish, that is to say the individual reaction to a common experience. As a result of deep thought he appeared to have discovered laws of the mind which other people ignore. He had in fact devoted years of study to this research, and even longer to maturing his conclusions.

'I have not read any books for twenty years,' he said, 'and I have burnt my papers. I cancel the living.'[3] This last rather fierce statement means that he does not wish to be bothered by the actual life around him. However, he retains what he wants. That is not hard; what is difficult is to retain what he will need in the future. 'I have tried to invent a mechanical mental sieve,' he confessed. 'For discovery is nothing. The difficulty is to assimilate what one has found.'

[1] Paul Valéry, *Monsieur Teste*, 17.
[2] *Ibid.*, 27: 'il avait tué la marionette.'
[3] Or, 'I cross out the living'—'je rature le vif.'

One of his special themes was 'the delicate art of duration,' the distribution and regulation of time, and how to spend it on well-chosen objects so as to cultivate them especially. He watched for the repetition of certain ideas. He 'watered them with numbers' and this helped him in the end 'to make a mechanical application of his conscious study.' He tried to sum up this task. He often said 'maturare,' realising that ripeness is all.

Evidently Teste had understood at an early age the importance of what his friend calls 'human plasticity' and he tried hard to discover the laws and limits of his own variations. For he always hoped to find some fundamental system, and to this end sought to master his thoughts. Moreover he had no opinions. He never laughed, and he never looked unhappy. In contrast to these refusals, he had special and precious qualities. He gave words new values: sometimes he would describe a material object by a group of abstract words, or by proper nouns. There was nothing to reply to what he said, even a polite assent seemed unnecessary. Conversations with him were prolonged by astonishing bounds. He was free from all guile and all wonder, believing that he could only arrive at real knowledge by freeing himself from other people. Therefore he did not read, or write, he was content to think and above all *to observe himself thinking.*

Thus Valéry draws the portrait of his intellectual robot, the embodiment of the desire to systematise his thought, who represents a state of consciousness aware of itself. We may say that absolute knowledge is represented in Teste as a living organism. He is a prosopopeia or personification of abstract thought. That Valéry succeeds in bringing him to life, while keeping him in the right perspective, is shown in the theatre scene, where his reactions are described in a remarkable passage.

> I can see him and the golden pillar standing together [says his friend]. He looked only at the audience. He was breathing in the great burning blast, on the edge of the pit. He was red.
>
> An immense copper girl separated us from a murmuring group beyond the glitter. Deep in the haze shone a naked bit of woman, smooth as a pebble. Many independent fans fluttered over the sombre and clear world that foamed right up to the fires above. My sight spelt a thousand little faces, fell on a sad head, ran along arms, on people, and finally burnt itself out.

Teste's friend then describes how each one was free to make small movements in his place, yet was part of a system of classification in the

85

almost theoretical simplicity of the audience, the social order. Everything in this vast space seemed to follow the same laws: to flare up in
laughter in great circles, be moved in rows, and 'feel as a mass intimate
and even unique things,' while the same music moved them all, swelled
and then diminished.

In this description all conventional classifications are discarded.
There is a fresh interpretation of a familiar scene: people and light are
regarded as objects, and as part of a general whole which is given an
individual unity. Beings are things, and objects become beings: a
statue is an immense copper girl, a woman's shoulder is like a white
pebble polished by waves. The poet describes what he actually sees.
Even music has become an object that inhabits space, bubbles up and
runs over. Nothing of this scene is merely nominal. Yet at the same
time there is no fantastic invention in Valéry's description; there is a
transformation which is guided by a general reality.

Of all this animated scene Teste lost nothing and turning towards his
friend he said, 'discipline is not bad. . . . It is a small beginning,' adding in his low quick voice, 'Let them enjoy and obey!'

> He fixed his eyes for a long time on a young man opposite us, then on a
> lady, then on a whole group in the higher gallery, that overflowed the
> dress circle, in five or six burning faces, and then on every one, the whole
> theatre, full as the heavens, eager and fascinated by the stage which we
> did not see. The stupor of all the others revealed that something or other
> sublime was taking place.

They watched the brightness dying from all the faces; and when it
was quite dim, when the light no longer shone, only the 'vast phos-
phorescence of those thousand faces' remained. This twilight made all
those beings passive. Their attention and the obscurity growing together formed a continuous equilibrium; and Teste and his companion
were 'necessarily attentive to all this attention.'

'The supreme simplifies them,' said Monsieur Teste, 'I am ready to
swear they are all thinking more and more of the same thing. They are
all alike faced by the conclusion or common limit. But the law is not so
simple since it does not include me—and I am here.' After a pause he
added, 'The light holds them.' 'You too,' replied his companion laughing. 'You too,' repeated Monsieur Teste. To his enthusiastic friend it
seemed as if Teste were 'watching some experiment made at the furthest
limit of all the sciences.' Was he not in fact watching his universal Self?
Did not the whole audience represent the transmutation of different

'selves' into a single being focused on a unique conception—some phenomenon of life? Valéry does not say so, but it is certainly inferred.

Doubtless certain aspects of this scene may remind us of passages in Huysmans' *A Rebours*; and the method of evoking objects by their analogues had of course been used by Mallarmé, who had also written memorable passages about the theatre. We may compare in particular this dense image:

> In some amphitheatre, like a wing of human infinity, the multitude divides [bifurcates], startled in front of the abrupt abyss made by the god, man or type.[1]

Nevertheless Valéry reaches deeper strata of experience than his elders. Everything becomes for him expressive of the self found in all life. For the theatre symbolises an intelligence whose thoughts are concentrated on 'n'importe quoi de sublime,' and the reactions of the crowded audience are symbolic of the process of thought. In 'L'Introduction à la méthode de Léonard de Vince' the same image is used to suggest thoughts that crowd the mind.[2] Thus with a poet's insight Valéry creates his own world. It is a world in which the individual is not free from suffering: 'It is here that I should begin,' sighs Teste, 'for to suffer is to give supreme attention to something, and I am above all attentive.' And he tries to dissipate suffering by denying it this attention, and by concentrating on some other thought, apart from the zones, circles and poles of the geometry of pain.

Madame Émilie Teste is introduced to us by her letter to a friend, in which she describes her husband's more human qualities. The Teste *ménage*, as French critics have said, is symbolic of the union of life and knowledge, and Madame Teste forms a link between her husband and the everyday world. She is a mixture of *finesse* and simplicity, and shows discernment in the portrait she draws of Teste. He is, she says 'a mystic without God.' He has moods like other people, sometimes he is hard, sometimes gentle. Love, which he disdains, does nevertheless attach him to the ground. When he breaks away from his 'monstrous inhuman silences' his wife appears to him as a new world, a 'rock of

---

[1] Stéphane Mallarmé, 'Variations sur un sujet,' *Œuvres complètes* ('Bibliothèque de la Pléiade') (Paris: Gallimard, 1945), 393: 'A quelque amphithéâtre, comme une aile d'infinité humaine, bifurque la multitude, effarouchée devant le brusque abîme fait par le dieu, l'homme—ou type.' (Much of the force and music is lost in translation.)

[2] Paul Valéry, 'Note et digression,' *Variété*, I, 199.

life' and a real presence. At such moments he addresses her lovingly as 'Being,' 'thing,' 'oasis.'

She knows her rôle is to be null and useful, realising that she is a part of her husband's life, though not an essential one. She accepts his negations while declaring, 'He never tells me that I am stupid, which touches me profoundly.' With evident pleasure she describes the walks they take together in the Botanical Gardens at Montpellier: telling how they go slowly down through the stony and crooked streets of the old town to the ancient park where 'all thoughtful people, all those with cares, all those who talk to themselves go down towards evening, as water flows to the river, and necessarily gather together.' There are 'scholars, old men, the disillusioned, and priests, all absent-minded men of every kind,' who seem to be 'looking for mutual loneliness. . . . They must like to see and not to know one another, and their separate disillusions are accustomed to meeting each other. . . .'

Here in this secluded place where Valéry so often discussed poetry with Gide or Louÿs, Monsieur Teste and his wife walk slowly together enjoying the sun, the cypresses and the cry of birds, while Teste is amused by 'the rather ridiculous order of the plants' and delights in spelling out the baroque names: 'A garden of epithets,' he said, 'a dictionary and cemetery of a garden,' and after a time he added, 'learnedly to die. *Transiit classificando*,' with which joke Madame Teste's letter ends.

Madame Teste had said: 'there is not a grain of the supernatural in Teste,' and this point of view is borne out by the prayer with which the extracts from his Log-Book open:

> Lord, I was in limbo—in nothingness infinitely negative and peaceful. I have been disturbed in that state to be thrown into this strange carnival. . . . Endowed with unequal gifts necessary to grow, to enjoy, to understand and to be wrong about things.

He regards the master of this mystery as the 'Dark' from whence he came, and to whom he prays 'give me the supreme thought'; and then, characteristically, he demolishes the idea of such thought, confessing that he has made an idol of his own intelligence, because he found nothing else.

The notes that follow in the Log-Book give further impressions of Teste, who knows that truth is relative like everything else, and realises the part that chance plays in human existence.

New Fragments on Monsieur Teste, published in 1946, contain

Valéry's mature reflections on his hero, as those of the *Soirée avec Monsieur Teste* gave the ideas of his youth. In the first *Fragment*, 'La Promenade,' there is a description of a street near the Madeleine in the morning. Here, as in the theatre scene, it is the light that unifies the crowd, the traffic (it is still the time of horses), the houses and the sky. The subdued noises also help to reduce the indifferent general hurry to a sort of pulp. Teste and his friend feel that, in spite of themselves, they are only a part of the whole where 'a continual force of beginning and ending consumes beings, parts of beings, doubts, sentences that walk . . . even to the very moments annihilated in a strange void.'

In the 'Second Fragment,' a dialogue, we are again assured that Teste 'is not a philosopher or anything of the kind; not even a man of letters.' This is the reason why he thinks so much, for 'the more one writes the less one thinks'; and Valéry repeats his mistrust of philosophy and his disdain for literature. Teste is in fact neither good nor bad, neither cheat nor cynic. 'He is content to choose,' and this gives him the power to combine the moment and himself into a harmonious whole. Moreover he has the great advantage over other people of knowing himself, having substituted for that vague 'me' which changes all our calculations, a definite being, a well-defined and educated Self, sure as an instrument, sensitive as an animal, and consistent in everything as a man. Thus armed with his own image he knows at each moment his weakness and his strength.

'The infinite is nothing much,' he said, 'it is a matter of writing, the universe only exists on paper. No idea represents it, none of our senses reveal it—a question of words, that is all. . . .' Nor is he interested in what other men call 'destiny.' As for enthusiasm, 'learn to bottle it,' says Monsieur Teste, and he adds, 'all fools shout for humanity, all the weak cry for justice; empty words always at our disposal. For between men there exist only two relationships—logic and war.'

In the *Notes for a Portrait* (1934) Teste has become less a figure of romance: his thoughts and ideas are no longer those of a prototype, they are more strictly autobiographical. He is not only what his creator would like to be, but more exactly what that creator is—at least at certain moments. And this sequence of his thought is the only sort of autobiography of which Valéry approved. We may therefore follow his ideas knowing that the poet himself speaks to us.

Teste is 'a man watched and spied on by his own ideas; the contrary to a madman, for his aberrations and dreams are arranged and classified;

he can repeat the operations of his thought exactly, finding his way back by an infallible inverse operation.' Everything appears to him as a particular case of his mental functioning, and this functioning itself becomes conscious thanks to his strict training and habits. He thinks all the time, and on every occasion, 'according to given premises and studied definitions.' Above all he refers everything to himself, being a man of precision to whom the most vivid memories appear only as actual formations of his mind. Even the sense of the past is accompanied by the notion that 'the past is an actuality of the present giving colour to some image of the past.'

Teste would preserve art, while exterminating the illusions of artists and authors. He could not suffer gladly the pretensions of poets or the exaggerations of romancers. He considered that exact ideas on what one was doing led to much more surprising and universal developments than did 'humbugging tales about inspiration, or people's lives etc. . . .'

'Some Thoughts from Monsieur Teste,' with which this curious little book ends, evidently were written at a considerably later date. Here many theories concerning poetry are introduced. Teste now considers that 'sensibility is all, endures all and appraises all.' He has in fact discovered in growing older that the only hope for a man is to develop means of action which diminish his ills by giving his sensibility something to perform, on itself, and according to itself.

The final sayings of Teste as he draws near to death are very moving, more so now than when first written, for we know the poet to have himself passed through the drama he had imagined. Suffering and the control of suffering are considered with the same lucid attention as is given to thought, analysed and measured against human possibilities. The final words have a classic dignity. 'All that I do and think is only a specimen of my capacity,' says Teste. 'For man is more general than his life and his acts. He is capable of more eventualities than will happen to him.' Therefore his reserves, his possibilities, will not abandon him. But the evil in life mocks: what proof have you that you are still that which you believed yourself to be? 'I have not turned towards the world. I have turned my face to the wall. There is not the least thing on the surface of the wall that I do not know.'

'We have to pass from zero to zero—and that is life,' sighs Monsieur Teste, 'sight is not being, but implies the being.'

'Adieu,' he murmurs, 'very soon there will end . . . a certain manner of seeing things. . . . An intellectual end, a funeral of thought.'

Is Monsieur Teste anti-poetic? Many French critics have considered him to be so, opposing Valéry-Teste to Valéry-poet.[1] Certainly Teste is the manifestation of Valéry's revolt against literature, in his rôle of an intellectual taking a stand against other idols and representing a vigorous spirit of positivism and anti-literary principles. However this does not prevent him from being a poetic creation, a figure carved from the mind of his maker. Whether at the theatre, or in his own commonplace and simple room, there is poetry in the austerity of Monsieur Teste's thought, as well as of his person. Thus the bareness of his room is not a vain negation, for he sees, around him and always renewed, all the luxury of his treasures: 'the graceful groups of his words, the mirrors in which the consequences and the perspectives of his thoughts move and fade into the infinite; the lights of his reason, of his faith and his hopes. He is more truly at home than any other man. . . .'[2] And what could be more poetic than the description of falling asleep which is put into the mouth of Monsieur Teste. '*Je fais la planche*—I float, I feel an imperceptible rolling beneath me, an immense movement. I love this current of sleep, and the bed clothes which stretch and fold and crumble like sand.'

Here it seems important to recognise the difference which Valéry sees between poetry and literature. For the qualities which are essentially those of Monsieur Teste, and which he expresses, are also those that Valéry considers to be of the greatest value in the functioning of poetic creation:

> . . . Flexibility of thought, the mind's consent to consummate difficulties and constraint, and the perpetual triumph of sacrifice. . . . For exactness and style are needed to counteract the permanent dissipation of thought. For all thoughts, even the most beautiful, are shadows, and the phantoms here precede the living. It was never a fool's game to impose a little grace, a little clarity, and a little continuity on the instability of the things of the mind, and to change that which passes into that which endures.[3]

Again, 'Enthusiasm is not the state of mind of a writer.'

Thus the function of the poet is in reality one with that of the intellectual who questions and studies his thoughts, trying always to determine, in his own mind, for his own satisfaction, the relations

[1] See A. Berne-Joffroy, 'Valéry Présent,' *Présence de Valéry* (Paris: Plon, 1944), 90.
[2] Paul Valéry, *Mauvaises pensées* (Paris: Gallimard, 1942), 157.
[3] Paul Valéry, 'Au sujet d'Adonis,' *Variété*, I, 56–7.

between things. For it is the poet in the intellectual who animates his thoughts and gives life to his abstractions.

'I claimed to govern my thoughts,' said Valéry years later in speaking of the early days of Monsieur Teste. It is not difficult to see how such a state of mind led to the pride of being unique, and we find this attitude in several passages. 'Vanity is to pride what superstition is to religion; and veritable pride is the antidote to all vanity.' So Teste choses the pride of being unique rather than the vanity of being considered an artist. At the top of the ladder are *les hommes d'esprit*—men of intelligence, men of wit, 'those who are silent, the race of the unique Teste: the intellectual man, who should finally discipline himself consciously to refuse to be anything whatsoever.'[1]

In any account of Valéry's evolution, Teste is significant as the figure-head of the boat in which the poet, leaving poetry behind, set out to cross the sea of self-knowledge. The symbol of the pride of being intellectually unique, he is at the same time a symbol of humility through his honest pursuit of knowledge and purity. In subsequent pages I shall examine the intellectual background that gave actuality to this question, round which Valéry constructed his thought during the years of comparative silence following the creation of Monsieur Teste.

3. VALÉRY AND THE PHILOSOPHERS

Ce que Valéry a fait méritait d'être tenté.
(BERGSON)

From an early stage in his development Valéry's attitude towards philosophy was one of proud refusal. He continually denied that he had ever found any answers to his own problems in philosophical works. Speaking of the time when he first read Poe's *Eureka* he said: 'As for philosophers, I had frequented them but little, yet that little was enough to irritate me, because they never replied to any of the difficulties that tormented me. I found them merely exasperating and I never felt that they communicated any real power.'[2]

This statement tells us a great deal not only about Valéry, but also

[1] Paul Valéry, 'Note et digression,' *Variété*, I, 176.
[2] Valéry, 'Au sujet d'*Eureka*,' *Variété*, I, 116.

about the state of philosophy at that time, and the general feeling of revolt in the intellectual world against what had proved static in metaphysical methods. Human inquiry was changing its ground, or, to speak more exactly, it was approaching its problems from a different angle. Nor was this all: the problems also had changed. Humanity had reached the stage at which the mind applies itself neither to purely metaphysical ideas nor to preconceived beliefs, but to observation and classification of laws which regulate effects, that is to say, to the invariable relations of succession and similitude which all things bear to each other. A progressive development towards concrete reality, as demonstrated by positive experiment, largely independent of abstract and theoretical reason, characterised the nineteenth century. It had become a contemporary conviction that abstract knowledge, if it did not convey a corresponding effective power, could be considered of only secondary importance. To know everything was only worth while if such knowledge was the source of real power.

With this new scientific and positive outlook, came the realisation that the efforts of the intellect could no longer be regarded as converging towards any one spiritual limit or unique truth.[1] Knowledge of the universe had been the supreme aim of philosophers. The positive minds of 1890, however, had lost all belief in a unique image of the cosmos: it was disintegrating, and naturally enough so was philosophy. The riddle of the universe, such as it had existed in mens' minds, was impossible to solve. The mature mind of humanity now turned to other more immediate and urgent questions.

The passage from the age of pure reason to the age of experiment and reality had been bridged by Auguste Comte (1798–1857), who in tracing the progress of intellectual thought had shown that certain fundamental laws of evolution were confirmed in the history of man. Yet there was nothing essentially new in Comte's statement, and perhaps the greatest merit of his gigantic work was to have cleared the ground of the confusion between language and thought, as Descartes (1596–1650) had done in his time.[2]

The two all-powerful elements of Cartesian thought, the Self and mathematics, remained as essential instruments of future development.

[1] Paul Valéry, 'Léonard et les philosophes,' *Variété*, III, 151: 'L'effort de l'intellect ne peut plus être regardé comme convergent vers une limite spirituelle, vers un *vrai*. . . .' 'La politique de l'esprit,' *Variété*, III, 237: 'L'univers se décompose, perd tout espoir d'une image unique.'

[2] Cf. Schere, *Revue des deux mondes* (1861).

The Cartesian 'Self' was to form the basis of a new science of psychology, and mathematics were also to develop conceptual non-Euclidian ideas.

Speaking very generally, in order to summarise a complicated situation, one might say that *applied* philosophy had gradually replaced speculative metaphysics in the domain of modern thought, at least in so far as scientific statements, confirmed through experiment, had to be established in reference to reason. This being so, it is not surprising that mathematical thought, which most closely expresses scientific reason, should take new life and vigour from the ideas of transformation, correspondences and varied application, which constituted a veritable dialectical development, as a scientific language of constructive reasoning, more especially in the new aspects of non-Euclidian geometry.

Thus as if in preparation for Einstein's relativity, mathematics had assumed an immense significance in the evolution of scientific thought. And we may observe, in considering the growth of this scientific age, that Lobatchewsky's Pan-geometry bears something of the same relationship to Euclidian geometry as Einstein's Pan-astronomy was to develop in relation to the astronomy of Newton. In both cases the older sciences—Euclid's geometry, Newton's mechanics—as French scientists have pointed out, have not been abolished, but as it were englobed; a transformation has taken place, including them as particular cases in wider conceptions.

Thus while its basic ideas were enlarged, science had gradually become more and more specialised, enriched by succeeding discoveries which obliged scientists to become specialists each in his own line. So too philosophers found themselves obliged to adopt a more positive and realistic attitude.

It had, as we have noticed, remained for a philosopher, Auguste Comte, in his classification of the sciences and his laws of mental evolution,[1] to express a synthesis of humanity's progress, and incidentally to prove that classical philosophy had fulfilled its own destiny and bequeathed its inheritance to positive science. Indeed after the conclusions of the early eighteenth century, such as that of Locke that 'all knowledge is founded on experience and all experience is relative,' that we cannot know things in themselves but only as they affect us, metaphysical thinkers inquired as to whether there are any ideas independent of such experience, and the answer was that there are not. Thus the *a priori* principles on which philosophy had counted to ex-

[1] Auguste Comte, *Cours de philosophie positive*, 6 vols. (Paris, 1830–42).

94

plain essences and causes, in the magnificent endeavour to know all things, had gradually given place to specific inquiries as to the laws which govern phenomena. From this point philosophy continued to prepare the way for an intellectual psychology. This had been its parting message, at once a challenge and a welcome to the new age.

As natural phenomena had been taken over by science, philosophers now turned to explore more thoroughly the mind of humanity and the part it played in the universe. It was the so-called 'natural philosophers,' such men as Schnelling and Hegel, who, though they had not attempted to bridge the gulf between philosophy and science, had enlarged imaginative thought and provided fresh material for poets and even answers to their passionate inquiries.

Hegel (1770–1831), whose friends were Goethe and Schiller, influenced the poets of the nineteenth century perhaps more than any other philosopher. He was pre-eminently the philosophic guide not only of the Romantic poets such as Schiller and Shelley, but also of Villiers and Mallarmé, all of whom found in the abstract premises of his idealism the theories necessary to support their intuitive and imaginative conceptions of humanity's rôle in the universe. The question of Mallarmé's relationship with the ideas of Hegel has been admirably dealt with by Professor Mondor and L. J. Austin,[1] so need not be discussed fully here. It is sufficient for our purpose to note that Mallarmé had based on Hegelian idealism his conception of man's capacity of expression as being the highest consciousness in the universe; and had in particular established for himself the place of his own art in the universal scheme.[2] He had, as Valéry said, identified himself with an Absolute of expression.

Hegel had boldly stated that the Absolute was one with the Non-Existent—the Nothingness or *Néant*. Yet he affirmed that Nothingness exists because it is Thought in its pure state ('Das Nichts ist; denn es ist ein Gedanke'). This Nothingness (*Néant, Nichts*) is the same Thought as that of pure Being (*Sein*), that is, an entirely unconditioned Thought. Being and Non-Being are the same ('Sein und Nichts ist dasselbe'). These conclusions lead, through a 'poem of ideas,' to the paradoxical statement that knowledge and existence are one and the same. The principle of the identity of contrasts (severely criticised by Jean-Paul

[1] Henri Mondor, *Vie de Mallarmé* (Paris: Gallimard, 1941), 219–21, and L. Austin, 'Mallarmé et le rêve du livre,' *Mercure de France*, I (1953), 81–108.
[2] Mallarmé, 'Le Livre, instrument spirituel,' *Œuvres complètes*, 378.

Sartre[1]) is the basis of Hegel's method. His Logic is founded, as he himself says, on Empedocles' idea of the flux and reflux of all things.

In the delicate relationship between theory and imagination, the poet takes from philosophy only what he needs, and, through a personal interpretation of dogmatic statements, the poetic genius confers a psychological significance on the philosophical data which it transforms. Thus the more Hegel deviated from strict logic, turning from the dusty answer of certitudes, to contemplate a shining idealism, and the more imaginative he became, the more the poets responded to his thought. Just as Hegel's ideas had been fundamental in the development of Mallarmé's poetic creed, so too, through Valéry's friendship with Mallarmé, the same ideas helped to form the younger poet's principles of psychological poetics.

Such was the position of the intellectual world for a brief moment at the end of the nineteenth century, where we find Valéry almost unconsciously taking part in the contemporary development of the science of Psychology, which was a new name expressing a new attitude in the minds of contemporary thinkers.

Undoubtedly Victor Cousin[2] (1792–1867) had been the first to organise the *experimental* study of the facts of consciousness, and while he agreed with the eighteenth-century philosophers that men could only grasp instantaneously the actual knowledge of the Self, he gave to the study of such facts a quite different signification, believing that they could present the nature of things in a perspective which would be different from that given by the phenomena of the exterior world.

Thus where Condillac had seen only one class of facts—that of sensation—Cousin discovered three classes: feeling, voluntary acts and rational acts. It is of particular interest in relation to our subject, that he gave the two last divisions of consciousness a fresh and characteristically nineteenth-century interpretation. For in the voluntary acts of consciousness he saw acts of free will revealing a permanent power which was both the condition and subject of all consciousness that constitutes the *Moi*—ego or I, while in the third category, that of the rational, consciousness appeared to have the faculty of raising itself above itself to become identified with reason or a universal Absolute. Cousin insisted on the necessity of beginning the study of metaphysics

---

[1] J.-P. Sartre, *L'Être et le Néant* (Paris: Gallimard, 1948), 295–301.

[2] Victor Cousin, *Fragments philosophiques* (Paris, 1838), *Du Vrai, du beau et du bien* (Paris, 1840).

through psychology, or in other words, of progressing from analysis to reason. Then he turned to mysticism.

But where Cousin left the ground, the ground nevertheless remained, and it was evident that intellectual psychology was the right approach to metaphysical thought. Unfortunately, this idea, which had long been foreseen by philosophers, was vitiated and destroyed by the quasi-religious mysticism of Cousin's direct successors. With their emotional reasoning Valéry had no sympathy. In speaking of the difficulties that beset the modern man he said, 'A great part of our difficulties comes from the strong survival of a sort of mysticism or mythology, which is less and less in accordance with the facts, but from which we do not know how to detach ourselves.'

However, religious mysticism was not the only opponent of a metaphysical conception of psychology which would include abstract intellectual states. The Freudian doctrine of merely organic, sub-conscious animal instincts, allied to the psychiatrist's study of mental disease, was to be universally accepted. Yet in Valéry's youth the idea of an intellectual psychology was still valid. Indeed this conception is the basis of his idea of a super-consciousness capable of passing from the sphere of phenomena to the sphere of noumena as the object of meditation; for it is true that the existence of states known only to consciousness is more certain, to each of us, than the phenomena of the exterior world shown to us through direct sensation. And these states, contrary to Freud's teaching, do not correspond to the states of our organism, though some of them may be affected by it. By fixing our will on certain ends, we create a series of intellectual acts, a state of awareness that depends entirely on our own powers.

Although the analytical methods of modern thought, as developed by Victor Cousin and his contemporaries, were new, the fundamental ideas which they analysed were as old as philosophy itself. From Plato to Descartes the idea of an intellectual psychology had been —under different names—a part of metaphysics, and the Self or consciousness had assumed an increasing importance, to the point of being, for Descartes, the basis of all knowledge and the only ground of absolute certainty. Thus the intellectual necessity of the development and knowledge of the Self, expressing the need of a condition of thought ready to comprehend the acts of universal knowledge and art, at which Valéry aimed, had already been formulated. When Valéry asked himself 'que peut un homme?' and turned to his own mind in order to find an answer, he was intuitively repeating the question formulated first by Descartes, later by Locke, and finally by Nietzsche.

Descartes had also been the first to declare that psychological and mathematical methods were inseparable, consciousness being the only ground for certitude (*Cogito ergo sum*) and mathematics the only sure *method*. Three centuries before Valéry, he wrote:

> I entirely gave up the study of letters, and resolved to seek for no other science than that which I could find within myself.[1]

What had proved valid for Descartes remained so for modern minds, and we find Valéry repeating the same idea.

> I have never consulted anything but my Pure Self, by which I mean the absolute of conscience, and this is the unique and uniform operation of freeing myself automatically from all things.[2]

If Descartes had been the first philosopher to question deliberately his secret self, Locke also had patiently watched the operations of his own mind so as to surprise his fugitive thoughts and discover from them the secret of their combinations.

> To understand the soul and its affections, he did not study books; they would have misdirected him, he was content to descend within himself, and after having, so to speak, contemplated himself a long while, he presented in his Essay [*On Human Understanding*] the mirror in which he had seen himself. . . . In a word, he reduced Metaphysics to that which they ought to be, namely, the experimental physics of the mind.

So wrote D'Alembert on Locke.[3] Might not his words be equally well applied to Valéry? Moreover a careful inquiry into the origin of 'thought' had also led Locke to comment on the jugglery that takes place in language 'some of it conscious, some unconscious, but all pernicious.' And he said that 'vague and insignificant forms of speech had too long passed for mysteries of science,'[4] showing a philological interest of which Valéry must certainly have approved. Nor was it only seventeenth-century philosophers who had foreshadowed certain of Valéry's ideas. Kant too (1724–1804) had affirmed the necessity of the

[1] René Descartes, *Discours de la méthode* (Paris: Flammarion, n.d.), première partie, 8 (my translation).

[2] Paul Valéry, letter to the R. P. Rideau (1943) (also printed as Preface to *L'Introduction à la pensée de Paul Valéry*, by Émile Rideau); *Lettres à quelques-uns*, 243.

[3] D'Alembert, *Discours préliminaire de l'Encyclopédie*.

[4] John Locke, *Essay concerning Human Understanding*.

study of consciousness in his *Critique of Pure Reason*, though the conclusions of Kantian ethics were very different from those of Valéry.

Yet we may question whether Valéry had ever studied, or more than glanced at Kant's investigations into the origins of thought, or whether he had read Locke's *Essay*, or the dicta of Locke's critic Leibnitz. It is more likely that he had become familiar with certain of their basic ideas through Condillac, who in any case undoubtedly played some part in the formation of Valéry's thought. Extremely clear as far as style was concerned, Condillac advanced theories which were often erroneous, based, it has been said, on a misconception of Locke's conclusions. It may be that Valéry's mistrust of philosophy had its origins in what his critical intelligence had found unsatisfactory in Condillac. Nevertheless Valéry had found something to agree with in Condillac's statement, 'We shall not discover a sure means of conducting our thoughts as long as we do not know how they are formed.'[1]

We may note in ending this all too brief summary of the philosophical recognition of the Self, that Nietzsche's works were at one time Valéry's bedside books.[2]

The second fundamental idea that Valéry derived from philosophy was that of method. To philosophers a method had come to be of the greatest importance. It was regarded as one of the essential inventions of philosophic genius, and its function was to indicate a passage from concrete to abstract. Bacon had been the first to invent a method, but it was Descartes who established a deductive method as it is understood in modern philosophy. Comte, Locke and Kant had each in turn evolved particular systems.

Before considering Valéry's response to this philosophical principle, let us glance at one aspect of Descartes' achievement. At the age of twenty-three he had made the discovery of quantitative geometry, through which geometrical relations might be expressed by algebraic symbols, and conversely algebraic equations could be demonstrated by geometric figures. This was one of the greatest discoveries of philosophy. Thanks to the twofold nature, both psychological and mathematical, of Descartes' method, the future progress of science was indicated.

[1] 'Condillac est absurde mais ses éléments surtout.' Paul Valéry, *Cahiers*, I: *1894–1900* (facsimile) (Paris: Centre national de la Recherche scientifique, 1957), 150.

[2] See *Correspondance André Gide–Paul Valéry*, ed. by Robert Mallet (Paris: Gallimard, 1955), and *Quatre Lettres de Paul Valéry* (privately printed).

It was from this principle that the nineteenth century evolved a new conception of mathematical science, in which each mathematical organisation of experiment is characterised by a special group of transformations, as, for instance, Euclidian geometry is founded on the group of displacements. On this theory of group transformations Valéry founded his system: phases of thought were to be submitted to mathematical transformations, grouped according to their kind, and manœuvred according to given laws. Words were also to be dealt with in the same way in so far as they became the means of poetic expression.

The Valérian idea of method was also supported by the Quantum theory, which gives a scientific justification to considering the 'real' through its mathematical organisation. Through this means matter was to be sublimated to the furthest psychological aspect of mathematics. Thenceforth the universe was comprehensible only through the action of numbers.

Here is Valéry's explanation of his adaptation of mathematical propositions of classification as applied to his system:

> *Au fond c'est bien simple:*—you reduce everything to sensations and mental phenomena, you regroup these into two or three classes according to their properties of substitution, you look for a comprehensive relationship between all these factors of cognition, etc.; and you have in your hands a means of analysis entirely general and new. You may henceforth envisage in each particular case the properties of the totality of combinations relative to it. You hold the origin of all possible developments of that which is given: according to the use you want to make of it you adopt one of these ways, literature, philosophy, criticism or imagination etc., etc.[1]

Thus the general scheme of Valéry's theory is seen to be a system of transmutation, a sort of intellectual metamorphosis through applied laws which are common to number, language, and by extension of such means, to the whole faculty of thought.

Only through such progressive transformations could the Self achieve the pure acts of its own being. The idea of transformation thus becomes for Valéry the common denominator between the language of mathematics and the language of Self, which in turn becomes the final language of a poetry expressing the elements of consciousness through an exact and formal art.

The German critic Ernst Robert Curtius was the first to remark on

---

[1] Paul Valéry, letter to Fontaine (juin 1898), 'Notes et documents,' *Correspondance Paul Valéry–Gustave Fourment* (Paris: Gallimard, 1957), 243.

the fact that Valéry's art was founded on a theory of transformation. And Curtius, commenting on the use of a mathematical conception of a universal science of pure form which would comprise the laws of all inferior states, says:

> Starting from the elements of our experience, instead of starting from the elements of arithmetic, we may imagine a similar approach: through a series of abstractions and from accumulated generalisations, which would lead on the 'ego' until it became nothing more than a vacant and nameless consciousness, and which would reduce the universe to be finally nothing but a particular case of an infinite multiplicity of possible systems.[1]

This idea is demonstrated in *Monsieur Teste*, and completed in the final shadow of 'Le Solitaire' in *Mon Faust*. But Curtius, in his all too brief essay, though he gives an admirable generalisation of the Valérian method, does not speak of the machinery which Valéry was obliged to evolve in order to achieve his purpose.

Already Henri Poincaré had raised the question as to whether it was possible to give a mathematical explanation of the working of thought, and had suggested that such a process must inevitably be purely arbitrary.

In geometry, intellectual forms resembling each other are dealt with according to an unchanging order. Common notions, engaged in different propositions, serve as links to unite other concepts to which they were separately attached. There remains nothing of thought but its pure acts through which it is changed and transformed into an abstract of itself, until finally it extracts from its shadows the whole play of its operations.

In the same way Valéry proposes to analyse consciousness of thought—which consists in being aware of the relations between different intellectual phases. For we may classify thought according to our familiarity with it and finally reduce it to its own abstraction. To do this our thoughts must be grouped according to their difficulty, beginning with the simplest, in such a way that each leads on to the next; and as thoughts must be expressed in words, words acquire here the value of geometric symbols. Thus, language may be compared to geometry in the mathematics of thought; that is to say, as thought becomes mathematical in the measure in which it becomes abstract,

---

[1] E. R. Curtius, *Hommage des écrivains étrangers à Paul Valéry* (Bossum: Stools, 1927), 22.

words, which define it, must necessarily have the geometric qualities of defining exactly the interrelationships of such thought.

Evidently language, having grown from all sorts of needs and myths, is impure as a means of abstract knowledge. So for Valéry's purpose all words must be classified with accuracy. For what are numbers but the most simple words used as signs or symbols of calculation: simple because created for a unique end to serve the special act of calculation? Sometimes they become 'almost a kind of poetry of repetition in a strictly closed system.'

In the Dialogue of 'Eupalinos' we are told that the arts of music and architecture take effect through 'numbers and the relationship of numbers.' This may also apply to a formal conception of thought or of formal poetry, which—like other formal arts—becomes a structure of 'forms and laws,' bringing us into contact with what is durable, ordered and stable, while leading to all possible abstract combinations and conceptions. These may create from their new forms, and through their own laws, figures which become 'singular beings, half abstract, half concrete, veritable creatures of man and not the resemblances of sensible things.'[1]

Thus in many passages Valéry insists that words are to be 'manœuvred' as are geometrical quantities. It is easy to understand how valuable the idea of mathematical principles would be in bringing new power to imaginative language, and in giving form to analytical transformations in the composition of poetry. This idea becomes all the more significant when we remember that Valéry regarded mathematics as an art, and his definition beautifully elucidates his point of view:

> Mathematics is an art of consequence and of connection in a rigorously closed system of properties, a sort of poetry of pure repetition.

Of algebra he said:

> Algebra may be considered as a sort of morphology, a creation or formation to some extent organic of number, of which it defines the species, the transformations, and the structure.[2]

These definitions are important as showing how Valéry reacted to intellectual noumena. They seem to suggest that all mathematical

---

[1] Paul Valéry, *Eupalinos ou l'architecte, L'Ame et la danse, Dialogue de l'arbre,* (Paris: Gallimard, 1944), 58.

[2] Paul Valéry, 'Discours en l'honneur de Goethe,' *Variété,* IV (Paris: Gallimard, 1944), 114.

thought is founded on a comparison of integral values and on a series of transformations of such abstractions as allow for possible classifications.

Valéry had the modern scientific attitude towards thought. He did not wish to accumulate riches but to make actual the means of doing so. If art were to be universal in the sense of satisfying the whole of the poet's intellectual curiosity and employing all his mental powers, technical means had to be enlarged and reinforced. Only thus could poetry emulate pure mathematics and be animated by the totality of consciousness.[1] Thus Valéry conforms to the methods of modern science, in replacing the experimental stages of inspiration by arbitrary laws which establish the scale on which symbolic images are to be constructed.

Do not all thinkers at some stage stop breathless before the gulf between theory and practice; between *Vouloir* and *Pouvoir*? Valéry reports that Einstein had said, in speaking of his own conclusions, that the distance between theory and experiment was such that it was necessary 'to find the point of view of architecture common to both.'[2] By this, said Valéry, he meant that he trusted in the productions of his own mind, in the liberation of certain harmonies and sympathies, in the action of certain preferences, in the suggestion or perception of symmetries, of given responses of obscure origin but imperious enough.

Nature is happily supervised by a controlled imagination. The nature of intellect provides what the nature of things refuses. Then the thinker extracts from both natures those conclusions which transform all ideas.[3] So in spite of the fact that a scientific method applied to poetry can evidently be based only on the hypothesis of a scale of values which must rest on the poet's preferences, and is therefore to be considered as arbitrary, we may nevertheless accept the imaginative structure of a master mind. We may apply Einstein's argument to Valéry's formal scheme, an act of faith fully justified by poetic results in which the variety, changes and caprices of language, its unstable conditions of origin and development, are all submitted to intellectual order. And we perceive that the principles of form remain valid for the poet as for the scientist.

[1] Paul Valéry, *Cahiers*, I: *1894–1900*, 150.
[2] 'La distance entre la théorie et l'expérience est telle, qu'il faut trouver des points de vue d'architecture.' Reported by Valéry, also his explanations which I have followed closely. See Paul Valéry, *L'Idée fixe* (Paris: Gallimard, 1934), 181.   [3] *Ibid.*

Strongly attracted by physical science, Valéry pursued scientific studies and followed the developments of modern physics in its most complicated fields of action, interesting himself in the relativity of time and space, and the inquiry into atomic energy. Such men as Prince Louis de Broglie and Pasteur Vallery-Radot were his friends and expressed their admiration for his intelligence. Mathematicians paid homage to his understanding of mathematics; for without being himself a mathematician, in the strict sense of the word, he was able to penetrate the subtleties of mathematical thought, and to take all that he required from it for his own purpose. He had the sort of universal mind that grasped the intellectual problems which presented themselves to his infinite curiosity, and which he analysed with a Cartesian persistence:

> Patience, patience,
> Patience dans l'azur!
> Chaque atome de silence
> Est la chance d'un fruit mur!

4. AN INTELLECTUAL PSYCHOLOGY

Quand l'esprit est en cause, tout est en cause.

(P. V.)

In the year 1897, on the advice of Huysmans, Valéry entered the offices of the Ministère de la Guerre.[1] This employment was most uncongenial and he regretted the time lost on routine. It is amusing to note that an inspector reported that Valéry 'would make a good functionary.' This however was not the opinion of the poet, who complained to Mallarmé, 'Du fond des sales bureaux . . . on a le gros ennui de ne plus pouvoir songer à rien. Ici il y a trop à faire.'

We catch sight of Valéry on his way to the ministry on a morning in June 1897, when he met Gide who had just returned from Italy, and who with his bulging portfolio, his top hat and his frock-coat, appeared as the image of a cocksure civil servant, with whom Valéry says that he would willingly have changed places, even to becoming the author of *Les Nourritures terrestres*.

---

[1] May 5, 1897—as *commis-rédacteur* in the Direction de l'Artillerie.

Inside the office at his usual place, stirred by his meeting with Gide, Valéry remembers that *au fond* he is still a poet; he hears the clock repeat the theme of the hours and the quarters in E major, prelude to the chords of 'Infinite Time,' while the motive of *sommeil des dossiers* (sleep of the ledgers), of which the clerk is the hero *par excellence*, breaks through the orchestra, supported by the brasses that evoke an imaginary operetta, in which the daughters of Ink sing together:

> Gratte, gratte, gratte la page
> Lâche la tâche! Mâche la tâche . . .

in the palace of Documents where the mocking god of Urgency still jeers at Destiny. . . .[1]

Though Valéry was now completely detached from any idea of a literary career, and in fact from literature in general, poetic images still came to his mind as symbols of his thought. In January 1898 he sent Gide the beginning of a poem in prose, of which he said, 'it is too difficult, I shall never finish it.' This was 'Agathe ou La Sainte du sommeil.' 'Let us imagine,' he continued in the same letter, 'one of those women who sleep two, three or ten years at a time, and who dreams during all that time, and when she wakes can tell her dream, though she has had no sensations for years: thus the diminution or other aspect of the data with which she went to sleep is to be studied.' This work was never completed, though Valéry alludes to it from time to time in his letters to Gide, Louÿs and Fourment. Certain lines from drafts of this fragment were used in *La Jeune Parque* many years later.

Two years after the death of Mallarmé, the circumstances of Valéry's life in Paris changed. In 1900 he married Jeannie Gobillard, niece of Berthe Morisot and close friend of Geneviève Mallarmé. After his marriage he went to live at 40 Rue de Villejust (now Rue Paul Valéry) in the house built by Berthe Morisot on the western slope above the Arc de Triomphe. This became his home for the next forty years, until his death in 1945. He had three children, to whom he was a devoted father. Some months after his marriage, he left the Ministère de la Guerre to become private secretary to the director of the Agence Havas, Edouard Lebey, who was old and infirm, and to whom he became guide, philosopher and friend. It was only a short distance from the Rue de Villejust to the Avenue du Bois where Edouard Lebey lived; and Valéry went there for four or five hours every afternoon.

---

[1] Paul Valéry, letter to André Fontainas (1 juin 1897), *Lettres à quelques-uns*, 57.

His chief duty was to read aloud the news of the Bourse, events from the daily papers, or the sermons of Bossuet and of Bourdaloue; of the latter, Valéry said, 'he was very pure and scarcely anything more than that,' and confessed that he sometimes skipped the dullest pages. . . .

Valéry's days were now passed in the quiet routine of a studious life. Since 1895 practically the only continuous form of expression which he had allowed himself was his Cahiers de Notes, a sort of journal, not of events of his daily life but of his ideas. In the 'Avant-propos' to the first published selection of these notes, Analecta (1926), he said:

> For the last thirty years I have kept a journal of my ideas. Hardly out of bed, at dawn in that pure and profound hour between the lamp and the sun, I have the habit of writing down whatever comes into my head. The idea of anyone else, of a reader, is altogether absent at these moments.[1]

The Note-Books, therefore, were only for himself; he had no idea of creating through them a form of literature. Their function, he tells us, was to fix 'a provisional truth' that he wished to retain for 'possible future use: an instantaneous truth, more or less true, which would not exclude contradictions in the form of other detached statements.' This way of working would be most useful in obtaining statements valid in themselves which would permit their author to classify and build up his thought, starting from its first statement, and thus obtain 'that real value of speech which only appears through its verification.'[2] All that was of significance could in this manner be easily divided from what did not add to the progress of the Intellectual Self. 'I write for the future of my thought,' he said, 'and not for its past . . . in order to advance and not to look back. . . . I write to test, to construct, to specify and to prolong, and not to double what already exists.'[3] And again in 'Analecta' he says, 'my principal object has been to figure to myself as simply and as exactly as possible the functioning of my whole being. I am world, body, thoughts,' and he adds, 'this is not a philosophical purpose.'[4]

[1] Paul Valéry, Analecta (1926), in Tel Quel, II (Paris: Gallimard, 1943), 201.
[2] Paul Valéry, Tel Quel, I (Paris: Gallimard, 1941), 7.
[3] Paul Valéry, 'Propos me concernant,' Présence de Valéry.
[4] Paul Valéry, Analecta, in Tel Quel, II. Except when stated otherwise, the quotations in this chapter are taken from the published selections of the Note-Books. The general theories are derived from the Note-Books or from the Variété series, where they are often repeated. The chief points of Valéry's psychology are from L'Idée fixe and Les Cahiers (published in facsimile by the Centre national de Recherche scientifique).

Of the 254 Cahiers only small portions were published during the author's life. These consisted of several selections of aphorisms, meditations, fragments and disconnected thoughts (which are discussed below on page 211). In some of these published selections we find the latent idea of a Method, while others express thoughts on a wide range of subjects. Valéry says, in the preface from which I have already quoted, that the purely theoretical ideas of his system are not included in the published Notes, and this applies to the subsequent Selections published during his lifetime.

Although all the volumes of the *Cahiers* in facsimile have not yet appeared, the general lines of Valéry's thought are sufficiently apparent to enable us to establish the theoretical ideas of his system which he defined as the essential of his invention. The first volume of the *Cahiers*, published in 1956, covers the period 1894–1900; and the second volume published in 1957, goes from 1900 to 1902. In the first Notes of 1894, the author fortifies himself with the thought that 'la régularité est l'aimant de l'esprit,' (regularity is the loadstone of the mind), and that 'la pensée réfléchie est une véritable expérience.'

The *Self Book* (1895) and the *Log-Book* (May–October 1896) follow with their pen-and-ink drawings, and ideas, and remind us of Leonardo's conception of notation. The *Log-Book* was used for the Log-Book of Monsieur Teste, with whom Valéry identified himself, and throws light on the growth of the Universal Self through this abstract being, in such Aphorisms as 'L'Abstrait est la possibilité d'un Tout.' Here we find thoughts derived from scientific data; equations used to combine transformations—arbitrary for the most part; observations on aspects of art or of life, sometimes personal, on the whole clever, and occasionally profound. These notes often express a contemporary trend of thought, and at other times flat contradictions of generally accepted concepts.

The really significant contents, however, consist in continuous efforts to refer all things of the intellect to mathematical formula—in a *mathématique de l'intelligence*. On one hand the intellectual data are dissected and classified, and thus almost achieve a separate existence through their own abstractions; on the other, the algebraic equations are worked out, arriving, we may conclude, at the same values in the poet's mind. In fact we may say with Valéry that 'all the elements are there,' with drawings and diagrams to illustrate the mind's progress.

For the rest, the theory and analysis of language as a source of poetry, together with the elements of an intellectual psychology, are noted and codified, particularly in the second volume (1900–02). These I shall deal with in due course.

One truth, known to certain painters and poets, is confirmed in Valéry's *Cahiers*: that what the poet perceives intuitively through his art can be stated with extreme precision through the medium of mathematics.[1]

We should notice here that the *methodical* presentation of Valéry's theories would necessarily have consisted in their final co-ordination and combination, and it was precisely this final arrangement which was never carried out to any significant extent by their author. Thus in 1901 we find Valéry writing to his brother:

> I work as I can but I really think that I shall never get through with it, and that I have undertaken too great difficulties. . . . It is even strange to have all, or almost all, the elements and not to be able to build, when it only remains to superimpose and join up. Unfortunately, or fortunately, I have reduced the practice of writing to an exact number of clear and direct operations. But once they are performed in my head, writing them down becomes extremely boring.[2]

Then fifteen years later, speaking of the Notes in a letter to Albert Coste, he says that he had spent his time 'on more or less abstract speculations difficult to define' from which there had resulted 'some kilos of registers,' and he adds, 'I have tried not to become a specialist even in the speciality of writing, but nevertheless to state my thoughts more and more clearly.'[3]

Undoubtedly as he grew older, Valéry lost faith in strictly methodical demonstrations of that intellectual activity which was always a necessity for him. The pure joy of creating took on a wider sense, and fortified by a lifelong discipline, classical expression, and all that it implies, became for him the spontaneous reaction of a method of thought, so that he could maintain that: 'les belles œuvres sont filles de leur forme qui est née avant elles.'

Thus the idea of completing the system which he had formulated was gradually abandoned. 'The mind has not the faculty of finishing off

---

[1] Théodore Roussel (1847–1926) formulated and prepared in advance all the tones for his painting the *Reading Girl* (Tate Gallery); he used the same method (chromatic analysis) for printing original etchings in colour.

[2] Paul Valéry, letter to Jules Valéry (1900–1901), in *Paul Valéry vivant* (Paris: Cahiers du Sud, 1946), 263. By permission of M. Ballard.

[3] Paul Valéry, letter to A. Coste, *Lettres à quelques-uns*, 103.

its works,' he said, and in the 'Note et Digression' (1919), commenting on the early idea of a mathematical method, he condemns the brilliant schema proposed for his Universal Man as impossible: 'Impossible dirait maintenant la raison.'

Nevertheless, and despite the fact that it was never completed, I hope to show that Valéry did invent a psychology for poets, and a linguistic system which governs his poetics. I propose to deal with those two aspects of technical method in two parts. In the first I shall consider the purely psychological aspect of the formation of the abstract Self, which constitutes a sort of intellectual psychology. In the second part, in a later section, I shall examine the system of poetics, which is based on similar principles, and whose function was to express through poetry the progress towards an absolute of consciousness.

In considering Valéry's psychology the first thing to notice is that he proposed to define and classify *mathematically* the mental operations of the intellect. Mental phenomena were to be grouped and classified according to their variations. These *states* were to be considered as limited in their operations and therefore definable—since they could be measured. By this means a sort of mechanism of the intellect could be established. This was to be the basic principle of a new intellectual psychology, which was founded on, and became the final outcome of his 'Arithmetica universalis,' to which, about 1900, he used to refer. Thus in a letter to Gustave Fourment, (1897) he says, 'I do not consider the mental states in themselves, they are infinite, discontinuous, etc.; but it is possible to believe that their variations or their conditions might be better known. . . .' And again: 'In the same way take mental phenomena of no matter what nature, images, interior phrases, sentiments etc., etc., all these phenomena are as it were equal in regard to certain states. Thus oblivion overtakes them all equally, sleep impairs them, and they can be reproduced. . . . They can be more or less grouped in classes according to the treatment which we accord to them. . . . I think that there are only a limited number of operations to which these complex phenomena, so difficult to understand, may be submitted.'[1]

'I tried,' he said, 'to make for myself a philosophical language arising from my own observations and from my real and personal

---

[1] *Correspondance Paul Valéry–Gustave Fourment*, Introduction et notes par Octave Nadal (Paris: Gallimard, 1957), 141.

needs.'[1] In order to do this, he rejected all problems outside his own sphere, organising only those ideas which were useful to him. In the pursuit of this research he evolved his own drama, declaring that all that is dramatic in life and history was of secondary interest as compared with the intellectual desire for knowledge.

It is evident that, in developing this inner mental drama, Valéry had to create his own terminology: terms which he kept for his own use. And he liked to compare himself to a 'Robinson' of the intellect, making his own tools adapted as closely as possible to his way of thinking and of combining the elements of his thought,[2] while in reality he was enlarging the field of human inquiry.

One aspect of this new terminology is of special interest. For its terms, some of which we are about to consider, define certain states which hitherto had never been described exactly, but which nevertheless exist and are recognisable as part of human experience; thus Valéry was the first to isolate certain phases and processes of thought.

Whatever the professional psychologists and psychiatrists or others may decide about the general value of Valéry's terminology, the fact remains that it is valid for poets, because it defines phases or states of intellectual consciousness through which all artists who advance to a certain mental level must inevitably pass; and the realisation of such states of consciousness serves to guide the progression of thought towards its own expression and final abstraction.

In this endeavour to extend the range of consciousness to its utmost mental limits, Valéry touched on a new poetic Relativity, in so far as abstractions now became fundamentally relative to their own symbolic expression, thus partaking of a relationship or unity in a manner somewhat analogous to that of space and time.

Starting with the mind itself, Valéry considers it as both that which contains and that which is contained. He defines the unifying element as 'the *Functional*'—a mental mechanism whose expense of energy is

---

[1] Paul Valéry, 'Propos me concernant,' *Présence de Valéry*, 27, and letter (mai 1921) in *L'Arche* (octobre 1945), 26: 'Une part immense à demi utile de mon travail fut de me faire des définitions. Penser au moyen de mes propres définitions ce fut pour moi une espèce de but.'

[2] Paul Valéry, *L'Idée fixe*, 33: 'Une idée est un moyen, ou un signal de transformation.' Of his terminology Valéry modestly says, 'des amusements sans conséquence,' but adds, 'la plupart des notions dont on use en psychologie ne sont pas beaucoup plus précises.'

limited to an exact circuit.[1] The mind is the centre of such functioning, it is the mill or mould through which all perceptions, sensations and images are transformed and regrouped, passing through a series of *Phases* each of which is complete in itself. It is thus that definite progress becomes possible, a progress in which words may replace mathematical figures in a continual transmutation of consciousness which may be pursued until a state of pure being is attained: until all exterior confusion has been eliminated, and all contact with the background and with the outer world has been absorbed and surpassed. So the pure moment may be finally reached in which all relevant powers of the mind are concentrated to an instantaneous state of complete unity. This moment of the pure Self may well be the moment of its expression in pure poetry.[2]

In this universe of creative values the function of thought is to co-ordinate and organise itself. It deals with the matter that it receives through sense perception; a profuse and often chaotic material which thought examines, sifts and classifies.

According to a law which Valéry calls *Plein Mental* the mind must have contact with material from the outer world on which to work.[3] So, too, whether the medium of thought be mathematical figures, tones as in music, or words as in poetry, the strictest correlation is necessary between the degrees of its internal progress. The realisation of this progression enables one to avoid all confusion between thought and the physical brain which provides the necessary energy for thought's development.

All that the senses offer flows into the mind as material to be tried out, to come into contact with the sixth sense of intellectual awareness through which the mind selects what it needs for its own purpose; it chooses. And may we not say that all art exists on this basis of *selection*, of combinations, acceptances and refusals, and all that the judgement of choice implies?

Starting from what he knows he can find, state and explain, Valéry

---

[1] Paul Valéry, *L'Idée fixe*, 33: 'En somme, une idée du fonctionnement d'ensemble. . . .' *Ibid.*, 35: 'C'est une mécanique tout particulière où les questions de temps jouent un rôle essentiel. . . .'

[2] Paul Valéry, 'Poésie et pensée abstraite,' *Variété*, V, 129: 'a pure and ideal voice . . . capable of communicating an idea which will express a Self that is miraculously superior to the Moi [I or me].'

[3] Readers should consult Mme. L. Julien-Cain, 'L'Être selon Valéry,' *La Nef* (janvier 1946). Mme. Julien-Cain was the first, so far as I know, to comment on Valéry's psychological terms.

proceeds towards an exact or intense expression—and exact and intense are not the same thing—and he defines this mental action as 'resolving a Nebula.'[1] We may recall that Jules Laforgue places the origin of his poetic dreams in a cosmic Nebula:

> O fleuve chaotique, ô Nébuleuse-mère
> Dont sortit le Soleil, notre père puissant.[2]

Valéry's Nebula however is 'a confused mass on the confines of the moment.'[3] It may be changed into a system of exact ideas, or it may remain in a state of cloud, a formless impression of unorganised intellectual presentiment. This mental Nebula, this invisible cloud of witnesses, may be recalled; shadows of ideas, every shade of thought, may return to the memory to be reconsidered, evolved and resolved into precise formula. It may be regarded as the material of memory, as the contents of the containing mind.

The work of selection from the Nebula implies a series of operations determined by a capacity of comparison which Valéry calls the *Pouvoir*, a power which directs the intellectual application of the movements or operations of thought, controlling and guiding them to a state of perfection. This power is in fact a sensitive critical faculty which leads to the first elements of form. It is moreover the power with which the poet constructs from such elements the pillars of formal art:

> Si froides et dorées
> Nous fûmes de nos lits
> Par le ciseau tirées,
> Pour devinir ces lys![4]

Thus classical form can live only through a continuous mental transformation. The *Pouvoir* is therefore a fruitful power which owes its fruitfulness to discipline, and which regulates the laws and liberties of poetic creation. For creation cannot take place under the reign of arbitrary rules, or under the rule of automatism; and Valéry's psychology, in this concept of *Pouvoir*, recognises the part played by the

---

[1] Paul Valéry, *L'Idée fixe*, 87: 'Il s'agit de procéder à partir de ce que je sais pouvoir, trouver, exprimer . . . c'est résoudre une nébuleuse. . . .'

[2] Jules Laforgue, 'Crépuscule de dimanche d'été,' *Poésies*, I (Paris: Mercure de France), 36.

[3] Paul Valéry, *L'Idée fixe*, 104; *Cahiers*, II.

[4] Paul Valéry, 'Cantique des colonnes,' *Charmes*, in *Poésies* (Paris: Gallimard, 1933).

voluntary organisation of aesthetic values which govern the poet's mental life.

However, the mind has its own limitations; it cannot apply itself indefinitely, beyond a certain limit, to the same idea. Valéry explains this incapacity by a law of continuity of mental change which he calls *Self-Variance*.[1] By means of this Self-Variance ideas become at once the signal and the means of a transformation: the tension of the mind has to change into an act, into words or into a phrase. Thus Self-Variance is the motive-power of all the future transmutations by which Valéry builds his system.

'L'œuvre de l'esprit n'existe qu'en acte.'[2] The working of the mind exists only in an act, and this mental act is the passage from one idea to another. Thus every work which is the result of the mind's action is also a transformation, and has for its object a transformation, and it can be nothing else. This law of change or progression governs and directs the whole range of intellectual thought. It represents for Valéry the working of his thought in general, and the development of the Self in particular.

Nor is this all, for the prime object of such laws being the systematic development of consciousness, this in turn supposes a law of cosmic change. Valéry goes so far as to suggest that one might consider the universe as a gigantic work implying an immense 'operation of transformation,'[3] and that such work would have for its secret goad or incentive the search for greater consciousness through which this thinking universe might attain to a certain supreme thought—'on the threshold of the all.' Such thought Valéry defines as *Omnivalent*[4] and universal, linked with everything and linking all things.

This exact and profound mental metamorphosis—and it is sometimes easier to be profound than exact—finally brings consciousness to its ultimate purity, and to the conclusion that all things are equal. That is to say that intellectually 'all things may be substitutes for all things,' and Valéry adds, 'might this not be the definition of things?'[5]

---

[1] Paul Valéry, *L'Idée fixe*, 34 et seq.

[2] Paul Valéry, 'Cours de Poétique,' *Variété*, V, 309.

[3] Paul Valéry, *L'Idée fixe*, 51: 'Cet univers en travail n'a peut-être pour fin— et pour aiguillon secret—que la recherche de la conscience, et par là d'une certaine pensée—suprême pensée.'

[4] *Ibid.*, 54 et seq. 'Idée omnivalente . . . omnivalence . . . s'accroche à tout, est accrochée par tout. . . .'

[5] Paul Valéry, 'Note et digression,' *Variété*, I, 201. All things are equal for *l'homme d'esprit*: 'Tous les phénomènes . . . apparaissent dans une certaine

It is significant that Valéry advances his ideas—his transformations from Phase to Phase—by a system which he calls *Tropism*: a figurative method of manœuvring his thought and co-ordinating its different Phases. Thus the knowledge of the workings of the mind begins with the analysis of the intellectual Phases of thought, which hitherto had appeared as mere undefined variations. For now these Phases have become isolated and complete states, being the outcome of successive transpositions from one thought to another. Thus the consciousness that we have of thought, *qua* thought, consists in being aware of this sort of equality and similarity, which at the same time permits us to make comparisons through which we recognise the equivalent variations of a common substance. Here the conception of a *Phase* is exceedingly subtle. Through the figurative and therefore metaphorical use of language, in the Valérian schema, each Phase may present a complete state of unity in which the Self is undivided; such as being newly awake, or a condition of complete mental attention.[1] Such Phases may be symbolised, in their condition of indivisibility and surety, by such universal constants as sea, sky, or some collective or representative phenomenon or object of perception.

Here we should not overlook the element of purification, which alone can make such metamorphosis valid as an instrument of thought. Valéry notes that there are states of 'non-attention' in which unrelated thoughts succeed each other in confused incoherence. Thus the process of thought can be methodically valid only in states of *attention*. For to know more is to be more, and Valéry was well aware of this essential aspect of change; in his search for abstract knowledge and pure expression this is self-evident.

équivalence . . . tout cela est égal. . . . Toutes choses se substituent, ne serait-ce pas la définition de choses?' This idea, dating from Anaxagoras master of Socrates, has been re-established by modern science. It reappears in the theory of Leibnitz (*repraesentatio multitudinis in unitate*) and in Lotze's theory of microcosms—not to speak of its development by the Mystics. The German romantic Novalis first proposed the idea of universal analogies found in Baudelaire's 'Correspondances' (*Les Fleurs du mal*). It is a fundamental idea of Symbolism. See Poe for aspects of this principle. See also Sorensen, 'La sémantique de Paul Valéry,' *Hommage des écrivains étrangers à Valéry* (Bossum: Stools, 1927).

[1] State of being newly awake: 'L'Ame, saisie d'une fraîcheur intime, d'une crainte, d'une tristesse, d'une tendresse qui l'opposent encore à tant de puissance croissante, se tient un peu à l'écart, dans une réserve inexprimable.' Paul Valéry, *Mauvaises pensées* (Paris: Gallimard, 1942), 135. See also Paul Valéry, 'Les Pas,' *Charmes*, in *Poésies* and cf. 'Second Poetic Period: 5. Time of *Charmes*,' below p. 184.

Thus the mind gradually builds up its own powers. It both sets its own course and conforms to its own laws. It aims at a future and greater consciousness. In each new Phase it increases its power of action.

The resources of energy that consciousness thus acquires may however remain potential, and this capacity of greater knowledge may remain in a state which Valéry defines as the *Implex*, 'that by which and in which we are eventual.'[1] The Implex is not at all the same thing as the Freudian subconscious, which it replaces. Valéry considered that the accepted 'subconscious, by which men mean all the hidden springs and the minute forces that work within us,' was one of those high-sounding words which he repudiated as having been too often used and misused. In any case he would have dismissed the elements of Freud's definitions as merely organic and animal reactions which did not necessarily govern mens' actions.

Nor is the Implex the same as the complex of current psychology. Valéry gives it an extended and intellectual significance, insisting that this capacity for feeling, searching, doing and understanding, is the faculty through which sensory knowledge passes into the world of thought, producing those so-called spontaneous ideas that hitherto have been generally dismissed as 'inspiration.' This is one of 'the laws of the mind' which men ignore and in which Monsieur Teste delighted. Variable and only more or less perceived, essentially unstable, the Implex remains for the individual the means of realising the most elevated thoughts, thus constituting a reserve of possibilities from which to reconstruct the whole functioning of the intellectual being.

The necessity of controlling the powers which might be antagonistic within his own mind led Valéry to divide those faculties into two groups. On the one hand there are those which are *transcendent* or *irrational*, evaluations or judgements without cause, or unexpected instantaneous clarities—'all that makes us centres of surprise to ourselves' and which includes aspirations and dreams. On the other hand there is the sense of logic—the relations which progress without missing a single degree of the operations in hand, or any moment of transformation which develops from equilibrium to equilibrium—and finally willingness to foresee and to co-ordinate all the properties of the design one wishes to construct.

Realising that sensibility is capable of becoming a valuable

[1] Latin *implexus*: 'Implex est capacité. Notre capacité de sentir, de réagir, de faire comprendre. . . .' *L'Idée fixe*, 106.

intellectual quality, to the point of animating the whole universe of thought, Valéry considered such sensibility as the creative force which makes all philosophers artists in their own sphere, and which, if rightly disciplined, should go to make all artists lovers of wisdom in their own art.

All Valéry's theories lead us back to his central theme of consciousness, or the Pure Self, and we may consider this constant aspect of his thought in following him through what he calls 'the temptation of the spirit.' Thus he tells us that through a process of elimination, by denying an infinite number of beliefs and also an indefinite quantity of elements, having controlled and composed its own variations, the Self becomes the result of its imposed discipline. Moreover the Pure Self is the unique and continuous element in each being, that loses and rediscovers itself, inhabiting the intelligence as some grave motif persists throughout a symphony. It is that 'profound note of existence'[1] which, from the moment we cultivate it, dominates the whole complication of circumstances and changes in our lives. Nor can we fail to observe, when we venture into the realms of transmutation, the constancy of this potential awareness—and Valéry said that he had chosen it as his objective because of its 'resistance to the flight of thought.' The Self that he elevated to such a high degree was not 'the cherished ego,' since his intention was to replace the ego by a Self without name or history. He compared this final state to 'the precious zero of mathematical language to which all algebraic expression is equal.'

Thus the Pure Self is assumed to be 'the direct heir to that being without face or origin on whom weighs the whole endeavour of the Cosmos to which it is related,' until at last it seems

> Que l'univers n'est qu'un défaut
> Dans la pureté du Non-être.[2]

A little more, says Valéry, and the Self will admit as necessary existences only two entities, both essentially unknown: itself and x, both of them abstracted from everything, implicated in everything and implicating everything, equal and consubstantial. The 'Solitaire' in *Mon Faust* is the final symbolic figure who expresses this state:

> A moi Splendeurs du pur, à moi, peuple superbe,
> Puissances de l'instant, Sainte diversité!

[1] Paul Valéry, 'Note et digression,' *Variété*, I, 204.
[2] Paul Valéry, 'Ébauche d'un serpent,' *Charmes*, in *Poésies* (1933), 166.

Venez! Hautes Vertus, sourires sans visage;
Sonnez! Voix sans parole et Paroles sans voix. . . .[1]

And a passage in *La Jeune Parque* evokes the sacrifice of life to pure consciousness:

O n'aurait-il fallu, folle, que j'accomplisse
Ma merveilleuse fin de choisir pour supplice
Ce lucide dédain des nuances du sort?

In these texts a cosmic consciousness, towards which all thought tends, is suggested, and Valéry might almost be said to be playing on the motif of Hegel's ideas of Being and Non-Being, in an attempt to establish his Absolute of Self as the final point of abstract purity.

Now that the Self has attained this pure state, it feels that it is only in contact with living shadows. It is no longer concerned with its own development, having absorbed and transformed all the variations of its own being, and 'all its genius was no more than the means of reaching this last simplicity.' Characteristically, Valéry insists that even the most powerful mind finds nothing better to contemplate than itself, 'there being no act of genius that would not be less than the act of being.' This is also the conclusion of *La Jeune Parque* as she turns to life:

Alors, malgré moi-même, il le faut, ô Soleil,
Que j'adore mon cœur où tu te viens connaître. . . .

Yet according to Valéry life is not an end in itself. It has to serve the purposes of the mind. It has to be composed and transformed to its furthest limits, perfected through a universal science of transformations in which all arts and sciences will be finally combined and unified in a single Cosmic Conception. This seems to me to be the conclusion which Valéry's doctrines suggest, since the most general group of the mind's transformations, which includes all sensations, all ideas, and all judgements, allows for a Constant, or in other words, leads to a pure and complete state of sensitive abstraction. It is no exaggeration to add that such a state would be the most probable approach to a further transmutation towards universal knowledge.

[1] Paul Valéry, *Mon Faust* (Paris: Gallimard, 1946), 227.

IV

The Poetics

1. THE RETURN TO POETRY

*Toute une existence de poète construite sur une
même thème.* (L. GILLET ON DANTE)

DURING THE YEARS of poetic silence, Valéry patiently constructed his
intellectual universe. He reached a state of detachment in which consciousness of Self, liberated from all ordinary preoccupations and
events, learned to refuse to be 'anything whatsoever.' This state might
be described as a condition of intellectual beatitude, a potential condition of awareness, a clarity that excludes any mystical revelation.
The Self, so deliberately cultivated, had in 1910 reached its maturity.[1]
Thought, conscious of itself, now represented a potential force capable
of calling up a state of readiness and comprehension: a moment of
intellectual enlightenment. But now a new problem arose: to what
clear end was this acquired power to serve, through what medium
could it find adequate expression?

Valéry had come to the limit of his elaborations and classifications,
to the end of self-analysis, in the effort of organising and directing
mental forms so as to establish fixed points in the chaos of his mind.[2]

---

[1] Paul Valéry, 'Propos me concernant,' *Présence de Valéry* (Paris: Plon, 1944),
43.

[2] Paul Valéry, 'Cahier B,' *Tel Quel*, I (Paris: Gallimard, 1941), 215: 'Il y a un
moment où tout penseur est la victime de la fin de son effort fini, et de sa propre
transformation. . . .' See also Valéry, 'Mémoires d'un poème,' *Variété*, V (Paris:
Gallimard, 1945), 112.

However, the creation of a transcendental order which included everything, having absorbed in advance the accidental, remained an abstraction which had not yet found its expression. To know that he possessed
this force of perception, and at the same time not to be able to find its
adequate and formal assertion, was almost intolerable. For too long his
mind had turned over the difficulties that such problems presented,
making for itself a sort of Dantesque inferno through which it wan-
dered. 'I was a prey to great anxiety . . . and to the humiliation and bitterness of feeling myself vanquished by intellectual matters,' wrote
Valéry. 'In vain I tried to reduce my ideas to the state of ordered
thought, the effect was only momentary. . . .'[1] For now the Pure Self
was like 'a beautiful fragment of perfection,' and the vanity of all that
could intrude upon it seemed a mere hindrance, a breeze that would
shatter the vision of an abstract Narcissus.

'I cannot recognise myself as a finished figure,' Valéry lamented,
'and the self flies always from my mind which however it delineates in
flying from it.'[2] Again, 'Teste is bound in chains. He knows so much,
and he is so sure of so many connections that he speaks no more.' And
he confesses, 'I don't even think any more, having the presentiment, as
soon as an idea rises, that an immense system gets started and enormous
toil is called for, and that I shall never go as far as I know it is necessary
to go.' He noted that he would have liked to have classified and to have
given precision to his own mental forms and 'to think through them in
such a way that each thought would bear the visible marks of the
whole system which it expressed, and which would clearly be a modification of a definite method'; and he added, 'in regard to this men are
still in the state of savages.'[3]

This amounts to a regretful farewell to his central scheme. Was it
then an impossible task to lay all his notes on the table and sort them
out, combining and associating the different parts? Was the essential
motive power lacking for this proposed flight into the stratosphere of
abstractions, as it had been for Leonardo's flying machine?

Valéry has described his state of intellectual anxiety at this period.
In the first morning light—'a light more obscure than the whole night'
—he wakes to a calm which lets all thought be seen through a lucid

[1] Paul Valéry, *L'Idée fixe* (Paris: Gallimard, 1934), 13.
[2] Paul Valéry, 'Cahier B,' *Tel Quel*, I, 187.
[3] *Ibid.*, 202: 'Je voudrais avoir classé et rendu nettes mes propres formes,
penser en elles . . . de sorte que chaque pensée porte les marques visibles de tout
le système.'

state, still simple, flexible and distinct: 'first resignation, clarity, well-being as if in a sort of primitive bath.' The early morning exists for him like a uniform sound. But soon all that he has not done, all that he never will do, surrounds him with regrets that are as strong and tenacious as a dream and as clear as waking. He feels 'the stupidity' and at the same time 'the truth of such moments.'

This was no mood for meditation. The only thing to do was to get up and go out; to wander among the dust-bins of early morning Paris, which so aptly symbolised regret, and in walking make the effort of leaving 'even torture unfinished.' What bitterness and disillusionment are betrayed in these words: 'Only suffering seems true,' he noted. 'The best seems a sign of the worst. . . . For suffering is always new.' Now the torment which was 'the revenge of useless and stationary thoughts' appeared as his real vocation: 'Angoisse, mon véritable métier,' he cries from the depth of his despair.[1] This crisis has been referred to by Valéry as a sort of mental *retour d'âge*; and here he again repeats the experience of Descartes, who at the same age had started to record the fruits of his years of meditation.

In reality Valéry had obtained the essential from his system, since the consciousness of a Pure Self had now become second nature and was ready to be transmuted into the form of poetry. Thus though he is still depressed, he begins to consider means of communicating his thought:

> Late this evening, shines more plainly that reflection of my nature: instinctive horror, and lack of interest in this particular human life. Dramas, comedies, novels, even strange ones and above all those which say they are intense, loves, joys, torments, all the sentiments appal or bore me; and the appalling does not exclude the boring.[2]

A strangely literary approach to life from one who had so long scorned all 'literature.' Yet here the interest lies in Valéry's preoccupation with such matters; for those rejected types of literature were forms in which he could not find his ultimate expression.

In drama he seems to have seen only his own conflict; and though such conflict has a universal significance, it is not enough that the dramatist is torn to pieces by his own inner drama, which he must act out to the end. For if he does not transpose this interior struggle, linking it with the wider problems of humanity, his drama remains a monologue. Valéry's drama is either a monologue or a dialogue between

---

[1] Paul Valéry, 'Cahier B,' *Tel Quel*, I, 213.   [2] *Ibid.*, 187.

different aspects of his Self—authentic but necessarily limited. Nevertheless when we examine this statement we are bound to admit that there are two principal ways of expressing man's universal tragedy: through the vast Shakespearian constellation shining in a sky of infinite consequences; or through the Valérian radiance of a single star lighting the same void between separate consciences. Fundamentally the drama is the same, since everything has to pass through the poet's mind and be felt, suffered, controlled and organised to become art. 'Connaissez donc en vous le fond de mon discours'[1] might as well have been said by Shakespeare as by Valéry.

The first signs of a return to poetry appear about 1910. Though Valéry still insisted that he was not a poet 'or anything like that,' his notes of this time show a fairly constant concern with critical considerations on poetry. 'There are more chances that a rhyme should produce a literary idea than that the rhyme should come from an idea,'[2] he noted, and then follows this confession which seems to re-establish the 'idea': 'Here are paper, ink, words, even cadence—all nothings which are more lasting than the essential.' The 'essential' was of course that moment of perception which should have both 'order and illumination,' gifts which often enough opposed each other in the poet's mind. 'For what use is a too brief flash, or what use is an ordered afternoon without it? I shall not have the courage to enter into this flash which instantaneously illuminates the years,' he noted, and then added, 'Ah, to think? . . . to think, that is to lose the thread.'

It seemed now rather ridiculous to pretend to explain anything, since he had proved to himself that the only real truth is instantaneous, imposed by the lucidity of the moment on that 'diversity which one calls man.' Music still appeared to be the only perfectly constructed example of method, and the poet's ideal would be to construct 'the scale and system of harmonic chords of which thought in general would be the music.'[3] Such ideas brought with them new courage and life, for there is a part of our minds that can only be satisfied when composing or making something. 'I invent therefore I am,' he wrote.

[1] Paul Valéry, 'Le Philosophe et la Jeune Parque,' in *Poésies* (Paris: Gallimard, 1942).

[2] Paul Valéry, 'Cahier B,' *Tel Quel*, I, 203.

[3] Paul Valéry, letter to A. A. Coste, *Lettres à quelques-uns* (Paris: Gallimard, 1952), 108: 'Mon idéal serait de construire la gamme et le système d'accords dont la pensée en général serait la musique.'

'For the general march of inventions belongs to this general type: a series of successive deformations, almost continuous, of the given matter, and then a doorway—a sudden preoccupation in the future of one of those states.' The future, that is to say the utilisable value, unique and significant, was, and could only be, the 'future' of poetry.

And now, brushing aside all the anxious self-questionings, in the unbroken solitude of dawn, who is it who steals in 'without waking the dog'? Who stands behind the poet's chair and calls softly 'C'est toi —Moi qui est aussi toi'—the most constant, the most obedient—who if not Poetry? Who if not Laure,[1] that delightful companion of silence, the mistress of dreams, too long neglected?

'Laure is with me since dawn,' Valéry recorded some time later, 'in a unique world of our own': in this closed sphere of solitude where all things are alive; in this first hour, neither night nor day, in which everything around the poet participates in his presence. The walls of his room seem to him to be constructed by his will; while the light of the lamp seems itself to be like a closed circle of time. The white sheet of paper before him (not to repeat Mallarmé's page) 'seems lucid and peopled as a sleepless night,' and the 'whole group of each instant' is felt by him.

For Laure to appear, everything must be like this and all the circumstances must make the poet ideally alone:

> Laure exacts and inhabits this silence which is armed with anticipation, where sometimes I become what I wait for. She watches for what is murmured between my desire and my demon. Her pale face is rather vague, but not her gaze. What a precise power! Wherever my sight rests it carries hers with it.[2]

And may not 'the veritable Laure who was flesh,' and who 'rises from the void,' be in reality those inspired moments of the youthful poems, and the first love which Monsieur Teste had banished, belonging to that ardent time that Valéry called the 'age of fire' and to which in the 'age of ice'[3] he now returns?

No poet ever had a more ideal dream-mistress, for Laure is nothing else than pure poetry. One thinks of Dante's Beatrice, of Petrarch's

---

[1] Valéry, 'Cahier B,' *Tel Quel*, I, 204: 'Tu m'appelles doucement et derrière moi.'

[2] Paul Valéry, *Mauvaises pensées et autres* (Paris: Gallimard, 1942), 131: 'Laure dès l'aube est avec moi dans une sphère unique au monde. . . .'

[3] Paul Valéry, *Analecta*, in *Tel Quel*, II (Paris: Gallimard, 1943), 266: 'Age de glace.'

Laura; but for all her abstraction, Valéry's Laure seems most poignantly real, perhaps because the poet's very existence depends on her presence and because she excludes for the moment the loves and troubles of everyday life. Valéry wrote only one short poem directly addressed to her; it is called 'La Distraite.'

> Daigne, Laure, au retour de la saison des pluies,
> Présence parfumée, épaule qui t'appuies
> Sur ma tendresse lente attentive à tes pas,
> Laure, très beau regard qui ne regarde pas,
> Daigne, tête aux grands yeux qui dans les cieux t'égares,
> Tandis qu'à pas rêveurs, tes pieds voués aux mares
> Trempent aux clairs miroirs dans la boue arrondis,
> Daigne, chère, écouter les choses que tu dis . . .[1]

Whether or not this interpretation of Laure is the right one, one thing is certain. The invisible presence of Laure foretold the return to a period of poetry, and a creative awareness replaced the bitterness and negation of sterile refusal. For now certain turns of speech, and forms of language, haunted the frontiers of mind and voice, demanding to be given life: 'Delicious moments when the stirrings of intimate and expressive invention begin to live'—like the tuning up of an orchestra, which is full of promise, a preparation for a miraculous unity.

In numerous essays and notes Valéry commented on his return to poetry, which he considered as the completion of the circle. 'I have observed in mental things,' he said, 'that if we are sometimes able to reach our antipodes, afterwards we can hardly do anything but return again. It is only a matter of time, for all further changes can only bring us back to the beginning.' So now after twenty years and more spent on 'all sorts of analyses, and the interior formations created or adopted for their furtherance,'[2] Valéry returned to poetry armed with certain invincible qualities: 'I have employed,' he said in 1919, 'an apparatus a hundred thousand times more precise, to observe the same thing that I observed in 1891. The degree of precision transforms a question, and sometimes a fourth decimal changes the whole idea that one had just before of a world.'[3]

Thus in one sense there was no complete break in the progress of his

---

[1] Paul Valéry, 'La Distraite,' in *Poésies* (1942), 168. By permission of Librairie Gallimard.

[2] Paul Valéry, 'Mémoires d'un poème,' *Variété*, V, 112.

[3] Paul Valéry, letter to Marius André (août 1919), in *Lettres à quelques-uns*, 132.

thought, which was now to be employed in the service of an art that he wished to make as perfect as possible to express the mature development of his mind. 'I thought of a certain purity of form,'[1] he said, amused anew by syllables and images, by similitudes and contrasts. Again, he found incomparable contentment and a theme of infinite question in poetic composition, realising through it the expression of the Self that had for so many years occupied him in its most abstract form.

It was therefore a happy coincidence, that while this metamorphosis of the abstract into poetry was gradually taking place in Valéry's mind, exterior circumstances were favourable to its development. These circumstances were as follows. In 1911 Gaston Gallimard sent André Gide to ask Valéry to allow the 'Nouvelle Revue Française' to collect and publish his early poems. This permission Valéry refused. Nevertheless the N.R.F. collected the poems that had appeared in various reviews and sent a typed copy to Valéry, who read them with some displeasure, finding that his taste had changed. Nor did he feel any special interest in a stage of his development which he had long since outgrown. He was quite sure that he did not wish to publish them.[2]

As for the Notes, and the ideas contained in them, which he had gradually accumulated, he declared them to be merely the material for his own mental exercises which for many years had given him an 'almost animal satisfaction' in the working of his mind. Yet since we have seen from his published Notes that he had returned to the consideration of poetry, we must take his word that he had done so only for his own satisfaction and mental necessity, without any idea of publication.

However, it was his disapproval of the early poems that induced him to make corrections and rewrite lines; and this led to the consideration of all sorts of new problems. From this it was a short step to start a poem, which he at first intended to be about forty lines in length and which was to be his farewell to verse. Here was a task to which the full force of his powers could be applied, and the theme that inevitably imposed itself was the genesis of the Self.

This poem was *La Jeune Parque*, the astonishing masterpiece on which Valéry was to work for five years at the rate of about a hundred lines a year. The coming of the war in 1914—with its foretaste of later

[1] Paul Valéry, 'Mémoires d'un poème,' *Variété*, V, 113.
[2] *Ibid.*, 77.

disaster—spurred him on to aim at perfection in this work. For in the dark period of war, with difficulties on every side, he felt that he had lost his spiritual liberty. The only solution was to continue to write his poem, making it as perfect as he could. The French language, he thought, was in danger; he would submit himself to its strict rules, building his art on classical French metres, rather than destroying them as others were doing. His poem would be a monument to the great French tradition of language and verse, the final expression of a heritage that was now threatened. *La Jeune Parque* was not—as some critics have supposed—the outcome of sublime indifference, but the expression of an 'anxious resistance and profound perturbation.'

It was Pierre Louÿs who, during this difficult period of completing the poem, sustained and encouraged Valéry. Here only a poet could provide that rare criticism which is in its turn creative. Unfortunately, part of the correspondence between the two poets is lost, although fifteen of Valéry's letters, sold after Louÿs' death, were privately printed.[1] In the remaining letters, which date from October 1915 to after the publication of the poem in 1917, Valéry speaks of the difficulties of the 'language of the mind.' He tells how in 1916 he read three hundred lines of his poem to Gide, who did not criticise it. And Valéry insists on the necessity of Louÿs' help if the poem is to be successfully finished. 'I have to get it finished,' he wrote, 'and I cannot do so without advice on different points. . . . I have only you to depend on, your ear, your taste and your experience, your difference from me, and your resemblance to me.'

Pressed by Gide and Louÿs, Valéry consented to publish *La Jeune Parque* with the N.R.F. In 1917 it was brought out in a small edition of six hundred copies, which was sold out in three months. Its success was immediate. Valéry was at once acclaimed as a poet. This was partly due to the enthusiasm of Pierre Louÿs, who recommended the poem to Paul Souday, critic of *Le Temps*, in the following terms: 'May I mention to you a really beautiful poem by Paul Valéry. I think it is a masterpiece of our literature.' Paul Souday responded with a long article in *Le Temps* on *La Jeune Parque*.

In May 1917, almost immediately after the publication of the poem, Valéry wrote to Louÿs explaining that 'nervous exhaustion' and 'certain torments' had prevented him from replying sooner; that, except for a few letters, the poem had brought him nothing but bother and fatigue; and that he bitterly regretted the loss of the shadow which he

[1] Paul Valéry, *Quinze Lettres à Pierre Louÿs* (1916–17) (Paris: Monod, 1926).

had been pursuing while the work was in progress, 'for the shadow is worth more than the prey.' This is a characteristic point of view. As for the 'torments,' it seems that with the re-establishment of the idol of poetry another idol had also reappeared, as if the heart too had imposed its reasons.

However in June of the same year he wrote more cheerfully: 'I begin to return to the delight of writing what I want, as it comes, and without thinking of going into print. Oh, how wise I was up to 1917. How well I foresaw things, and my own in particular, in 1892! . . .' Now the fruits of much labour were to be picked at choice and become the material for 'Le Cimetière marin' (published in 1920), and for the lyrics of *Charmes* (1922).

2. THEORY OF COMPOSITION

Mais lui s'était fait des clartés toutes personnelles.

(P. V.)

When we consider Valéry's second poetic period, in which the doctrines formed during the years of silence became a veritable system of poetics, we may start from his statement that his poetry is founded on analysis and music, and that its object is purity: that is to say, the expression of an absolute of Self. 'There are two things that count,' he said, 'that ring true on the table when the mind plays its game against itself. One, which I call analysis, has purity for its object, the other, which I call music, composes that purity making something from it.'[1]

His aim was to make language do what it had not previously done, and to make it appear to do so in perfect freedom. The effort of acquiring this liberty led him to apply his 'method'—in classifying his chosen language, and evolving a theory of composition, of works composed in all their parts as in music. The Greeks had shown an example of such an enterprise by dividing language in two parts: formal logic and rhetoric. Valéry wished to continue the work of analysis, for 'syntax is a faculty of the mind.'[2]

If we define a writer as one for whom there is an affinity between a certain state of mind and a certain sensibility to language, we may easily

[1] Paul Valéry, 'Propos me concernant,' *Présence de Valéry*, 34.
[2] Paul Valéry, *Choses tues, Tel Quel*, I, 25.

understand how the mere thought of composition becomes the most poetic of ideas: of composing all that is most rare yet most authentic in both thought and expression, so that, through their rhythmic relationship a spiritual exercise is created and leads to a poetic revelation.

The idea of form is fundamental in all Valéry's theories of composition; it leads to the conception of 'formal poetry' on which his poetics are based. Observing in the arts of music and architecture a wealth of combinations and regular developments comparable to those of mathematics, his constant endeavour was to introduce similar qualities into his poetry. For in both music and architecture 'the union of the different parts and the relation of the detail to the whole is always exacting and is always felt.'[1] These two arts therefore seemed 'the most apt to embrace and express the essence of things, and to be the most abstract and pure means of expression.'

In various essays Valéry spoke of the idea of composition and pointed out how rare such an idea was in poetry. By 'composed' works he did not mean either those constructed on a succession of events, or those which simply followed a logical scheme. Every composition, in the Valérian sense, should be one in which the internal relations are indissoluble.[2] This unity gives a special significance to his insistence on classical prosody. 'Every time I think of writing,' he says, 'the same idea comes to my mind. I fancy that I progressively find my composition starting from pure conditions of form, more and more studied, and in fact defined to a point of almost proposing a theme—or at least a group of themes.'[3] And these conditions of form,

> Belles chaines en qui s'engage
> Le Dieu dans la chair égaré,

are the expression of a poetic intelligence and an awareness of the means at the poet's disposal in the execution of his poem.

There are two aspects of this theory which must be expressed through laws of syntax: the psychological and the musical. The first reveals an analytical approach with a given end in view—the development through progressive figures towards the ultimate Self, or some

---

[1] Cf. Valéry, 'Propos me concernant,' *Présence de Valéry*, 55.

[2] Paul Valéry, 'Reflections sur l'art,' *Bulletin de la Société française de philosophie* (1935), 74. Cf. Valéry, 'Au sujet du Cimetière marin,' *Variété*, III (Paris: Gallimard, 1936), 70: 'Cependant la seule pensée de constructions . . . demeure pour moi la plus poétique des idées: l'idée de composition.'

[3] See below p. 136, 'Theory of Language,' also Paul Valéry, 'Poésie et pensée abstraite,' *Variété*, V, 130 *et seq*.

dramatic episode of such development. In the musical presentation there is a whole range of euphonic values which constitute a fresh application of musical effects, to which I shall return.

This formal poetry is neither 'encumbered nor obstructed by anything arbitrary or superficial taken from self-evident reality,' and it must also be free from too obvious reproduction of concrete forms of life, and from types of thought or expression already worn out. Thus all heterogeneous elements of the outer world, foreign to the notion of composition, must be rejected. The idea of exact synthesis—light reflected in a diamond—is inherent in this conception.[1]

From this it will be seen that Valéry's idea of poetic composition is far removed from the notion of poetry as spontaneous expression, from which it differs in the same way as the scientific treatment by analysis of a question of physics differs from the mere noting of the preliminary observations. Scientific treatment implies the reconsideration of the phenomena concerned; the scientist is obliged to create the methods of a new computation.[2] And this is a fairly apt description of what Valéry does in composing his poems.

If poetry is to express a conception of intellectual sensibility, the nearer it approaches an abstract symmetrical synthesis, while keeping its emotional appeal, the more completely will it fulfil the ideal of its own perfection, and Valéry summed up this view when he said:

A pure art would be one which would include nothing except the functions of sensibility, excluding their application to the facts of practical life which implies the incoherence of the real. Such an art tends to create an absolute system or at least to give the impression of one, a closed system, which at the same time is the most general, containing all the possibilities in virtual state.

The 'composition' of this formal poetry consisted in 'infinite operations on language.'[3] In a valuable statement on his theory of composition Valéry said:

Scientific language and lyrical language are both symmetrical manifestations of a desire for power through purity, which, starting from ordinary

[1] Cf. Paul Valéry, 'Avant-propos' (for *La Connaissance de la déesse* of Lucien Fabre), *Variété*, I (Paris: Gallimard, 1924), 107: 'L'algèbre et la géométrie sur le modèle desquelles je m'assure que l'avenir saura construire un langage pour l'intellect.'

[2] Paul Valéry, *Eupalinos ou l'architecte.*

[3] Paul Valéry, 'Situation de Baudelaire,' *Variété*, II, (Paris: Gallimard, 1929), 156.

language, whose domain and operations are established, works to enlarge that significance which utilitarian life only conserves and reproduces.

In this realm of 'poetic significance' one of the principal acts of such composition will evidently consist in the transmutation of ideas into metaphors or figures, and images, and Valéry's conception of such figures is the centre of his idea of transformation through which they become the means of increasing the range and intensity of expression, and of conveying ideas which cannot be adequately stated in prose. Such ideas are only possible in a rhythmic and instantaneous movement of intuitive thought.

In attempting a synthesis of Valéry's ideas on metaphorical language, we may say that a metaphor is the result of a leap beyond concrete knowledge of things, a reaching forward towards an abstraction tending to an absolute of expression which transcends the flat reality of a prose statement. This is one aspect of metaphorical figures.

To symbolise the 'unshakable themes' of his thought (those abstractions which were absolutes), Valéry preferred to use, as 'figures,' the 'substance' of things that are not merely accidental—as incidents in landscape are interchangeable—but have a sort of universal nature—such as water, rock, fibre of bark or leaves, the 'pulp' of natural objects. On the same principle he differentiated between images and figures. A typical example of the use of figures and images occurs in the opening lines of 'Le Cimetière marin' where the image 'Ce toit tranquille, où marchent des colombes,' introduces the figures of 'Midi le juste' and 'La mer, le mer, toujours recommencée!' Here 'des colombes' are 'des focs' (the sails) of the last line of the poem.

Thus he suggested that 'figures' should convey some idea of a universal reality, and would be chosen instead of more casual 'images,' which he took as representing fugitive or fanciful states or things. He always tried to strengthen his composition by replacing such images by figures reduced as far as possible to their essential properties, so as to unify automatically the physical and psychic worlds.[1]

Therefore these figures will become all important as 'constants' of poetic significance; while in the group of substitutes or transformations, images will be considered as 'variables' of indeterminate value to be in general avoided as a less sure means of transmutation. This nice distinction suggests new aspects of composition. Indeed, Valéry declares that metaphorical figures are essential to poetry as the

[1] Paul Valéry, *Analecta*, in *Tel Quel*, II, 226.

profound properties of formal sensibility, for the poet who multiplies his figures is in reality creating for himself language in its first stages, since 'the metaphor is a natural production of the mind and its rôle is capital even in all scientific figures.' [1]

The relation of poetry to music was never far from Valéry's mind, and holds an important place in his theory of composition. Fully aware that poetry had its own distinctive harmony, he realised that such harmony could be renewed and enriched by extending the alliance which Mallarmé had so admirably created between the two arts. Like Mallarmé, he insisted that 'a musical condition is absolute'—and if the author has not reckoned with it, 'we can only despair of the man who wishes to sing without feeling the necessity of doing so.'

The difference between the music of the verse of the two poets comes from the fact that Mallarmé always looked for an effect of orchestration, for the contrapuntal power of different instruments playing together, while Valéry sought the effect of a classical recitative, a pure song, a single voice. Certainly Mallarme's lines have the density of orchestral music. Both sound and content are orchestrated, composed of harmonies and their overtones, and so demand the attention from readers that a full orchestra exacts from listeners. For example:

> A quel psaume de nul antique antiphonaire
> Ouï planer ici comme un viril tonnerre
> Du cachot fulguré pour s'ensevelir où?
> Sauf amplificatrice irruption ou trou
> Grand ouvert par un vol ébloui de vitrage.[2]

Observe how these lines are packed with musical significance, subtly contrapuntal, rich in overtones.

Then listen to the lyrical purity of Valéry's song:

> O n'aurait-il fallu, folle, que j'accomplisse
> Ma merveilleuse fin de choisir pour supplice
> Ce lucide dédain des nuances du sort?[3]

[1] Paul Valéry, *Tel Quel*, II, and *Calepin d'un poète* (Paris, Gallimard: 1933), 185–6.

[2] Stéphane Mallarmé 'Inédit,' cited by Henri Mondor, *Vie de Mallarmé*, (Paris: Gallimard, 1941), 792, also in Mallarmé, 'Notes et Variantes,' *Œuvres complètes*, ('Bibliothèque de la Pléiade') (Paris: Gallimard, 1945), 1445.

[3] Paul Valéry, *La Jeune Parque*, line 381, in *Poésies* (1933), 381.

The singing quality of such lines has rarely been surpassed. The fact that Valéry almost always wrote his poems in the first person adds to their intimate and lyrical effect.

In the conception of both poets there is a musical sensibility that guides the construction and design of their poems. Both should be read as we read classical authors, for their work is designed and meditated, *voulue et réfléchie*, as carefully composed as its absolute poetic conditions permit. Yet in both cases it is poetry free from rhetoric, deeply felt, in which passion is sublimated, and which is perpetually controlled by its own laws and musical conditions.

Although Valéry's *Jeune Parque* is written in the same metre as Mallarmé's *Hérodiade*, that is in alexandrines, the use that each makes of this verse form has very different results: each pursues a different effect. Mallarmé looks for every device to free his verse from the regularity of classical metre. He avoids the accepted rhythm of the alexandrine, merely using this form as a sort of framework. His harmonics are individual, his words, uniquely placed, are often unusual and always right though unexpected, and their sequence is infallibly musical. We may recall what Valéry said of the Symbolists—that 'irregular rhythms, curiosities of vocabulary and continually changing figures were all invented to orchestrate their poetry.'[1]

It is not surprising that Valéry was inspired by classical recitative in planning his longer poems. Speaking of *La Jeune Parque* he said that his aim had been to compose a sort of discourse in which the sequence of the verse would be developed in such a way that the whole piece would give an impression similar to that of the recitatives of classical opera, such as those of Gluck's *Alcestis*. Indeed, he actually composed whole passages of *La Jeune Parque* while with one finger he picked out at the piano a recitative of Gluck.[2] There exists a copy of *La Jeune Parque* that Valéry had marked as a musical score.

This application of musical methods on lines equivalent to those of *modulation*, in transition from one passage to another, as from key to key, presented considerable difficulties and led to the discovery and the consideration of definite problems of style. Valéry realised that, while pursuing an end which did not greatly differ from that of the musician, the poet was deprived of the advantages and possibilities latent in the means of traditional harmony. Yet he claimed for poets the right to develop and organise their means, as did classical composers, through the

[1] Paul Valéry, 'Avant-propos,' *Variété*, I, 96.
[2] Paul Valéry, 'Le Prince et la Jeune Parque,' *Variété*, V, 120.

use of methods approaching those of the mathematician: he considered that poets should impose on themselves a task comparable to that of a serious composer, or of a scientist elaborating a theory.

Thus poetic 'modulation' implies not only the means of transposition from one rhythmic phrase to another, but also the blending of spirit, sense and shape in a harmonious whole. It is therefore a necessary element in pure poetry, representing those Valérian transformations which may be expressed only 'through the mysterious virtue of imperceptible modulations.'

Undoubtedly such methods are capable of enriching the possibilities and widening the scope of prosody if treated on a high level of imaginative experience. The temptation of going to the very end of a problem was a danger against which Lefebure had warned Mallarmé, in regard to philosophy, almost a generation earlier.[1] But perhaps it was because Valéry had worked so thoroughly to solve the most abstract problems that he was now able to treat his poetic language in the dimensions which characterise musical compositions.

Valéry's laws of composition do not stop at syntax, for they also govern the poet's mind and 'compose' the transformations through which it passes. Just as his material undergoes a transformation, so the poet is himself transformed through a special disposition for concentrated attention. He must pass through many successive stages, each marking a further separation from the outer world of external life, so as to free his mind from the average undifferentiated state which serves for ordinary use. 'All sorts of perceptions, emotions and ideas from without intrude upon the mind making a familiar chaos which confuses and blurs poetic vision, while the Self tends to slide into the usual association of ideas.'[2] Therefore the Self of the instant, of immediate sensibility, considered as merely functional, is transcended and transformed into the creative Self who discovers ideas, and who must in turn pass to the Self who judges, compares and combines. These successive transmutations must continue till a state of spiritual sensibility is attained. Since poetry comes from these ecstatic moments of being, such consciousness is evidently the ideal soul which should quicken the ideal shape. We may therefore define the content of Valéry's poetry by paraphrasing Aristotle's statement that 'the soul is the shape' and say that the Self is the shape—always with strictly Valérian reservations as to what 'Self' implies.

[1] Henri Mondor, *Vie de Mallarmé*, 241.
[2] Cf. Paul Valéry, *Variété*, IV, 111.

Valéry has compared these different transformations to a series of mirrors which lead to the ultimate state of seeing oneself through one-self. It is thus that he arrives at an absolute of consciousness whose expression is absolute poetry.

This conception of 'composed' poetry is, as Valéry himself says, a conception of an almost inaccessible type, an ideal limit of the desires, efforts and powers of the poet. It can be created only at the extreme point of contact of rational and dream—like that point in space to which Baudelaire compared eternity.

In fact even the greatest minds can grasp the complete poetic significance of things only at certain moments. Their consciousness is not always alert; it may actually need a shock or an intrusion from the outer world to waken it to action and to full awareness:

> J'ai grand besoin d'un prompt tourment:
> Un mal vif et bien terminé
> Vaut mieux qu'un supplice dormant.[1]

Thus the constantly renewed assaults of the outer world, while threatening the inner Self, afford it a 'means of saving itself,' by bracing all its forces to be for an instant one with and equal to all the movements and all the forms of which it receives the impression. After this first shock the mind then retires within itself to impose intellectual order on the chaos of its responses. The poet must then create for himself that silence to which poetry in the form of a pure line or a luminous idea replies, for 'un silence est la source étrange des poèmes.'[2] In this state of concentration the verse seems to compose itself from an inner necessity in which the poet's whole being is concerned, and which is at the same time the integral element of memory, action and perception— a fresh vision and also an organised function.[3]

The passage from thought to poetry, as from speech to song or from walking to dancing, is made up of act and dream. The necessarily abstract poetic condition may depend on a favourable state of mind such as is sometimes found when waking from sleep, or it may be suggested instantaneously by a sensual impression of sound, sight or touch. But such a state is more often led up to by patient preparation— a united effort of sensibility and intellect from which arises 'a state comparable to that of dancing, voluptuousness in self-mastery in

[1] Paul Valéry, 'L'Abeille,' *Charmes*, in *Poésies*, (1933), 122.
[2] Paul Valéry, 'Le Philosophe et la jeune Parque,' in *Poésies* (1942), 180.
[3] Paul Valéry, *Calepin d'un poète*, 183.

which poetic awareness takes charge of the mind.' For poetry, like dancing, is an end in itself. It pursues an ideal state, a supreme moment of being and perfection of expression; and the outcome of this poetic state will be the art of 'composition,' of giving form and style to thought which by its nature lacks both those qualities. That is why Valéry speaks of poetry as an exercise which must be carried out according to set rules and in complicated conditions. These conditions include all that is implied in the word 'exercise,' which should not be given the derogatory sense of routine, trick or puzzle.

The qualities necessary to sustain this theory of composition tend to lose their spiritual significance, and to be neglected, during periods of decadence, when poets find it safer to keep as near to prose as possible, having no higher necessity. But for Valéry it is the poetry that matters. In prose, words are exchanged for a definite idea; in poetry, it is the sound, the rhythm, the placing and the interrelation of words, their effects of induction, their mutual influences dominating and supervening in a unique form, which are the poet's concern: 'L'expression seule me conquiert.'[1]

Such poetry is therefore as classical as it is possible to make it. The term 'classic' implies voluntary and deliberate acts which modify a natural production in conformity with a clear and rational conception of man and art. Thus classical art is characterised by the existence and fulfilment of certain conventions, whether they be the three unities, conceptions of prosody, or restrictions of vocabulary, and these rules, which appear arbitrary, constitute at once its strength and its weakness.[2]

It is not surprising that Valéry turned with a fresh impulse to the masters of French classical verse, and when we consider his approach to Racine, we find that the influence of this master, which in other circumstances might have appeared as a mere return to academic principles, became for Valéry the means of expressing a new rhythmic conception and a fresh vision. As in higher mathematics, the thinker must conform to the rules of the game if he is to reach those altitudes where abstract thought becomes effective, similarly, through classical means, the poet was to enter into a new region of intellectual experience.

[1] Paul Valéry, letter to André Gide (Montpellier, novembre 1892), *Correspondance André Gide–Paul Valéry*, ed. by Robert Mallet (Paris: Gallimard, 1955), 139. By permission of Librairie Gallimard.

[2] Cf. Paul Valéry, *Calepin d'un poète*, *Variété*, I–V, *Tel Quel*, I–II, *Mauvaises pensées et autres* (all Gallimard, Paris).

If we may judge from certain passages in the 'Narcisse parle' of the *Vers anciens*, Valéry had long been familiar with La Fontaine's Adonis,[1] and he had noted that this poem had probably been a model for the younger poet Racine, who was on intimate terms with the fabulist. Racine had gone further in formal art than any dramatic poet since the Greeks. The complete unity of form and content gave a spiritual perfection to his tragedies portraying humanity as the victim of its own passions. Valéry for his part was untouched by any exterior conditions of dramatic consequence, but his particular aim and personal approach made it possible for him to adapt to his own needs many of Racine's technical qualities.

Two different incidents had helped to focus his interest on Racine. The first was a report, in an article by Adolphe Brisson in *Le Temps*, of a brochure by Prince George of Prussia, which gave a careful analysis of the range and musical effect of the voice of Rachel in the plays of Racine. Here every detail of the great actress's diction was considered, even to the length of pauses, and the rhythm of her breathing. Valéry had found this article quite by chance, when, discouraged by the difficulties of his work, he had gone for a walk, and stopping at a café had picked up a copy of *Le Temps*. Some time later he was amused to find that Pierre Louÿs had been equally impressed by the same article, and had carefully marked certain passages. This had awakened Valéry's interest in the musical qualities of Racine's verse.[2]

The second circumstance which incited Valéry to study Racine is described in a letter to André Fontainas, written probably in 1915.

A strange thing, the influence of the childrens' lessons: making them recite the dream of Athalie taught me the most unsuspected things— which at once solved all the difficulties to which I was a prey.[3]

Here Valéry is referring to the period of writing *La Jeune Parque*. There are many references to Racine in the prose works, and always the most enthusiastic praise. 'Le jour n'est pas plus pur que le fond de mon cœur' was, for Valéry, a perfect line; and he comments on the admirable technical qualities and the economy of means and general perfection of the great dramatist's art, where, as in Valéry's own works, the greatest scope is the result of the greatest rigour.

[1] See Paul Valéry, 'Au sujet d'Adonis,' *Variété*, I.
[2] Paul Valéry, 'Le Prince et la Jeune Parque,' *Variété*, V, 119.
[3] Paul Valéry, letter to André Fontainas, in *Réponses: Lettres de 1917-1928* (Saint-Félicien-en-Vivarais: Le Pigeonnier, 1928).

Of all the French masters, Racine approached nearest to music, as Valéry noted: 'Racine whose periods so often give the idea of recitatives, hardly less "singing" than those of lyrical works'; 'Racine whose lines and movements seem to be the immediate transformations of the lovely forms and pure developments of Gluck'—which, however, they anticipated.

In recent years much has been written in favour of short poems, but Valéry's theories of composition are all in support of a design sustained throughout long ones. To construct a whole poem by pure means, distinct from the ordinary mixture of thought and word, and to establish a system of reciprocal relations between ideas, images, means of expression and an emotional state, were the major problems of composition as he saw them, and were what he implied when he insisted on the purity of all the elements of a poem. Poetry was to be an original synthesis obtained through analysis, and constituting the harmony which he called music.

3. THEORY OF LANGUAGE

Notre langage est terriblement limitatif et incomplet (CH.-N. MARTIN)

'Literature is, and can be nothing else than a sort of extension and application of certain properties of language.'[1] This statement serves to introduce us to the theories of language which form the substance and means of Valéry's poetics. In everything he wrote about the science of poetry, he was always more concerned with stating various problems than with resolving them through any dogmatic doctrine or creed; the ideal object of his life of thought having always been to realise and experience his own act and effort to the point of discovering the invisible conditions of his powers and their limitations. His intention was to raise poetry to the intellectual level at which it might become a necessary part of himself, as he said, to make him more real to himself, more penetratingly actual; and he considered that the unique value of art lay in its power to do so. He proposed to use all the means at his disposal in order that the whole of his intellectual powers should come into action in creating his poetry.

[1] Paul Valéry, 'Enseignement de la poétique,' *Variété*, V, 289.

When in 1911, after re-reading his youthful poems, he started to write poetry again, he applied to his new work the method which had grown from his 'meditations, observation and precisions.' Of his method he tells us two things, confessing that he would find it difficult to say more. The first necessity is 'to acquire the greatest conscious-ness,' and the second is 'to choose pure means and to recapture and hold this poetic moment of pure perception so as to retain with the will of consciousness some results analogous to the interesting "finds" which mental chance grants us among a hundred thousand hazards of all sorts.'[1]

'The greatest possible consciousness, and pure means': here is all Valéry in a phrase, the statement of an immense endeavour, a definition of high poetic aims. For when a state of poetic awareness takes charge of the mind, it is not enough in itself to make a man poet. The action that fills this transitory state is what counts, the mental activity which creates from the poet's sensibility, a poem, a work of art. Ideas and perceptions are not alone in the making of poetry, they have to combine with and inhabit, and even give new life to language. Con-sequently language must become the 'pure means' of which Valéry speaks.

His special complaint against current language was its want of power, clarity and precision. All the qualities necessary for the expres-sion of pure thought were, he complained, lacking in that maid-of-all-work, everyday speech. In the essay on 'Poésie et pensée abstraite,' to which I have constantly referred, he tells us that he begins by 'clearing the verbal situation,' and he notes that the first words that come to the mind are generally suspect. But in speaking of 'Les Cantiques spirituels'[2] he says that when the mind is by itself, and 'speaks to itself, from time to time between two silences, it uses only a small number of words none of which is extraordinary.'

Valéry starts by rejecting all words that he considers vague or pre-tentious: all such as can only blur one's perceptions. For instance, he says of the word *temps*, 'caught on the wing it is perfectly clear, but when we consider the number of uses it is put to, we become convinced that the number of meanings is far in excess of its functions.' And he amusingly points out that 'formerly it was only a means, it has now become an end—the object of a terribly philosophic desire.' For the same reasons he criticises *vie, idée, force, simple, neuf*, and there are

---

[1] Paul Valéry, 'Mémoires d'un poème,' *Variété*, V, 102.
[2] Paul Valéry, 'Cantiques spirituels,' *Variété*, V, 176.

other words that he carefully avoids using in any thought born of personal experience. Having killed off all the *perroquets*, that is about three in every six words, he employs the others with all possible circumspection.

Faced with the problem of poetic language we must first free our minds from the idea that romantic or fine words are what we mean by the term 'poetic.' Not that, on the other hand, quite plain speech, suburban or worn-out words, over-used terms, prose cut into sections—whether rhythmical or not—are any better or more expressive. Both such methods have been too much exploited. In both, Valéry's analysis has not taken place. Unfortunately the very word 'poetic' has been debased; it has almost come to mean something sentimental or affected. To save this useful word from the gutter I protest that poetic language is a language which is expressive of real poetry, and that to achieve this end, it must be used in an individual way and at the same time according to a given sense of composition.

We may ask ourselves, what is a poetic word? Valéry's answer would be that it should have two simultaneous values of equal importance: sound, and instantaneous psychic effect. This definition might also be applied to the line or phrase of poetry in which the word occurs and which by its musical and its psychic efficacy wakes in us the magic of a deeper state of consciousness.

Therefore the poet separates certain words from their ordinary conditions of usage. He submits them to the process of secret transformations. He brings together the variable semantic and the variable phonetic: he meditates on both sense and sound. All this and more, yet the first definition still remains valid.

One essential quality of the poetic word is resonance, the power of creating a prolonged vibration or reflection of sensation and perception, together with the attribute of harmoniously combining vowels and consonants that awake echoes in other words: as musical chords suggest a melodic sequence of overtones; as in the back-wash of a wave, or the undertones of a storm. I shall return to this *état chantant* in considering the extension of lateral effects. For the moment I shall only notice the actual application of verbal means.

This aspect of the poetic word is all important in relation to the other words with which it is concerted. For example, take the first verse of 'L'Abeille':[1]

[1] Paul Valéry, 'L'Abeille,' *Charmes*, in *Poésies* (1933), 122.

138

Quelle, et si fine, et si mortelle,
Que soit ta pointe, blonde abeille,
Je n'ai, sur ma tendre corbeille,
Jeté qu'un songe de dentelle.

Observe the part played by the first word 'Quelle' which through its sonority introduces the dominant harmony of the whole poem, of which the key word is 'abeille.' Notice also the freshness and animation given by the division of the usual form of *Quelle que soit* making a direct lyrical attack. This example shows that any word, if used constructively in a poem, acquires a poetic significance.

According to Valéry, one makes a poem by the analysis of its parts; therefore one begins by the choice of words. Here there are many interesting considerations, technical for the most part, in which verbal contacts are composed to poetry, and here assonance and dissonance are both essential. For certain combinations of words are capable of producing, as others are not, a specific type of poetical emotion through which all things are intensified, harmonised and almost recreated. 'I look for a word, says the poet, a word which is feminine, of two syllables, containing P or F, ending in a mute, synonymous with a break or disintegration, and neither learned nor rare. Six conditions at least.'[1] Examples of such a word are found in 'Un fleuve sans coupure' (*Poésies*, p. 99), 'Cette lumineuse rupture' in 'Les Grenades' of *Charmes* (*Poésies*, p. 143). (The word *rupture* also occurs in 'La Pythie.') Although English-speaking poets have slightly different considerations, the principle of analysis and music remains the same in all languages.

Valéry had not a particularly wide vocabulary, nor did he look for rare or technical terms, but he was sensitive to the significance of each word and to the possibilities of every shade of meaning, and of each syllable of sound. He is reported to have said that in *Charmes* he had exhausted the particular vocabulary that he had used there. From this we may conclude that the words carefully chosen for their quality of resonance and their symbolic value were considered to have fulfilled their poetic destiny in these lyrics.

This idea of a special vocabulary is allied to the notion that the poet is an architect of words, and Valéry's Socrates, in the Dialogue of Eupalinos, says:

[1] Paul Valéry, 'Autres Rhumbs,' *Tel Quel*, II, 153.

139

One must adjust one's complex words as if they were irregular blocks; speculating on the chances and the surprises that arrangements of this kind reserve for us; and we give the name of poet to those whom fortune favours in this work.

Every detail depends on and takes its special value for Valéry from the inner sense which the words symbolise. But he rightly considers that the esoteric centre of his art is no immediate concern of his readers. He has even said that the longer the secret is kept the better it is for the poet.

Valéry's whole conception of symbolism is of vital interest: his poetry rests on it. He is perhaps the only completely symbolic poet, since his use of this means is total and englobes the whole of his poetic expression. We have seen that the intellectual and psychological motif of the poems is the Self which undergoes endless transformations to reach a state of pure being, and each stage of its development may be expressed only through an integral symbolism to which the same principle of transmutation has been applied, so that the symbols themselves have become formalised to express intimately the spiritual states of the Self. And as Bossuet said, the spiritual is the intellectual.

Thus every poem in *Charmes*, as well as *La Jeune Parque*, symbolises some state of the poet's intellectual life through some corresponding aspect of his sensual and visual outer world. Sun and light always symbolise intellectual power; the sea conveys the idea of life; the wind suggests emotion; the swan, as for Mallarmé, represents poetic inspiration; *l'abeille* is the word. This consistency or use of constants in his symbolism allows Valéry to create a world of his own in the universe of nature.

This world of transmuted intuition is one of cosmic grandeur. The sun lights all with intellectual consciousness; the stars, those powerful strangers, are analogous to pure ideas. The sea is the mysterious source of all life, of which the wind is the eternal plaint. The islands of thought, the flowers of fancy, all are there. And the poet's mistress is the poem whose mysterious footsteps are the long-awaited, ultimate words. Trees are given a significant place: their roots are emblems of man's earthly state; the trunk is the force of his endeavour; the spreading branches bear the leaves of his aspirations; and the complete tree suggests the transformation of his whole being into spiritual power and intellectual acts.

Valéry never uses the term 'ornament' in the sense of 'decoration,' for him it is not something added to a composition, or to a shape, with the idea of beautifying it. On the contrary, he sees ornament inherent in language, and this idea is always latent in his work. Combined with the theory of geometrical or exact construction, which I have noticed in discussing his theory of composition, this conception of ornament is also a reason for using chosen words to give what he calls style to those thoughts which he wishes to reveal as constant or absolute. So that language, inseparable from what it expresses, must follow a sequence tending towards a final abstraction.[1]

Thus certain words are considered as constants (or key vocables) and are compared to 'those precious quantities that mathematicians handle so lovingly.' The key words have far-reaching qualities, the first of which is their symbolic value; they must also have euphonic and etymologic attributes for which they are specially chosen. Each key word has its own group—or groups—of variables or harmonics which knit together the fabric of the poem. Thus in the poems of the second period the verses are constructed round the key words and their accompanying vocables as in a musical composition.

This system derived from the 'group theory' is applied throughout *Charmes*, and the last poem of this collection, 'Palme,' provides a good example of the method. For the basic harmony of the poem is constructed round the word *Palme*, together with its 'similitude amie' *calme*. The open *a* predominates in such words as *grâce*, *éclat*, *table*, *plat*, *pâle*, *âme*, *sable*; and its melodic mode or form is echoed in the closed *a* of *ange*, *pain*, *ample*, *s'attendre*, *main*, *grains*, etc. The other letters in the key word follow the same principle, and other key words, in so much as they are constant symbols, serve as counterpoint to the melodic theme. Thus the words *soleil*, *or*, *compose*, *azur*, all occur in this poem, because of their symbolic significance.

It is important to notice that key words are always symbols, but symbols are not necessarily key words; though they may generally be considered as constants there are exceptions to this rule. Thus the word *ange* is used in 'Palme' to symbolise a state of beatitude, though in '*Mon Faust*,' in the line 'Moi qui sus l'ange vaincre,' it symbolises a religious faith which Faust has rejected. Again, in 'Le Cimetière marin' (verse 2)—

> Éloignes-en les prudentes colombes,
> Les songes vains, les anges curieux!

[1] For this aspect of Valéry, consult Victor E. Van Vriesland, 'Le Verbe dans la poésie de Valéry,' *Hommage des écrivains étrangers à Paul Valéry* (Bossum: Stools, 1927).

'les anges curieux' are emblems of religious mythology as carved on the tombs. In the prose poem *L'Ange*, however, Valéry tells us that his angel represents the absolute of the Self contemplating 'sorrow in a human form.' We may note that for Mallarmé the angel is the poet: 'Je me mire et me vois ange,' he says in 'Les Fenêtres,' and in 'Tombeau d'Edgar Poe' the poet is the angel who gives 'un sens plus pur aux mots du tribu.'

There would be no particular virtue in making an exhaustive list of Valéry's key words. It is the principle that is significant, the application of the theory that leads to the association and pattern of poetic images. I shall therefore comment only on his choice of words and his characteristic use of them.

'Le mot "pur" ouvre mes lèvres,' Valéry tells us, and he notes that it replied to the most intimate and sometimes the most indefinable aspirations of which it is both a symbol and an ideal representation. Almost always used as an absolute, this word represented for him a unique expression of universal perfection, having a symbolic, musical and formal significance. In an instructive passage he says:

> The word pure is so beautiful that it carries the mind far beyond any definite signification. Accompanying the mysterious word 'poetry' it arouses, by a kind of resonance, an intellectual astonishment, a marvellous awaking of all the superior powers of our being—a thirst for that which promises all that we feel to be the most exalted within ourselves.[1]

What better statement of the *effect* of pure poetry could we have than this 'intellectual astonishment and awaking' that the poet proposes.

We need not dwell here on the 'Moi pur,' which I have discussed elsewhere, but we may remind ourselves that both 'pure poetry' and the 'pure Self' are absolutes of consciousness, or, to be more exact, that the former is the expression of the latter. The complete unity of sound and sense that the word 'pure' carries makes it an admirable 'constant' in the composition of a poem. Musically it is allied to a wide group of assonant words, which in their turn suggest a poetic sequence. Actually each letter wakes an echo in other resonant words such as *murmur* and *rumeur* for the *u* sound, and *profonde* for the *p* and *v* in such lines as

> Trouveras-tu jamais plus transparente mort
> Ni de pente plus pure où je rampe à ma perte

[1] Cf. Valéry, 'Avant-propos,' *Variété*, I, 104.

Que sur ce long regard de victime entr' ouverte?
Pâle que se résigne et saigne sans regret. . . .[1]

The composition of these lines gives an excellent example of verbal music. Notice the value of the word *pâle* which resolves the alliteration of the 'pente plus pure. . . .'

In certain passages the meaning of *pur* is slightly modified, and this is frequently the case with words which Valéry uses to denote psychological and intellectual realities. Thus in 'L'Ébauche d'un serpent' he speaks of God as 'L'Être vieil et pur' and as being 'Comme las de son pur spectacle.' A striking example of such modification occurs in the same poem: 'le long pur d'un dos,' which might be translated as 'the long purity of a back'—or 'the pure length'—but neither would convey the synthesis of Valéry's line. In 'Le Cimetière marin' there is a concentrated, heaped up sense in the phrase 'Entre le vide et l'événement pur.'[2] Other more usual applications are found throughout the poems, as in the 'Fragment du Narcisse': 'Que tu brilles enfin, terme pur de ma course.' In *La Jeune Parque* we have 'Loin des purs environs je suis captive,' and also the more simple meaning of 'actes purs,' 'un bras très pur.'

Absence is another particularly Valérian word of which Mallarmé had already enriched the sense. For both poets *absence* like *présence* partakes etymologically and metaphysically of being; and Valéry extracts the deepest poetical meaning from it. Sometimes he uses it as an image of sleep: 'Dors, ma sagesse, dors. Forme-toi cette absence . . .;[3] and he refers to sleep as 'Mon absence peinte,' and also says

D'une absence aux contours de mortelle bercés
Par soi seule.

Many years later, in the lyric 'Neige,' there is the surprise of 'Oh! combien de flocons, pendant ma douce absence.'[4] *Absence* is also used in the sense of being dispersed or changed, as in 'Le Cimetière marin,' where it occurs in two good images:

Comme le fruit se fond en jouissance
Comme en délice il change son absence . . .

Ils ont fondu dans une absence épaisse.

---

[1] Paul Valéry, *La Jeune Parque*, lines 384 *et seq.*, in *Poésies* (1933), 96.
[2] Paul Valéry, 'Le Cimetière marin,' line 45, *Poésies* (1933), 185.
[3] Paul Valéry, *La Jeune Parque*, line 457, *Poésies* (1933), 100.
[4] Paul Valéry, 'Neige,' in *Poésies* (1942), 163.

In this poem the full poetry of *absence* is also expressed in the nostalgic sense of 'La vie est vaste, étant ivre d'absence,' and in 'Au Platane' (*Charmes*) speaking of trees:

> Ils vivent séparés, ils pleurent confondus
> Dans une seule absence.

The same word occurs in a characteristic verse in 'Fragment du Narcisse,'

> Mais moi, Narcisse aimé, je ne suis curieux
> Que de ma seule essence
> Tout autre n'a pour moi qu'un cœur mystérieux
> Tout autre n'est qu'absence.

Many are the examples of such uses of this far-reaching word. *Absence* has become an imaginative state expressing and imposing an original poetic idea, and constantly bringing the reader to the mysterious threshold of the temple of poetic thought—*au seuil battu de tempêtes*;[1] while in the composition of the verse it has the constructive force of a mathematical quantity.

Another word to which Valéry gives special attention, and a particular psycho-mathematical significance is *composer*, which represents for him the art of making something out of a given material, be it music, poetry or architecture. He composes his poems, his systems and his thoughts. In his verses he makes fine use of this strong word. In 'Le Cimetière marin':

> Midi le juste y compose de feux
> La mer, la mer, toujours recommencée!

and also

> Ce lieu me plaît, dominé de flambeaux,
> Composé d'or, de pierre et d'arbres sombres.

The harmonious vocable *abeille* always symbolises word or language, and Valéry allies it with *corbeille* in the verse I have already quoted from the poem for which it serves as title; it occurs also in the second verse of 'Aurore':

> Salut! encore endormies
> A vos sourires jumeaux,
> Similitudes amies
> Qui brillez parmi les mots!

---

[1] Paul Valéry, 'Naissance de Vénus,' *Album de vers anciens*, in *Poésies* (1933), 15.

Au vacarme des abeilles
Je vous aurai par corbeilles. . . .[1]

A desire to reach the highest point of intellectual awareness leads to the effective use of superlatives, of which Valéry is very fond, and to the adverbial, adjectival, or nominal use of such intense words as *extrême*, as in 'Sur le bord d'une extrême merveille' ('Un Feu distinct'); and in the poetic prose of 'L'Ame et la dance' we find 'L'étonnante et l'extrême danseuse, Athikté!'

Extrême is also used to great effect and in a more extended sense in the musical opening lines of *La Jeune Parque*:

Qui pleure là, sinon le vent simple, à cette heure
Seule avec diamants extrêmes? . . . Mais qui pleure,
Si proche de moi-même au moment de pleurer?

It appears again in the second movement of the same poem—

une secrète sœur
Brûle, qui se préfère à l'extrême attentive . . .

and in 'Aurore' also:

Toute l'âme s'appareille
A l'extrême du désir. . . .

Candeur is sometimes used by Valéry in its current sense, but he also employs it with fresh intention as in 'Mais la candeur ruisselle à mots si doux,' or as in 'Platane'—speaking of the tree—where it occurs twice:

Mais ta candeur est prise et ton pied retenu
Par la force du site. . . .

A Latin sense is sometimes given to *candeur* and *candide* as in the 'Cantique des colonnes,' where 'Vois quels hymnes candides' suggests an extended sense of purity and of form. In *La Jeune Parque* also we have

et si l'onde
Au cap tonne, immolant un monstre de candeur . . .

describing the glory of breaking waves.

This faculty of giving new life and the force of an extended meaning to language is one of the remarkable aspects of Valéry's genius: almost every word proper to his purpose is made to express its utmost sense,

[1] For comments on poems, see below p. 179, 'The Time of Charmes.' Paul Valéry, 'Aurore,' *Charmes, Poésies* (1933), 108.

or one might almost say, its own abstraction. Each word has for him the virtue of living speech, yet its fundamental properties are respected. Such is his use of the word *perdu* which enlarges the meaning of *lost* to that of being diluted or dispersed as in 'Perdu ce vin, ivres les ondes' ('Le Vin perdu') and 'Douce perte, arome ou zéphir' ('Ébauche d'un serpent'). And La Jeune Parque cries, 'Grands Dieux! Je perds en vous mes pas déconcertés.'

Generally, it is not from the Latin or Greek usage that Valéry takes the effective sense of his words, but from the seventeenth-century French, where the meaning was very much nearer to English usage than it is today, and therefore presents no special difficulty to English readers.

Such words as *singulier*, in 'Les âmes singulières' ('Le Cimetière marin'), and many other words, are given the sense in which Voltaire and writers of his time used them. Thus from forgotten or archaic words new harmonies and meanings are formed, which appear fresh when used by a poet who has perfect possession of his means and a transcendent theme to express. We should look at these words in their context, in the relationship to other words that the poet gives them, as well as in the full understanding of his aim, for sometimes words, like precious stones, require a new setting according to the poet's purpose and the taste of each age. Nor should we belittle a poet, or dismiss him as dated, because our roving and superficial eye happens to pick out from his verses words which we have seen or heard in writers of other ages. Rather we should ask him, 'De quelle profondeur songes-tu de m'instruire?' We should be equally wrong were we, on the other hand, to dismiss words as anti-poetic because we have not met them before in poetry, for words are as notes in music: modulation is all.

Faites, Maîtres heureux, Pères des justes fraudes [1]

This modification of the word *fraudes* (the same word in English) by the adjective *justes* is a favourite device of Valéry's to determine a new poetical effect. He uses it also in 'Le Cimetière marin': 'Le beau mensonge et la pieuse ruse.' There are many other examples in his poems of the meaning being modified by forcible juxtaposition of opposites both in sound and sense, as the harmony is also governed by the position of each vocable.

In this renewal of poetic diction Valéry's neologisms, often auda-

[1] Paul Valéry, 'Fragments du Narcisse,' line 280, *Charmes*, in *Poésies* (1933), 146.

cious, are at the same time so apt that they appear to be classical. They are generally the result of adopting, from all the variations of sense which a word has acquired in its course, that which sums up its most significant attributes; so that such words possess a greater density of substance and a greater evocative force. A marginal note of Valéry's on the word *durée* (duration) illustrates my meaning and helps to make clear his approach to language: *durée*, he notes, 'comes from *dur* (hard) and this incidentally amounts to giving double values to certain visual, tactile or mobile images, or any combination of them.' English readers may compare the word 'endure' from the same Latin root, and Scots may think of 'dour,' meaning stern or hard.

Other typical neologisms of the first period are such words as *épeurer* in 'Et le pied pur s'épeure comme un bel oiseau/Ivre d'ombre . . .' ('Épisode'). And *anxieux*, anxious, in the sense of longing for, in 'Anxieuse d'azur, de gloire consumée . . .' ('Air de Sémiramis'). *Éploré*, which is generally used as a past participle, occurs in a poem of the first period as an active present in

> Son sourire se forme, et suit sur ses bras blancs
> Qu'éplore l'orient d'une épaule meutrie . . .

These examples are typical of Valéry's use of neologisms.[1]

It is rare to find structural modifications in Valéry's verse. By this I mean that his harmonic schemes do not often impose changes in the usual order of words. This is one of the chief effects in Mallarmé's orchestration, where the density of the line is all important; Valéry needs the lyrical clarity of the human voice to express pure states of thought. He prefers to be as simple as possible when he uses concrete terms to infer the abstract, *pour figurer les lois 'inhérentes au Cosmos.'* This implies a classical conception of the aspect of things, and he uses abstractions of essential qualities in place of descriptive passages or too intimate effects. This is noticeable in his use of colour. Generally the only colours introduced are the formal ones of heraldry—such as *or*, *azur, pourpre, rose, vermeille, blanc*—which have a universal or abstract value. The word *pourpre* has a double signification: it may mean purple but it is often used in poetry as a glorified form of red. In his *Theory of Colours* Goethe says of *red*: 'because of its high dignity we have often designated this colour as purple.' Ronsard uses *pourpre* in this sense in speaking of a rose: 'Les plis de sa robe pourprée'; and Flaubert speaks

[1] Readers should consult Albert Henry, *Langage chez Paul Valéry* (Paris: Mercure de France, 1952).

of 'Une gorge pourprée' in describing Mme. Schlesinger in *L'Éducation sentimentale*. In *La Jeune Parque* we have: 'Dans quelle blanche paix cette pourpre la laisse'; and, referring to her body, 'cette blonde pulpe' and 'gorge de miel'; *doré* in the line 'Je pense sur le bord doré de l'univers'; and *azur* in 'L'azur de la sainte distance.' Perhaps the line with the most colour in this poem, where the favourite word *émeraude* occurs, is 'Et trempe à l'émeraude un long rose de honte.'

Adjectives are often abstract, particularly in *La Jeune Parque*, where we find 'invincibles armes,' 'inévitables astres,' 'enfers pensifs,' 'attente infinie,' 'l'innocence anxieuse,' 'front limpide.'

Language has thus become the instrument of the poet's deepest consciousness, suggesting the inner significance of things and conveying those abstract analogies that are the acts of intellectual poetry. Yet when he wishes Valéry can be as direct and actual as nature itself, as when he sums up all summer of Provence in one phrase of 'Le Cimetière marin':

> L'insecte net gratte la sécheresse
> Tout est brûlé, défait, reçu dans l'air.

Attentive to the harmonies that rise spontaneously in his mind, Valéry often starts his poems from a 'given' phrase. Thus 'La Pythie,' he tells us, began with an eight syllable line that came by itself, and round which the poem was written:

> Pâle, profondément mordue . . .

This line implied a phrase and 'this phrase once found implied other phrases.' Characteristically, he considered this approach to his poem as a problem 'of a kind that admits of a number of solutions, only limited by the metrical and musical conditions.'[1] To those conditions he strictly adhered, while developing and renewing classical form. He is the most spiritually and technically classical of modern poets, both because of the universal significance of his constant symbolism and because of his use of classical prosody, and in particular of Racinian alexandrines. To remain oneself, keeping the free movement of one's thought, while wearing the heavy armour of classical tradition, is no light task. And we may observe in certain poets, such as Péguy, how their religious thought, when expressed in biblical language, leads them to imitate too closely liturgic and traditional rhythms, awaking an uneasy comparison in their readers' minds.

[1] Paul Valéry, 'Poésie et pensée abstraite,' *Variété*, V, 161.

If the supreme end of the poet's art is the power to bend words to unexpected ends without breaking the consecrated forms, the capture and possession of subtle thought is the very soul of this endeavour. Both operations exact the simultaneous control of syntax, harmony and ideas; for the poetic universe is not revealed and sustained only by its density of figures and images, of assonance and dissonance, of sequence and turns of phrase, of rhyme and rhythm, in all of which it has its being; its thought too should have, or tend towards, a universal significance, and should be incarnated in the melodic progress of the poem. So thought, systematised to a personal synthesis, is capable of giving the poet a constellation of possibilities known only to his own consciousness, which he can employ, through the use of symbols, without any other reference to the exterior world.

This poetic thought is often a sort of flash-back to a direct impression, or it may be a progressive meditation. Moreover, there is the interchange of two parallel themes, that of symbols conveyed directly through figures and images, and that of the thought that illuminates the poet's spiritual life. It follows that the closer a poem conforms to poetry the less can its thought be prose; for the ideas suggested by the text are one of the means that should unite with rhythm, verse forms and grace of structure to provoke and sustain a certain exaltation, and a state of mind in which ideas and words become adjusted to the general degree of sensibility.

> Between voice and thought, thought and voice,
> Presence and absence, the pendulum
> Of poetry forever oscillates. . . .[1]

In Valéry's poetic universe, ideas change their value. They become linked in an associated relationship, and what he calls 'musicalised,' affecting one another with a mutual vibration through which their intellectual harmony finds its expression. Consequently, thought may remain abstract and at the same time become poetic, since both sense and sound have this poetic quality of resonance, creating an emotional or intellectual vibration in the reader's mind. Thus poetry may be considered as the modification of a mental and emotional balance in which all the possibilities of thought and language are called upon to play a harmonious part. To this task the poet brings a spiritual energy which reveals him to himself in certain 'moments of infinite consequence.' It is at such moments, thanks to his powers of concentration and poetic

---

[1] Paul Valéry, 'Poésie et pensée abstraite,' *Variété*, V, 153.

consciousness, that words are used to convey beyond their apparent sense a second significance which is the extension of their function of resonance.

These lateral effects are extremely subtle. They are allied to the central symbolism but are not to be confused with it. They have a sort of spiritual sonority whose vibrations serve as a means of intellectual modulation; they are therefore a means of transition. Known only to certain poets, they express a dimension of their own. I can think of no better way of explaining them than by saying that they express a sort of relativity of sound and sense, comparable with the idea of space-time, and capable of giving us the power of a fresh perception, by showing us an aspect of the world of imaginative thought 'Ayant l'expansion des choses infinies.'[1]

This idea of lateral effects finds new expression in Valéry's poetry. Yet it is not a new idea, although it has taken on a fresh significance for modern readers. Poe had said that two things were invariably required in poetry, 'first some degree of complexity and secondly some degree of suggestiveness, some under-current, however indefinite, of meaning.' Although Poe does not actually speak of what Valéry implies by lateral effects, these might well be included in this wide statement.

We may compare this conception with that of the mediaeval symbolists, which Dante adopted, of the four different meanings of a poem: the literal or historic sense, the moral sense, the figurative or allegorical and finally the anagogic, mystic or transcendent sense.[2] 'Four readings of one text which are four different aspects of the face of reality.'[3]

Valéry in his function of creative poet sublimated the idea of meaning in poetry, so as to express an imaginative state tending towards a pure abstraction, which would be an Absolute of poetry. For the real virtuoso is one in whom the development of his means is so advanced, and also so thoroughly identified with his own intelligence, that it becomes possible for him to think and invent through his habitual way of working, starting from his method itself. By this means art becomes nature, for 'spontaneous art is the fruit of conquest'; this is the result of training, habit and constant vigilance which lead to the capacity of taking a work of art to the point of perfection. Thus the poet or artist

---

[1] Baudelaire, 'Correspondances,' *Les Fleurs du mal* (Paris: Lemerre, 1888), 108.

[2] Dante, *Convivio*, II, ep. xiii.

[3] Louis Gillet, *Dante*, (Paris: Flammarion, 1941), 142.

finally tends to become 'the effect of his work' and acquires the gift of improvising through 'an immense and continual reflection.'[1]

Valéry had noted that other poets and hundreds of amateurs had expressed immediate emotions; but no French poet had dealt with the epos and pathos of the mind. No Lucretius or Dante had appeared in France. Yet what poetic material could be richer than that of the intellect and the conditions of thought which lead to a transcendental consciousness? Did not these constitute an incomparable lyrical universe, and a complete drama in which neither adventure nor passion, nor any human attributes, were lacking? In this domain of intellectual sensibility, Valéry saw a new dramatic theme on which he founded his Intellectual Comedy, expressed in his poems, commented on in his prose.

There is a poetry of inexhaustible resources in the thirst to understand and to create; in the moments of mental action; in the anticipation of the 'gift' of a form or of an idea; in the simple word that changes the impossible into something achieved:

> Quel pur travail de fins éclairs consume
> Maint diamant d'imperceptible écume,
> Et quelle paix semble se concevoir!
> Quand sur l'abîme un soleil se repose,
> Ouvrages purs d'une éternelle cause,
> Le Temps scintille et le Songe est savoir.[2]

These finely symbolic lines sum up, as no prose could, the life of the mind: that meditation which is the highest form of activity. Here the symbolism is profound but clear; the universe of the mind has been harmoniously transposed to a figure of cosmic grandeur.

Valéry is the poet of spiritual adventure, of those extraordinary moments of which he has spoken: such as that sudden isolation and solitude which all at once, even in a crowd, falls round a poet, like a veil under which the mystery of an immediate revelation takes place.

[1] Paul Valéry, *Pièces sur l'art*, (Paris: Gallimard, 1934), 175.
[2] Paul Valéry, 'Le Cimetière marin,' *Charmes*, in *Poésies* (1936), 185.

V

The Second Poetic Period

I. 'LA JEUNE PARQUE'

. . . J'appartiens à l'effort.
(LE PHILOSOPHE ET LA JEUNE PARQUE)

THE THEME of *La Jeune Parque* is the drama of the pure Self, the incarnation of a special consciousness, the being and non-being of an intellectual life that looks with astonishment on its own awakenings:

> Harmonieuse MOI, différente d'un songe,
> Femme flexible et ferme aux silences suivis
> D'actes purs! . . .[1]

Triumphant in the power of such knowledge,

> . . . J'étais l'égale et l'épouse du jour
> Seul support souriant que je formais d'amour
> A la toute-puissante altitude adorée . . .

In this light of intellectual consciousness we follow the life of the mind,

> Poreuse à l'éternel qui me semblait m'enclore,

which animates the whole poem.

So, too, the different phases of the movements are steps in the mind's progress. Thus in the second movement a new Self is evolved:

[1] Paul Valéry, *La Jeune Parque*, lines 102–4. The following quoted lines (in order of quotation) are 107–9; 113; 48–9; 37; 50–1; 101; 508–9; in *Poésies* (Paris: Gallimard, 1933).

> Dieux! Dans ma lourde plaie une secrète sœur
> Brûle, qui se préfère à l'extrême attentive.

The *secrète sœur* is the further projection of the isolated mind that defends itself against the Serpent—symbol of temptation:

> J'y suivais un serpent qui venait de me mordre.

In the third movement it is this new Self who repulses the tempter:

> Va! je n'ai plus besoin de ta race naïve,
> Cher Serpent . . .

Again in the fourth movement,

> Adieu, pensai-je, MOI, mortelle sœur, mensonge . . .

leads to a different 'Harmonieuse MOI.' In this continuous metamorphosis of the Self to greater consciousness lies the whole secret of the poem, 'for the real subject,' says Valéry, 'is the painting of a sequence of psychological substitutions and in the main the change of consciousness during the length of a night.'[1] 'I have tried,' he continues, 'and at the cost of unbelievable effort, to explain the modulation of a life.'

In a letter to M. Lafont in 1922, Valéry called his poem a reverie, 'with all the ruptures, all the renewals and surprises of a reverie. But at the same time a reverie in which the conscious consciousness is both the subject and the object.' 'Imagine,' he wrote, 'someone waking in the middle of the night, and the whole of his life appearing and speaking to him about itself . . . sensuality, memories, emotions, sensations of the body, the depth of memory and the light of former skies seen again. . . . Of this knotted thread, which has neither beginning nor end, I have made a monologue, on which I imposed, before I began, conditions of form as severe as the substance was free.'[2]

The action of this dramatic sequence lies in the dualism, the opposition between a state of mind which looks for an absolute of consciousness, whose strength is in its isolation from ordinary life, and the impure attitude of mind which accepts life and action and all its delights, while constantly and inevitably changing, renouncing the ideal of perfect integrity found in the first state to let itself be seduced by constantly varied intrusions of life.

[1] Quoted by E. Noulet, *Paul Valéry: Études* (Bruxelles: Renaissance du Livre, 1951).
[2] Paul Valéry, letter to Aimé Lafont (septembre 1922), *Lettres à quelques-uns* (Paris: Gallimard, 1952), 143.

This was, as we have seen, the intellectual and æsthetic problem which constantly preoccupied Valéry: a problem first stated during the night of storm at Genoa, and from which the method attributed to Leonardo and the person of Monsieur Teste had both grown. Such a problem has a universal application, for as soon as man's awareness is fully awakened, he begins to feel himself isolated and exiled from the world to which he is attached by all his senses, and by part of his intellect, but which must always remain strange to him. It is no longer possible for thoughtful men to escape from this dualism. Therefore man's destiny is to compromise, to look for a middle way between the spirit and the material preoccupations which invade it from the exterior world, while using the outer world to stimulate, and also to symbolise, the different phases of his interior life. So that finally the complete Self triumphs in full recognition of its own existence of which knowledge is the light:

> Alors, malgré moi-même, il le faut, ô Soleil,
> Que j'adore mon cœur où tu te viens connaître . . .

In this sensitive intellectual poetry, La Jeune Parque, the youngest of the Fates, meditates retrospectively on her conflict with life. She is a being of extremely responsive perceptions whose attributes are universal and scarcely feminine, an image of the poet's mind, through whom he meditates on the substance and reality of his intellectual consciousness.

It should be clear to the reader that the inner world evoked is not a moral or ethical conception, but rather one of poetic intuition, always aspiring to the prolongation of a lucid perfection. Nor does this 'absolute' exist in the function of an uncertain being, who would be *ourselves*, but in the future of a being of universal attributes.

The difficulties inherent in the creation of such a poem must have raised many problems, chief among which would be that of the functioning of the mind. But we need not fear that we shall be led into a maze of psychological terms, for Valéry's psychology is as far from the accepted ideas of current usage as his poetry is from prose. Everything is transposed into sure and dense poetry in which only figures that have a universal significance are used: such as sea, stars, sky, dawn and light, and always a wide horizon as the background of thought.

'Those who know how to read me will read an autobiography in the form,' wrote Valéry, 'for the substance matters little . . . it was from language that I started, at first, to make this poem the length of a page.'[1] We have seen in considering his poetics, what importance he gave to the idea of form as the real substance of poetry, since it is that by which it is primarily differentiated from prose; in *La Jeune Parque*, as always for Valéry, the idea of form is twofold: a designed construction of thought expressed through a designed structure of language.

The poem was also an investigation into what might be attempted in poetry, and a study of poetic modulation. It was modestly described as an exercise, in which the poet had imposed upon himself 'laws and observations which constituted its veritable object.' Valéry's ideal was not only to write regular verse but to do so 'with cæsuræ, without run-on lines and without weak rhymes.' 'I wanted,' he said, 'to try to be more abstract than modern usage tolerates. I had a hard time with *words*. . . . I made about a hundred drafts. The *transitions* cost me infinite trouble. In short it was a difficult exercise.'[2]

Nothing interested him more than those transitions implying change of mood, tone and time, to denote the progress of the mind; they corresponded to the mental transformations of his system, and were all-important in the construction of the poem. He noted that all such considerations were ignored by his contemporaries. The figures and images throughout the poem rise directly from emotional necessity, to express the different phases through which the poet's thought passes by means of such transformations. These phases are not linked by explanatory passages but appear to grow from an interior impulse, so that they form a complete unity sustained by the melodic progress of the whole composition.

The verse form is the classical French alexandrine, and the resources of this line of twelve syllables are enlarged and renewed. The rhymed couplets also follow the classical Racinian usage. There are sixteen movements of varied length, consisting of recitatives often composed of a single period, or periods alternating with lyrical passages. The changes of tone depend on the nuance of the melody and the texture of the language.

In his vocabulary, as well as in the structure of his verse, Valéry sometimes follows Racine very closely, as in the lines:

> Elle sait, sur mon ombre égarant ses tourments,
> De mon sein, dans les nuits, mordre les rocs charmants.[3]

---

[1] Paul Valéry, letter to André Fontainas (1917), *Réponses: Lettres de 1917–1928* (Saint-Félicien-en-Vivarais: Le Pigeonnier, 1928).

[2] Valéry, letter to Aimé Lafont (septembre 1922), *Lettres à quelques-uns*, 143.

[3] Paul Valéry, *Le Jeune Parque*, lines 55–6. For further examples see, Octave Nadal, *MS. Autographe de la Jeune Parque* (Paris: Club du Meilleur Livre, 1957).

Here indeed are Racine's *péchés mignons—tourments, sein, charmants*. However, Valéry generally uses a more personal idiom. His use of alliteration and assonance would alone redeem a too classical vocabulary. In regard to purely technical means, there were two things which made it possible for him to revert to traditional forms. The first was the extended significance which he gave to words of his own choice; and the second was his use of ellipse and synthesis, which Mallarmé had so admirably developed, and to which Valéry added his own lyrical clarity, thus assuring an individual technique with which to express his unique theme.

Before attempting a brief commentary on the text, I should say at once that it is impossible to describe or translate the spiritual and musical act of such poetry. A critic can only indicate the path leading to the imaginative world of dream and thought in which Valéry delights. I have therefore only tried to suggest the inner meaning which the images symbolise, and I do so without any dogmatic claims to special knowledge. The understanding of minds other than our own can be only intuitive and tentative.

Valéry himself condemned all attempts to record in prose the themes of his poems. He knew that to judge poetry by what it is about was as trivial and useless as to judge pictures by their subject. He always insisted on the necessary mental effort of the reader as well as the author. All that he wrote about his own work is of value in showing us the right approach, and in making clear the significance of a desired technical perfection.

Each reader should first enjoy the music of the verse, which will inevitably bring him to his idea of the sense, according to his capacity and sensibility. His first impression will be that of a sustained and yet infinitely varied musical effect and the balanced perfection of each part, while he gradually assimilates the poetic significance of sound and sense. Thus the reader is transported into a world where everything has been transformed by the miracle of poetry.

The title of the poem is comprehensive, for in the pure Self Valéry had evidently found a new Fate. (Pierre Louÿs had generously offered the title of his own poem 'Psyche,' but Valéry refused this offer, since not only Pierre Louÿs but also La Fontaine had already used it.[1]) The actual images present no difficulty. La Jeune Parque, a statue come to life, wakes on some remote Thessalian shore. Her waking thoughts and retrospective meditations, her walks through flowering

[1] Paul Valéry, letter to Pierre Louÿs (27 juin 1916), *Lettres à quelques-uns*, 117.

grass, her reactions to the world around her, her horror of the serpent and her desire for purity are easy to understand.

The opening lines of the prelude, or first movement, evoke the awakening of La Jeune Parque, and the clear vowels with the harmonies of the contrapuntal consonants propose the theme. In the grand sweep of the first chords the sense and emotion are one, as in the music of Gluck's Overture to Alcestis from which they were conceived:

> Qui pleure là, sinon le vent simple, à cette heure
> Seule avec diamants extrêmes? . . . Mais qui pleure,
> Si proche de moi-même au moment de pleurer? [1]

We are at once charmed by the interplay of the *eu* in 'pleure,' 'heure,' 'seule,' with the shorter *e*'s, and the echo of the consonants *pl*, where each sound is significant. Notice also the urgency given by the harmonious repetition of 'mais qui pleure'; and how 'pleurer' is used in the third line to carry the musical movement which describes the waking, to the possibility of different destinies, of La Jeune Parque, whose tear symbolises regret for unfulfilled desires:

> Cette main, sur mes traits qu'elle rêve effleurer,
> Distraitement docile à quelque fin profonde,
> Attend de ma faiblesse une larme qui fonde,
> Et que de mes destins lentement divisé,
> Le plus pur en silence éclaire un cœur brisé.

Now the signs of the exterior world become apparent:

> La houle me murmure une ombre de reproche,
> Ou retire ici bas, dans ses gorges de roche,
> Comme chose déçue et bue amèrement,
> Une rumeur de plainte et de resserrement . . .

The savage jostling of the swell is echoed in the music of 'reproche,' 'gorges de roche' and in the general motion of the whole passage.

How actual and at the same time how abstract this poetry is: nothing is described but everything is suggested with strict economy of words. Valéry brings us to the rocks of a lonely shore in the hour before dawn. He links the images—a hand, a tear, the cavernous rocks, the pluck and sigh of the sea—with the torment of reviving thought. Beneath the unfamiliar sky before dawn, the waking mind,

[1] Throughout this section the quotations are taken from *La Jeune Parque*.

the Psyche, feels herself linked with the still visible stars, with what grandeur in the lines

> Je scintille, liée à ce ciel inconnu . . .
> L'immense grappe brille à ma soif de désastres.

There follows a recitative of great beauty, an invocation to the stars:

> Tout-puissants étrangers, inévitables astres
> Qui daignez faire luire au lointain temporel
> Je ne sais quoi de pur et de surnaturel;
> Vous qui dans les mortels plongez jusques aux larmes
> Ces souverains éclats, ces invincibles armes,
> Et les élancements de votre éternité,
> Je suis seule avec vous. . . .

There is a sort of universal order in the images, difficult to define, partly due to their essential nobility, a cosmic quality such as we find in certain passages of Milton's *Paradise Lost*. Here nature is never merely pretty or picturesque. The intimate communion with the universe of stars, sun and sea never suggests that they are either gentle, or sympathetic towards man. They are majestic, or sombre in their large indifference, but never comfortable or kind. They remain isolated in their own grandeur.

Alone before such cosmic purity La Jeune Parque turns to question her memories: what reality or what dream had come to trouble her:

> J'interroge mon cœur quelle douleur l'éveille,
> Quel crime par moi-même ou sur moi consommé? . . .

And the Valérian self-questioning, familiar to us through Monsieur Teste, is expressed in the symbolic cry:

> Je me voyais me voir, sinueuse, et dorais
> De regards en regards, mes profondes forêts.

The first movement ends with the introduction of the serpent:

> J'y suivais un serpent qui venait de me mordre.

The second movement takes up the theme of temptation with its disordered treasures and undisciplined ideas and desires which wake a longing for clarity:

> Quel repli de désirs, sa traîne! . . . Quel désordre
> De trésors s'arrachant à mon avidité,
> Et quelle sombre soif de la limpidité!

Passions without object poison the mind, tormenting and wounding the Self.

> Le poison, mon poison, m'éclaire et se connaît.

So from anxious questioning a further Self is projected:

> Dieux! Dans ma lourde plaie une secrète sœur
> Brûle, qui se préfère à l'extrême attentive.

Through torment and uncertainty the mind wakes to greater consciousness, rejecting the temptations of the other world of the senses. Born of the resolution to be free from all idols, this new Self defies temptation:[1]

> Va! je n'ai plus besoin de ta race naïve
> Cher Serpent. . . .

> Laisse donc défaillir ce bras de pierreries
> Qui menace d'amour mon sort spirituel. . .

> Rappelle ces remous, ces promesses immondes . . .
> Ma surprise s'abrège, et mes yeux sont ouverts.

This brings us very close to the young man, who twenty years earlier, in his lonely room in Genoa, had battled with his own tormented spirit, aware that the passion, which his imagination had nourished, was one of the idols which he must overthrow. Vain hopes and vain words must be rejected so that the mind alone may triumph:

> Tout peut naître ici-bas d'une attente infinie.

The serpent, symbolising the world and carnal desires, must be driven out:

> Va chercher des yeux clos pour tes danses massives.
> Coule vers d'autres lits tes robes successives,
> Couve sur d'autres cœurs les germes de leur mal,
> Et que dans les anneaux de ton rêve animal
> Halète jusqu'au jour l'innocence anxieuse! . . .
> Moi, je veille. Je sors, pâle et prodigieuse,
> Toute humide des pleurs que je n'ai point versés,
> D'une absence aux contours de mortelle bercés
> Par soi seule . . .

---

[1] In apostrophe to serpent the poet talks to himself. The passage is actually a summing-up of the whole poem. See Paul Valéry, letter to André Gide, *Correspondance André Gide–Paul Valéry*, ed. by Robert Mallet (Paris: Gallimard, 1955), 448.

La Jeune Parque has taken her decision. Henceforth she must stand alone, governed not by her sensibility but by her intellect sustained by pride:

> Et brisant une tombe sereine,
> Je m'accoude inquiète et pourtant souveraine,
> Tant de mes visions parmi la nuit et l'œil,
> Les moindres mouvements consultent mon orgueil.

But this statement of the mind's attitude is only the beginning of the drama. For pride is not enough: the actual imperfections of the Self must be cast off.

The fourth movement explains this. It is short and beautifully modulated. The use of the past tense shows us that La Parque is meditating on her recent triumphant words:

> Mais je tremblais de perdre une douleur divine!
> Je baisais sur ma main cette morsure fine,
> Et je ne savais plus de mon antique corps
> Insensible, qu'un feu qui brûlait sur mes bords:
>
> Adieu, pensai-je, MOI, mortelle sœur, mensonge . . .

The last rhyme, 'mensonge,' carries the musical sequence to the fifth movement which begins with the lyrical

> Harmonieuse MOI, différente d'un songe,
> Femme flexible et ferme aux silences suivis
> D'actes purs!

in which a new Self exalts, in those moments that radiate thought—

> Poreuse à l'éternel qui me semblait m'enclore,—

memories of past triumphs and happiness. Youth feels itself to be immortal since time seems eternal.

> Mon amère saveur ne m'était point venue.
> Je ne sacrifiais que mon épaule nue
> A la lumière.

In this passage light symbolises the understanding and knowledge for which Valéry always looked.

The memory of walking in the wind through flowering fields inspires the lines:

> Heureuse! A la hauteur de tant de gerbes belles,
> Qui laissais à ma robe obéir les ombelles,
> Dans les abaissements de leur frêle fierté;
> Et si, contre le fil de cette liberté,
> Si la robe s'arrache à la rebelle ronce,
> L'arc de mon brusque corps s'accuse et me prononce,
> Nu sous le voile enflé de vivantes couleurs
> Que dispute ma race aux longs liens de fleurs!

Surely the first joys of early poetry are recalled here in 'tant de gerbes belles,' where,

> . . . dans l'ardente paix des songes naturels,
> Tous ces pas infinis me semblaient éternels.

This movement ends with fresh images to describe sleep:

> Si ce n'est, ô Splendeur, qu'à mes pieds l'ennemie,
> Mon ombre! la mobile et la souple momie,
> De mon absence peinte effleurait sans effort
> La terre où je fuyais cette légère mort.
> Entre la rose et moi, je la vois qui s'abrite;
> Sur la poudre qui danse, elle glisse et n'irrite
> Nul feuillage, mais passe, et se brise partout . . .
> Glisse! Barque funèbre. . . .

This illustrates Valéry's special use of *absence*, which is 'peinte' because referring to 'momie.'

In the sixth movement we return to the present where La Jeune Parque re-awakes to the problem of life. The line broken off at the end of the coming of sleep is taken up again in a moving autobiographical passage:

> Et moi vive, debout,
> Dure, et de mon néant secrètement armée,
> Mais comme par l'amour une joue enflammée,
> Et la narine jointe au vent de l'oranger,
> Je ne rends plus au jour qu'un regard étranger . . .
> Oh! combien peut grandir dans ma nuit curieuse
> De mon cœur séparé la part mystérieuse,
> Et de sombres essais s'approfondir mon art! . . .

But waking also brings the exasperation of limitations from which the thoughtful poet necessarily suffers,

> Loin des purs environs, je suis captive,

and bathed in the light of knowledge

> Je pense, sur le bord doré de l'univers,
> A ce goût de périr qui prend la Pythonisse
> En qui mugit l'espoir que le monde finisse.

This idea was fully worked out in 'La Pythie,' and found its final expression in 'Le Solitaire' of *Mon Faust*.

However the idea of the preparation and waiting for a poem counteracts here the full negation of such thought, as in 'Les Pas' in *Charmes*, which we may compare with these lines:

> Je renouvelle en moi mes énigmes, mes dieux,
> Mes pas interrompus de paroles aux cieux,
> Mes pauses, sur le pied portant la rêverie,
> Qui suit au miroir d'aile un oiseau qui varie,
> Cent fois sur le soleil joue avec le néant . . .

This is followed in the seventh movement by a clear reflection of the poet's mind, in which his capacity for feeling the boredom of living is transposed into poetry.

> Car l'œil spirituel sur ses plages de soie
> Avait déjà vu luire et pâlir trop de jours
> Dont je m'étais prédit les couleurs et le cours.
> L'ennui, le clair ennui de mirer leur nuance,
> Me donnait sur ma vie une funeste avance:
> L'aube me dévoilait tout le jour ennemi.

This thought also appears in 'L'Ame et la danse' where Socrates speaks of: 'this evil above all evils, this poison of poisons, this venom opposed to all nature . . . l'ennui de vivre.'

In the lyrical lines which follow there are echoes from the 'Episode' of *Les Vers anciens*.

> Osera-t-il, le Temps, de mes diverses tombes,
> Ressusciter un soir favori des colombes,
> Un soir qui traîne au fil d'un lambeau voyageur
> De ma docile enfance un reflet de rougeur,
> Et trempe à l'émeraude un long rose de honte?

In the eighth movement all the bitterness of memory and the mind's reaction are metamorphosed into music. The Self meditates on 'la pâle circonstance' of its early obsession (*pâle* because already fading into the past) and treats with severity the vain love of a former Self. The early poems are included in the last lines of this condemnation,

where 'le col charmant' is that of poetic inspiration, *le cygne* of
Mallarmé.

> Viens! que je reconnaisse et que je les haïsse,
> Cette ombrageuse enfant, ce silence complice,
> Ce trouble transparent qui baigne dans les bois . . .
> Et de mon sein glacé rejaillisse la voix
> Que j'ignorais si rauque et d'amour si voilée . . .
> Le col charmant cherchant la chasseresse ailée.

And the passage ends with regret for those very temptations which
have been rejected:

> O pampres! Sur ma joue errant en fils tenaces,
> Ou toi . . . de cils tissue et de fluides fûts,
> Tendre lueur d'un soir brisé de bras confus?

The ninth movement opens with La Jeune Parque's vow, and
refusal to be ensnared:

> 'Que dans le ciel placés, mes yeux tracent mon temple!
> Et que sur moi repose un autel sans exemple!'[1]
>
> Criaient de tout mon corps la pierre et la pâleur . . .
> La terre ne m'est plus qu'un bandeau de couleur
> Qui coule et se refuse au front blanc de vertige . . .
> Tout l'univers chancelle et tremble sur ma tige, . . .

Thus a new Self repudiates the world, with all the force and clarity of a
state of ecstasy. But, alas, such moments are rare and die of their own
perfection:

> La pensive couronne échappe à mes esprits,
> La mort veut respirer cette rose sans prix
> Dont la douceur importe à sa fin ténébreuse!

Death haunts all beauty, and despair shadows ecstasy.

> De moi-même si lasse, image condamnée!

The mind can renew itself only through contact with universal nature,
of which it is a part,[2] and the Self turns now to the secret movement of
the waking spring.

---

[1] Cf. Valéry's saying, that 'the *croyant* contemplates the sky, while the *savant*
considers it.'

[2] Cf. Paul Valéry, 'Dialogue de l'arbre,' *Eupalinos ou l'architecte, L'Ame et la
danse, Dialogue de l'arbre* (Paris: Gallimard, 1944), 183, and below p. 227, 'The
Dialogues.'

Le gel cède à regret ses derniers diamants . . .
Demain, sur un soupir des bontés constellées,
Le printemps vient briser les fontaines scellées:
L'étonnant printemps rit, viole . . . On ne sait d'où
Venu? Mais la candeur ruisselle à mots si doux
Qu'une tendresse prend la terre à ses entrailles . ...
Les arbres regonflés et recouverts d'écailles
Chargés de tant de bras et de trop d'horizons,
Meuvent sur le soleil leurs tonnantes toisons,
Montent dans l'air amer avec toutes leurs ailes
De feuilles par milliers qu'ils se sentent nouvelles . . .
N'entends-tu pas frémir ces noms aériens,
O Sourde! . . .

This triumphant recitative for spring was added after the rest of the poem. In it there is a change of tempo, an *andante* in the slowing down of phrasing and rhythm.[1] Born directly of images seen and felt there is nothing sentimental in this candid acceptance of nature: we are in the forest where the forcible rhymes—*entrailles, écailles, horizons, toisons*—are full of the turbulent winds of spring.

In the foreground La Jeune Parque meditates on her own substance and her relationship with universal life. Not without regrets, however, for who could resist the wild joy of 'la flottante forêt' where thought becomes music:

Quelle résisterait, mortelle, à ces remous?
Quelle mortelle?

Moi si pure, mes genoux
Pressentent les terreurs de genoux sans défense . . .
L'air me brise. L'oiseau perce de cris d'enfance
Inouïs . . . l'ombre même où se serre mon cœur,
Et roses! mon soupir vous soulève, vainqueur
Hélas!

These lines with their rather facile rhymes—*cœur, vainqueur*—admirably express the frailty of the flesh. How is La Jeune Parque to resist these desires, and all the joys of love?

Chers fantômes naissants dont la soif m'est unie
Désirs! Visages clairs! . . . Et vous, beaux fruits d'amour.

---

[1] For similar changes in tempo cf. the speech of Joad in Racine's *Athalie*, Act III, Scene 7.

Was she not formed by the gods to enjoy fully the glory of physical love?

> Pour que la vie embrasse un autel de délices.[1]

Yet all this must be lost if the life of pure intelligence is to be gained, for the mind must acquire a still greater spiritual freedom. The whole of this tenth movement, too long to quote in its entirety, is a veritable *agitato*, with its cries, its insistence, and repeated refusals:

> Non, souffles! Non, regards, tendresses . . . mes convives,
> Peuple altéré de moi suppliant que tu vives,
> Non, vous ne tiendrez pas de moi la vie! . . .
>
> Je n'accorderai pas la lumière à des ombres,
> Je garde loin de vous, l'esprit sinistre et clair . . .
> Non, vous ne tiendrez pas de mes lèvres l'éclair! . . .

Such is the poet, unsatisfied, rejecting all that is easy and too eloquent in poetry; such the youth ideally in love, renouncing sensual desires. This is the poetic expression of a deeply rooted asceticism which confirms Valéry's judgement on literature and his doubts as to its real value, his hatred of all that tended in the written word to exalt mere appearances above spiritual awareness. The conflict between what is natural, and therefore easy, and what requires real effort had for him the gravity of an ethical problem,[2] for he had disciplined himself to the conception and contemplation of a poetic absolute, which he expresses here.

So La Jeune Parque, symbol of the poet's mind, must reject all desires in order that only the pure emotion of pity, manifested by tears, should remain:

> Très imminente larme, et seule à me répondre. . . .

Valéry has often meditated on the gift of tears which lays so true a claim to poetry, and here he sings marvellously of the mystery of their source:

> Larme qui fais trembler à mes regards humains
> Une variété de funèbres chemins;
> Tu procèdes de l'âme, orgueil du labyrinthe. . . .
>
> Tendre libation de l'arrière-pensée!

[1] 'Tout ce qui est sexuel est surajouté, tel, le passage sur *le printemps* qui semble maintenant d'importance essentiel.' Valéry, letter to Albert Mockel (1917), *Lettres à quelques-uns*, 124.
[2] Paul Valéry, 'Lettre sur Mallarmé,' *Variété*, II, 229 (for 'la rigueur des refus,' etc.).

Tears also come to the aid of the human being who knows not why or whence comes his suffering.

> Mais blessure, sanglots, sombres essais, pourquoi?
> Pour qui, joyaux cruels, marquez-vous ce corps froid,
> Aveugle aux doigts ouverts évitant l'espérance!
> Où va-t-il, sans répondre à sa propre ignorance,
> Ce corps dans la nuit noire étonné de sa foi?

Thus consciousness considers its own drama.

Now the poet turns to the all-searching discipline of thought of which the earth is emblem:

> . . . Dureté précieuse . . . O sentiment du sol,
> Mon pas fondait sur toi l'assurance sacrée!

But here also the mind is assailed by difficulties, all the torment of conflict, the bitter questioning of existence; for there is no sure path, and thought may lead to the void.

> Non loin, parmi ces pas, rêve mon précipice . . .
> L'insensible rocher, glissant d'algues, propice
> A fuir (comme en soi-même ineffablement seul),
> Commence . . .

For even thought is treacherous:

> Hélas! De mes pieds nus qui trouvera la trace
> Cessera-t-il longtemps de ne songer qu'à soi?
>
> Terre trouble, et mêlée à l'algue, porte-moi!

The whole of this movement is an excellent example of Valéry's analysis and music. The constantly echoed *leit-motiv* of death, with its Wagnerian insistence, gives an epic grandeur to the difficult destiny chosen by the youngest and most sensitive of the Fates, and to the solitary destiny chosen by the poet.

> Mystérieuse Moi, pourtant, tu vis encore!
> Tu vas te reconnaître au lever de l'aurore
> Amèrement la même . . .

This opens the eleventh movement. The Self enters into a fresh phase, but the problems to be stated are still the same and temptation is always new:

L'ombre qui m'abandonne, impérissable hostie,
Me découvre vermeille à de nouveaux désirs,
Sur le terrible autel de tous mes souvenirs.

The ritual of living repeats its illusions and hypocrisy:

Tout va donc accomplir son acte solennel
De toujours reparaître incomparable et chaste,
Et de restituer la tombe enthousiaste
Au gracieux état du rire universel.

In a supremely lyrical period the gradual rising of dawn over the still dim islands is sung in the twelfth movement:

Salut! Divinités par la rose et le sel,
Et les premiers jouets de la jeune lumière,
Iles!...Ruches bientôt,...[1]

Here the intelligence symbolised by 'la jeune lumière' plays with the ideas, those islands which may become poems—'ruches bientôt'—hives which come to life in the growing light beneath the visible sky that is the elevation of our thought while words and ideas crowd the mind, born from the murmur of the sea (life), marvels of decorative expression but without living roots:

Rien n'égale dans l'air les fleurs que vous placez,
Mais dans la profondeur, que vos pieds sont glacés!

In this figure we may trace many lateral effects: a further condemnation of all that is futile in the 'hymnes d'hommes'; the changing Self and its ephemeral flowers; that disillusionment which lies behind appearances; and death which is at the foundation of all life.

In the thirteenth movement we are reminded that both the Self and its expression in poetry are in search of their Absolute; and the genesis of such a state is here the theme:

De l'âme les apprêts sous la tempe calmée,
Ma mort, enfant secrète et déjà si formée,
Et vous, divins dégoûts qui me donniez l'essor,
Chastes éloignements des lustres de mon sort,
Ne fûtes-vous, ferveur, qu'une noble durée?

---

[1] 'Quant à la petite invocation aux Iles, je ne sais pas s'il fallait y insister au point de faire trop voir.' Valéry, letter to Albert Mockel, *Lettres à quelques-uns*, 122.

Nulle jamais des dieux plus près aventurée
N'osa peindre à son front leur souffle ravisseur,
Et de la nuit parfaite implorant l'épaisseur,
Prétendre par la lèvre au suprême murmure.

After the refusal of all idols, only extreme fervour is acceptable as the basis of pure poetry. And the poet's renunciation and his return to poetry are transposed to admirable figures:

Je soutenais l'éclat de la mort toute pure
Telle j'avais jadis le soleil soutenu . . .
Mon corps désespéré tendait le torse nu
Où l'âme, ivre de soi, de silence et de gloire,
Prête à s'évanouir de sa propre mémoire,
Écoute, avec espoir, frapper au mur pieux
Ce cœur,—qui se ruine à coups mystérieux
Jusqu'à ne plus tenir que de sa complaisance
Un frémissement fin de feuille, ma présence . . .

But retrospection and regret are not enough to sustain the life of poetry; a further sacrifice must be made:

Attente vaine, et vaine . . . Elle ne peut mourir
Qui devant son miroir, pleure pour s'attendrir.

This movement in a minor key should be read with a perceptive and open mind, for the symbolism of the transformations of the Self has a double significance and gives those lateral effects of which I have spoken. The reader is directly impressed by the theme of life and death.

The fourteenth movement opens with a lyrical passage of rare beauty, of which Valéry was justly proud, and to which his mind returned during his last illness.[1]

O n'aurait-il fallu, folle, que j'accomplisse
Ma merveilleuse fin de choisir pour supplice
Ce lucide dédain des nuances du sort?
Trouveras-tu jamais plus transparente mort
Ni de pente plus pure où je rampe à ma perte
Que sur ce long regard de victime entr'ouverte,
Pâle, que se résigne et saigne sans regret?

Here English readers should particularly notice the value of the mute *e* in 'folle' and 'merveilleuse'; also the interplay of the *l*'s and *f*'s. The alexandrines admirably convey the strength and clarity of 'ce lucide

---

[1] I am indebted to Professor Mondor for this moving detail.

dédain' which expresses Valéry's Self in the altitude where he finds
his poems, having sacrificed everything to that which is 'à l'extrême
de l'être,' where 'elle se fait toujours plus seule et plus lointaine' till
the Self becomes part of universal consciousness:

> L'être immense me gagne, et de mon cœur divin
> L'encens qui brûle expire une forme sans fin . . .
> Tous les corps radieux tremblent dans mon essence! . . .

But why should this moment fade? Why should sleep, that false
death, break the thread of thought?

> Sombre lys! Ténébreuse allusion des cieux, . . .

Consider, cries La Jeune Parque, through what mysterious progression night brought you from death to daylight. Consider by what
action life called you back to its own reality, its impure state:

> Par quel retour sur toi, reptile, as-tu repris
> Tes parfums de caverne et tes tristes esprits?

For the serpent, the tempter within ourselves, is intimately present at
moments of intellectual lassitude. Sleep, for Valéry, symbolises a
passing from one sort of consciousness to another; and here the regret
that consciousness must give way to night, seems to be the motif of
this passage. Evidently these elliptic lines could be given various
interpretations, as variations on a theme.

The fifteenth movement sings of the betrayal of the Self overcome
by sleep:

> Mais le sommeil s'éprit d'une douceur si grande,
> Et nouée à moi-même au creux de mes cheveux,
> J'ai mollement perdu mon empire nerveux.

Here we are brought back to the night which had ended in the first
movement of the poem, in a meditation on the strange and sometimes
terrifying process of falling asleep, and above all the regret for that
Self which sleep has ravished.

> Au milieu de mes bras, je me suis faite une autre . . .
> Qui s'aliène? . . . Qui s'envole? . . . Qui se vautre? . . .
> A quel détour caché, mon cœur s'est-il fondu?
> Quelle conque a redit le nom que j'ai perdu?
> Le sais-je, quel reflux traître m'a retirée
> De mon extrémité pure et prématurée
> Et m'a repris le sens de mon vaste soupir?
> Comme l'oiseau se pose, il fallut m'assoupir.

For the spirit comes to rest inevitably as does the body:

> Ce fut l'heure, peut-être, où la devineresse
> Intérieure s'use et se désintéresse:
> Elle n'est plus la même . . . Une profonde enfant
> Des degrés inconnus vainement se défend,
> Et redemande au loin ses mains abandonnées.

On the words *se désintéresse* (1. 446), Thibaudet founded his argument that Valéry was referring here to the *élan vital* of Bergson, and declared that throughout his poem the poet had closely followed the philosopher.[1] Valéry, however, categorically denied any belief in the *élan vital*, insisting that he was merely describing the state of falling asleep when the mind is obliged to abandon those thoughts which are most profound when on the edge of the abyss; and for him the abyss consists of 'des mots sans fin, sans moi, balbutiés,' where the Self is absent.

> Dors, ma sagesse, dors. Forme-toi cette absence;
> Retourne dans le germe et la sombre innocence,
> Abandonne-toi vive aux serpents, aux trésors.
> Dors toujours! Descends, dors toujours! Descends, dors, dors!

Thus the gradual fading out process takes place when one is overcome by sleep, and the elements of thought must return to chaos.

The final movement opens with the poetic image of waking in the cool delight of fine linen sheets:

> Délicieux linceuls, mon désordre tiède,
> Couche où je me répands, m'interroge et me cède,
> Où j'allai de mon cœur noyer les battements, . . .

This brings us back to a double waking, for the Self of yesterday is replaced by that of today which in its turn must also die; for the new day already forms the substance of a tomb, each sunrise foretells its own setting, all thought has an end:

> Et ce jeune soleil de mes étonnements
> Me paraît d'une aïeule éclairer les tourments.

But sleep has an actual poetic and metaphysical value. While limiting our powers, it nevertheless is part of that strange necessity by which we partake of universal life and not merely our own individual

---

[1] Albert Thibaudet, *Paul Valéry* ('Les Cahiers verts,' 25) (Paris: Grasset, 1923), 118.

existence. This feeling of universal life, which is not necessarily sympathetic to the individual, permeates the whole poem, and finally triumphs, as it does also in 'Le Cimetière marin.' Here it takes the form of an irresistible approach to the sea at dawn, in which dreams are cast aside:

> Sur ce bord, sans horreur, humer la haute écume,
> Boire des yeux l'immense et riante amertume,
> L'être contre le vent, dans le plus vif de l'air,
> Recevant au visage un appel de la mer;

Here the symbolism is easy to follow, for the sea always represents life—how vividly here—with its immense and laughing bitterness.

Thus the Self accepts the pure source of all intellectual power, in the figures of the sun and the sea as image and substance of the poet's life; presence to which he must return, and in which he renews his creative forces:

> Alors, malgré moi-même, il le faut ô Soleil,
> Que j'adore mon cœur où tu te viens connaître,
> Doux et puissant retour du délice de naître,
>
> Feu vers qui se soulève une vierge de sang
> Sous les espèces d'or d'un sein reconnaissant!

André Gide, on re-reading this poem, thought that there was too much introspection. But since the theme is admittedly based on intimate self-questioning of the mind, this criticism seems scarcely valid. While admiring the musical qualities, Gide found that some parts of the poem were too close to Mallarmé,[1] and perhaps this observation is justified in so far as images and sequences are sometimes used which have also been used by the elder poet.

A comparison might be made between La Jeune Parque and Mallarmé's Hérodiade, fragmentary though the latter is, when we remember how greatly Valéry was moved at an impressionable age by these fragments. Indeed, the fact that the Hérodiade was not finished suggested the possibility of infinite splendour in the mind of the younger poet. It may well appear to us today that Valéry achieved in La Jeune Parque what Mallarmé had dreamed of doing, in creating a poetic Absolute. That high seriousness and purity for which Mallarmé had always striven in his poems had made it possible for Valéry to develop

[1] André Gide, Journal (1927) ('Bibliothèque de la Pléiade,') (Paris: Gallimard, 1940), 843.

his own sphere of being, which intrinsically directs its own expression to ever wider possibilities. Unexplored aspects of syntax had been revealed through an unequalled domination of language. This the master had achieved. It remained for the disciple by combined analysis and construction to evolve a further perfection of thought and word, constituting a future conception of a universal art.

While enjoying the strange beauty of Valéry's poem, the reader should consult the commentary made by the most valid critic, the poet himself who, in 'Le Philosophe et le jeune Parque,' assures us that

Qui s'égare en soi-même aussitôt me retrouve . . .[1]

2. 'LE CIMETIÈRE MARIN'

*N'aspire pas à l'immortalité, ô mon âme, mais
explore les limites du possible.* (PINDAR)

Of all Valéry's poems, not excepting *La Jeune Parque*, 'Le Cimetière marin' has been the most discussed, admired and translated. On its first appearance in *La Nouvelle Revue Française* in June 1920, it was at once received with enthusiasm. In the same year it was published by Émile Paul and two years later was included in *Charmes* (Gallimard, 1922). There was also a small and rare edition with an etching[2] by Valéry produced in 1926 (Ronald Davis).

Many commentaries were made on the poem during Valéry's lifetime. Professor Gustave Cohen described the work as a classical tragedy, not in five acts, but in four, a lyrical and dramatic dialogue between the three actors of Greek tragedy.[3] The protagonist here is Non-Being, the *néant* whose immobility is symbolised by *midi*—'midi le juste,' 'midi le feu'; the deuteragonist is the consciousness of the poet and of man; while the tritagonist is the author, at once actor and spectator of the drama which he passionately contemplates. There is for Professor Cohen a double significance, for *le soleil de*

[1] Paul Valéry, 'Le Philosophe et la Jeune Parque,' in *Poésies* (1942), 180.

[2] The etching is of a cemetery, with the oblong tomb of the Valéry family in the foreground, a mass of trees at the left, and the harbour seen in the distance below. It has no particular technical interest.

[3] Gustave Cohen, 'Essai d'explication du Cimetière marin,' *Nouvelle Revue Française* (février 1929).

midi is also for him eternity, and *la mer* represents consciousness, and so on.

Amused and curious, Valéry had listened to the first reading of this essay. His answer was cautious and tactful, and pleased everyone: 'My poems have the sense which their readers give them.'[1] Hence-forth this became the poet's reply to his learned friends' assertions or inquiries; it was at the same time a compliment and a means of self-defence. But it was Valéry himself who best commented on his own works, and to some extent he was obliged to do so in consequence of the pontifical attitude that had been thrust upon him. Thus his essay 'Au sujet du Cimetière marin,' which served as preface to the critical study of Professor Cohen, tells us of the origins and aims of the poem.[2]

Characteristically, Valéry's intention was not to say something, but to make something, and this was the *raison d'être* of the poem.[3] An immense amount of work had gone to the making of it, as L. J. Austin shows in an examination of the many drafts in which Valéry gradually built up the whole structure.[4] Valéry was working on this when Jacques Rivière insisted on taking it for *La Nouvelle Revue Française*.[5] It is therefore almost by chance that we have the poem in its present form. To a mind as scrupulous as Valéry's a poem was never finished, but was abandoned at a certain stage. Suspicious of all beginnings and of all that came to him easily, he considered that the spontaneous movements of his mind must be verified and examined; the idea of the 'first Self' must be scrutinised by another more critical, more difficult Self, as we have seen it to be in *La Jeune Parque*.

Like many of the poems, 'Le Cimetière marin' arose from a rhythmic figure which obsessed the poet. Noticing that this figure was decasyllabic, he reflected that this metre was very little used in modern French verse, and that it seemed poor and monotonous in comparison with the alexandrine, which several generations of great artists had

[1] Paul Valéry, 'Commentaires de Charmes,' *Variété*, III (Paris: Gallimard, 1936), 80: 'Mes vers ont le sens qu'on leur prête'; 'Au sujet du Cimetière marin,' *ibid.* 74: 'Il n'y a pas de vrai sens d'un texte.'

[2] Valéry, 'Au sujet du Cimetière marin,' *Variété*, III, 59.

[3] *Ibid.*, 64: 'La littérature ne m'intéresse donc profondément que dans la mesure où elle exerce l'esprit à certaines transformations—celles dans lesquelles les propriétés excitantes du langage jouent un rôle capital.'

[4] For drafts and variants see L. J. Austin, 'Paul Valéry compose le Cimetière marin,' *Mercure de France* (avril–mai 1953).

[5] Paul Valéry, 'Au sujet du Cimetière marin,' *Variété*, III, 64.

elaborated and enriched. 'The demon of generalisation,' he noted, 'suggested the attempt to carry this *ten* to the power of twelve.'[1] So he started on a poem to be composed of verses of six lines, each line of ten syllables, with contrasts and correspondences between the verses.[2] These conditions, he tells us, seemed to demand that the poem should be a monologue of the Self, in which the most simple and the most constant themes of his intellectual and emotional life would be united or opposed. These themes were associated with the sea, the the light and a certain locality on the Mediterranean coast—the marine cemetery at Sète. All this led to the theme of death and touched on pure thought.

The decasyllabic line was that of the *chansons de geste*. It is very close to the rhythm of the spoken word. The lines to be appropriate for Valéry's purpose had to be dense and strongly rhymed, for he was aiming at a monologue which should be as personal, and at the same time as universal, as he could make it. This type of line and the form of the verses were favourable to certain movements, allowing for changes of time and demanding a certain style. Thus the whole poem was gradually planned.

The main theme is the meditation of a certain Self transposed into a sentient, emotional and abstract poetic universe. The necessity of producing contrasts and keeping a sort of equilibrium between the moments of this Self led the poet to introduce at one point certain philosophical reflections. Thus the lines in which the famous arguments of Zeno of Elea are lightly touched on 'compensate by their metaphysical tone for the sensual and too human tones of the proceding verses.' This philosophic interlude, the reference to Zeno, does in fact give relief to a meditation in which the difference between being and knowing was becoming too cruelly felt. 'The soul [*l'âme*] naïvely wishes to exhaust the Infinite of the Elean.' However, the poet did not want to take from philosophy 'anything except a little of its colour'; and to this end the arguments are animated and broken up and 'sweep away all dialectics as hurricane gusts sweep away the rigging of a ship.'[3]

The scene opens on the immense tranquillity of mid-day, which admirably symbolises that silence from which poetry is born.

[1] Paul Valéry, 'Au sujet du Cimetière marin,' *Variété*, III, 72.

[2] The verses, of which there are 24 regular sextains, have the following rhyme scheme: *aabccb*.

[3] Valéry, 'Au sujet du Cimetière marin,' *Variété*, III, 72.

Ce toit tranquille, où marchent des colombes,
Entre les pins palpite, entre les tombes;
Midi le juste y compose de feux
La mer, la mer, toujours recommencée!
O récompense après une pensée
Qu'un long regard sur le calme des dieux![1]

The Mediterranean is evoked, the classic wine-dark sea of the world's
centre, the essential background of Valéry's thought,[2] with which he
identifies his universal Self:

Temple du Temps, qu'un seul soupir résume,
A ce point pur je monte et m'accoutume,
Tout entouré de mon regard marin;
Et comme aux dieux mon offrande suprême,
La scintillation sereine sème
Sur l'altitude un dédain souverain.

After the calm of the first four stanzas the idea of change is introduced. This is one of the high points of modern poetry, one of the most
musical images of the fragility of life and the mortality of the spirit
which is consumed as smoke when the body is dissolved, changing as
the waves change into sound on the shore. English poets may sigh for
the pure closed *u* which furnishes here such rich harmony with the
accompanying consonants.

Comme le fruit se fond en jouissance,
Comme en délice il change son absence
Dans une bouche où sa forme se meurt,
Je hume ici ma future fumée,
Et le ciel chante à l'âme consumée
Le changement des rives en rumeur.[3]

The idea of change now becomes the *leit-motiv*:

Beau ciel, vrai ciel, regarde-moi qui change!

---

[1] *Ce toit* is of course the sea, *les colombes* are the sails—*les focs* of the final verse
(a 'foc' is a triangular sail). Cf. Stéphane Mallarmé, 'sur un toit, ainsi que la mer,'
in 'Ballet, Deux Pigeons, (Crayonné au théâtre)' *Œuvres complètes* ('Bibliothèque
de la Pléiade') (Paris: Gallimard, 1945).
[2] Cf. Valéry, 'Inspirations méditerranéennes,' *Variété*, III, 245.
[3] Cf. a curious passage in Valéry, letter to P. Louÿs (avril 1910), in *Lettres à
quelques-uns*, 87 (concerning the funeral of Moréas).

That light which is pure knowledge now

> Suppose d'ombre une morne moitié

as life is shadowed by death. So the poet turns to contemplate his own secret reality in the presence of a universal fatality:

> O pour moi seul, à moi seul, en moi-même,
> Auprès d'un cœur, aux sources du poème,
> Entre le vide et l'événement pur,
> J'attends l'écho de ma grandeur interne,
> Amère, sombre et sonore citerne,
> Sonnant dans l'âme un creux toujours futur!

This is an essential moment for the poet, between the void of non-being and the initial consciousness, 'l'événement pur,' which is also the motif of his poem, that unique instant when the unconscious may become conscious, reflecting the waking of human intelligence in the poetic universe.

Death in the presence of this great light, this 'feu sans matière,' now fills the mind with questionings, death which makes man one with non-being. In a remarkable image the tombs in this quiet place are compared to a flock of sheep guarded by the sea.

> Chienne splendide, écarte l'idolâtre!
> Quand solitaire au sourire de pâtre,
> Je pais longtemps, moutons mystérieux,
> Le blanc troupeau de mes tranquilles tombes,
> Éloignes-en les prudentes colombes,
> Les songes vains, les anges curieux!

In the calm that reigns only the cigala is heard:

> Ici venu, l'avenir est paresse.
> L'insecte net gratte la sécheresse;
> Tout est brûlé, défait, reçu dans l'air
> A je ne sais quelle sévère essence . . .
> La vie est vaste, étant ivre d'absence,
> Et l'amertume est douce, et l'esprit clair.

So the dead dissolve into nothingness while

> Midi là-haut, Midi sans mouvement
> En soi se pense et convient à soi-même . . .

—an intelligence in which living man is the secret change, with his repentance, doubt and constraint, the only flaw in the 'grand diamant.' We may compare the similar idea in 'L'Ébauche d'un serpent.'[1]

As for the dead:

> Ils ont fondu dans une absence épaisse,
> L'argile rouge a bu la blanche espèce,
> Le don de vivre a passé dans les fleurs!
> Où sont des morts les phrases familières,
> L'art personnel, les âmes singulières? . . .
>
> Tout va sous terre et rentre dans le jeu!

There is nothing to hope for in death, not even the unreality of a dream. The spirit is porous to eternity, which absorbs it as the earth absorbs the body. *La Jeune Parque* has also expressed this idea. Even the immortality which religion may offer is an empty mockery: 'Le beau mensonge et la pieuse ruse!' The dead have become one with the earth; it is on the living that death feeds:

> Le vrai rongeur, le ver irréfutable
> N'est point pour vous qui dormez sous la table,
> Il vit de vie, il ne me quitte pas!

For death is so intimately concerned with life that everything living seems to belong to it:

> Ma chair lui plaît, et jusque sur ma couche,
> A ce vivant je vis d'appartenir!

At this point Valéry relieves the tension by introducing a philosophic interlude, which breaks and dissipates with sudden change the state of sombre reflection, and brings us back to the reigning splendour, summoning the philosopher Zeno to bridge the gap between life and death.

Zeno of Elea was the inventor of dialectics, from which all subsequent sophism and scepticism originated, and which has been defined as 'a refutation of error by the *reductio ad absurdum* as a means of establishing the truth.'[2] He declared real motion to be impossible since all substance is one; in the flying arrow there is only the appearance of

---

[1] Paul Valéry, *Charmes*, in *Poésies* (1933), 165.

[2] John Stuart Mill, *System of Logic* (London, 1872), II, 183. For source of this stanza see V. Bochard, 'Les paradoxes de Zénon,' *Revue de métaphysique et de morale* (1893), cited by Gustave Cohen, 'Essai d'explication du Cimetière marin,' *Nouvelle Revue Française*.

movement. His famous demonstration of Achilles and the tortoise was based on the theoretical subdivision of time.

> Zénon! Cruel Zénon! Zénon d'Élée!
> M'as-tu percé de cette flèche ailée
> Qui vibre, vole, et qui ne vole pas!
> Le son m'enfante et la flèche me tue!
> Ah! le soleil . . . Quelle ombre de tortue
> Pour l'âme, Achille immobile à grands pas!

Having thus invited the reader to meditate on the meaning of time, Valéry turns again to life, to the sea; and the poem ends in a hymn to being, magnificent in its force and simplicity, with the wind blowing through the final verse:

> Le vent se lève! . . . il faut tenter de vivre!
> L'air immense ouvre et referme mon livre,
> La vague en poudre ose jaillir des rocs!
> Envolez-vous, pages tout éblouies!
> Rompez, vagues! Rompez d'eaux réjouies
> Ce toit tranquille où picoraient des focs!

3. THE TIME OF 'CHARMES'

Nil in intellectu quod non erat primum in sensu.

Valéry's poetic genius reached its zenith in his lyrical *Charmes*, published in 1922. Most of these poems were written immediately after the completion of *La Jeune Parque*, that is towards the end of the war and in the years that directly followed. This was for Valéry a time of poetic research and lyrical activity during which he must have been almost happy. Had he not found the fulfilment of that long prepared state of grace, the synthesis of an authentic poetic experience? All he had cultivated, all he had exacted from himself now bore fruit.

In the summer of 1920 we find him enjoying that intellectual vitality which he rightly considered as the most enviable of states. In the rich green country near Avranches, where trees grew as grass, he spent three or four months, and wrote 'La Pythie,' and other *Charmes*.[1]

'L'Insinuant' was also written here, in the park where a tiny river

---

[1] Paul Valéry, letter to a friend, *Lettres à quelques-uns*, 160.

wound in and out and the tide came up in a single huge wave, a great distance from the sea, and could be heard long before it arrived:

> O Courbes, méandre,
> Secrets du menteur,
> Est-il art plus tendre
> Que cette lenteur?

'Au Platane' also seems to date from this time. Under the poet's window there were groups of lime trees, and copper beeches spread their wide branches to the ground:

> Le tremble pur, le charme, et ce hêtre formé
> De quatre jeunes femmes,
> Ne cessent point de battre un ciel toujours fermé, . . .

This is an admirable example of the force of *choses vues* on the poet's mind.

Every morning before sunrise Valéry crept out barefoot on the ice-cold grass. What an awaking for the poet of dawn, on whom the first moments of daylight had always exerted a strange power: when mingled sadness, enchantment and emotion brought a mental clarity which was so intense as to be almost painful. As soon as the sky became faintly coloured he returned to his room to write his poems: that book which Mallarmé seems to have foretold when, years before in a letter to Verlaine, he had spoke of 'an architectural and premeditated work, and not a collection of chance inspirations—no matter how beautiful.' Such was Valéry's *Charmes*. The Self and its poetic expression were the secret theme progressing from poem to poem, where all the fresh and sensual delight of the animated world of nature provided symbolic beauty, 'rêve, mais rêve tout pénétré de symétries, tout ordre, tout actes et séquences! . . .'[1]

The first poem 'Aurore,' sings of the moment of waking when a poem may take form. Originally this was planned as a single composition with 'Palme,' which tells of the final profusion of the poet's thought. In the earliest editions, 'Aurore,' 'Air de Sémiramis,' 'Palme' and 'Cantique des colonnes' were all included under the title 'Aurore.'[2]

---

[1] Paul Valéry, L'Ame et la danse,' in *Eupalinos, L'Ame et la danse, Dialogue de l'arbre* (Paris: Gallimard, 1944), 142.

[2] See E. Noulet, the first critic to state the interior plan of *Charmes*, in 'La Composition de Charmes,' *Paul Valéry: Études* (Bruxelles: Renaissance du Livre, 1951).

In its present form the poem begins with a synthesis of that sensation of waking so precious to Valéry and so carefully studied by him.

> La confusion morose
> Qui me servait de sommeil,
> Se dissipe dès la rose
> Apparence du soleil.
> Dans mon âme je m'avance,
> Tout ailé de confiance:
> C'est la première oraison!
> A peine sorti des sables,
> Je fais des pas admirables
> Dans les pas de ma raison.

This is the gradual return to consciousness, after which, words wake in the poet's receptive mind:

> Salut! encore endormies
> A vos sourires jumeaux
> Similitudes amies
> Qui brillez parmi les mots!
> Au vacarme des abeilles
> Je vous aurai par corbeilles,
> Et sur l'échelon tremblant
> De mon échelle dorée
> Ma prudence évaporée
> Déjà pose son pied blanc.

First of all he looks for words, which gradually awaken in groups:

> Quelle aurore sur ces croupes
> Qui commencent de frémir!
> Déjà s'étirent par groupes
> Telles qui semblaient dormir:
> L'une brille, l'autre bâille;
> Et sur un peigne d'écaille,
> Égarant ses vagues doigts,
> Du songe encore prochaine,
> La paresseuse l'enchaîne,
> Aux prémisses de sa voix.

Then follow ideas, whom the poet questions:

> Quoi! c'est vous, mal déridées!
> Que fîtes-vous, cette nuit,
> Maîtresses de l'âme, Idées,
> Courtisanes par ennui?

> —Toujours sages, disent-elles,
> Nos présences immortelles
> Jamais n'ont trahi ton toit!
> Nous étions non éloignées,
> Mais secrètes araignées
> Dans les ténèbres de toi! [1]

Thus ideas tempt the poet, for they have spun a whole 'toile spirituelle' while he slept:

> Nous avons sur tes abîmes
> Tendu nos fils primitifs,
> Et pris la nature nue
> Dans une trame ténue
> De tremblants préparatifs . . .

But he breaks their web:

> Leur toile spirituelle,
> Je la brise, et vais cherchant
> Dans ma forêt sensuelle
> Les oracles de mon chant.

It is in himself that he must look for his poem.

> Être! Universelle oreille!
> Toute l'âme s'appareille
> A l'extrême du désir. . .
> Elle s'écoute qui tremble
> Et parfois ma lèvre semble
> Son frémissement saisir.

This and the following verse are precious material of poetic auto-biography which reveal the instant of perception. Since Shelley watched the bees 'in the ivy bloom' there had been no more authentic witness of the birth of poetry.

> Voici mes vignes ombreuses,
> Les berceaux de mes hasards!
> Les images sont nombreuses
> A l'égal de mes regards . . .

[1] Cf. this verse with Mallarmé, *Œuvres complètes*, 56:

> Gloire du long désir, Idées
> Tout en moi s'exaltait de voir
> La famille des iridées
> Surgir à ce nouveau devoir.

Cf. Diderot 'Mes Idées sont mes catins.'

Toute feuille me présente
Une source complaisante
Où je bois ce frêle bruit . . .
Tout m'est pulpe, tout amande,
Tout calice me demande
Que j'attende pour son fruit.

Here we are at the source of poetic expression: and it is perhaps significant that it is of the lyrical poets, of Shelley and Keats, that we are reminded. Keats too listened to 'ce frêle bruit'—

That little noiseless noise among the leaves,
Born of the very sigh that silence heaves.

Nor do difficulties embarrass the poet, but rather brace him to greater effort:

Je ne crains pas les épines!
L'éveil est bon, même dur!
Ces idéales rapines
Ne veulent pas qu'on soit sûr:
Il n'est pour ravir un monde
De blessure si profonde
Qui ne soit au ravisseur
Une féconde blessure,
Et son propre sang l'assure
D'être le vrai possesseur.

In the last verse the image of the Mallarméan *cygne*[1] completes the poem it foretells:

J'approche la transparence
De l'invisible bassin
Où nage mon Espérance
Que l'eau porte par le sein.
Son col coupe le temps vague
Et soulève cette vague
Que fait un col sans pareil . . .
Elle sent sous l'onde unie
La profondeur infinie,
Et frémit depuis l'orteil.

The second poem, 'Au Platane,' symbolises the mind imprisoned in the limitations of the body:

[1] See above p. 140, system of poetics in 'Theory of Language.'

> Ce front n'aura d'accès qu'aux degrés lumineux
> Où la sève l'exalte;
> Tu peux grandir, candeur, mais non rompre les nœuds
> De l'éternelle halte!

Here the varied length of the lines expresses the feeling of frustration and limitation. There is however a certain lack of concentration in the eighteen verses, which might well have ended with the sixteenth:

> Je t'ai choisi, puissant personnage d'un parc,
> Ivre de ton tangage,
> Puisque le ciel t'exerce, et te presse, ô grand arc,
> De lui rendre un langage!

The 'Cantique des colonnes' pursues, in audaciously pure syntax, the creative stages of a poem. In the treatment of the main figure, and the images, as well as in the content, it is one of the most original of the *Charmes*. A triumphant hymn in six-syllabled lines grouped in quatrains, it sings the virtue of restraint as a condition of liberty, and the beauty of classical form.

> Nos antiques jeunesses,
> Chair mate et belles ombres,
> Sont fières des finesses
> Qui naissent par les nombres!

It is amusing to note that this poem is dedicated to Léon-Paul Fargue, the 'poète d'une belle incohérence' as he modestly said of himself. To appreciate Valéry's treatment of his theme—the transposition of concrete into abstract—we may compare the 'Cantique' with Théophile Gautier's 'Art' which deals very differently with the same subject.

With 'L'Abeille' we come to the poet's choice of words, as a stage of development in the growth of his poem. The title-word awakes the poem, followed by the fine harmony of the opening lines:

> Quelle, et si fine, et si mortelle,
> Que soit ta pointe, blonde abeille,
> Je n'ai, sur ma tendre corbeille
> Jeté qu'un songe de dentelle.

Here the force of words gives the stimulus coming from the outer world, stinging the poet to action:

> Soit donc mon sens illuminé
> Par cette infime alerte d'or
> Sans que l'Amour meurt ou s'endort!

In 'Poésie' the poet invokes 'ma mère Intelligence,' as classical poets called upon their Muse, for intelligence must nourish him and be the source of his inspiration:

A peine, dans ton ciel sombre,
Abattu sur ta beauté,
Je sentais, à boire l'ombre,
M'envahir une clarté!

Yet like the Muse, she may withhold her treasures.

In 'Les Pas,' the poet describes how, with extreme attention, he waits for the rhythmic words which come through the silence to announce his poem, like the footsteps of a loved mistress.

Tes pas, enfants de mon silence,
Saintement, lentement placés,
Vers le lit de ma vigilance
Procèdent muets et glacés.

In the last verse the formal *vous* subtly indicates the meditative attitude before the fulfilment of the poem:

Car j'ai vécu de vous attendre,
Et mon cœur n'était que vos pas.

We may compare this with 'L'Amateur de poèmes,' where Valéry says, 'I feel each word in all its force through having waited for it indefinitely,' and with the Jeune Parque's words:

Mes pas interrompus de paroles aux cieux,
Mes pauses, sur le pied portant la rêverie . . .

This lyric, coming immediately after 'Poésie,' ('O ma mère Intelligence'), seems to infer that a passive attitude of receptive patience is more propitious than the state of active inquiry indicated in the former poem.

The classical symbol of love's abandonment in 'La Ceinture' expresses the gift of a poem to the world:

Cette ceinture vagabonde
Fait dans le souffle aérien
Frémir le suprême lien
De mon silence avec ce monde . . .

Mallarmé had also used this symbol in the figure 'A leur ombre enlever encore des ceintures.'

In the next lyric, 'La Dormeuse,' a sleeping girl represents the un-written poem, or rather its form, which waits in the poet's mind:

> ta forme veille, et mes yeux sont ouverts.

This sonnet is more mature than 'Anne' of *Les Vers anciens*; Alain compared it to Proust's description of Albertine asleep.

In this first part of *Charmes*, which ends with 'La Dormeuse,' the poet has symbolised his preparation and initiation in the approach to his poem, and, through the poem, to the instances of his Absolute of consciousness. A passage in 'Eupalinos' refers to this moment:

> Imagine a mortal . . . pure enough, sufficiently subtle and tenacious to meditate to the very extreme of his powers, and therefore to the extreme of reality, this strange bringing together of visible forms with ephemeral groups of successive sounds. . . . To join together ecstasy and analysis would be the most precious faculty that a poet could possess. . . .

And Eupalinos the architect continues:

> . . . I become quite a different person, all is clear and seems easy. Then my syntheses [*combinations*] take form and are perpetuated in my intelligence. I feel my need for beauty, equal to my unknown resources, create for itself alone the figures which content it. I desire with all my being. . . . These powers advance through illusion to reality. I call them into being through my silence. There they are, loaded with error and with light. . . .[1]

What better commentary on the poems could we have than these confidences in which the poet speaks directly of his own powers and what he desires from them: 'to join together ecstasy and analysis'?

> Que tu brilles enfin, terme pur de ma course!

So begins the 'Fragments du Narcisse' which opens the second part of *Charmes*. Here the poet has arrived at the stage of self-analysis and ecstasy. Now the silence of concentration must remain undisturbed, for the least interruption, the least sound

> . . . suffit à rompre un univers dormant . . .

Silence and solitude are necessary:

> Je suis seul! . . . Si les Dieu, les échos et les ondes
> Et si tant de soupirs permettent qu'on le soit!
> Seul! . . . mais encor celui qui s'approche de soi
> Quand il s'approche aux bords que bénit ce feuillage . . .

[1] *Eupalinos ou l'architecte*, pp. 40–1.

And a fine rendering of evening light follows:

> O douceur de survivre à la force du jour,
> Quand elle se retire enfin rose d'amour,
> Encore un peu brûlante, et lasse, mais comblée,
> Et de tant de trésors tendrement accablée,
> Par de tels souvenirs qu'ils empourprent sa mort,
> Et qu'ils la font heureuse agenouiller dans l'or,
> Puis s'étendre, se fondre, et perdre sa vendange
> Et s'éteindre en un songe en qui le soir se change.[1]

Here the poetic resonance is extraordinarily rich.

Certain verses of 'Narcisse parle' are repeated in this later poem, but here the structure is stronger, more sinuous and varied than in the early work. It has been said that the similarity between the 'Narcisse' and Mallarmé's *L'Après-midi d'un faune* is striking, and that at any point verses might be transposed from one poem to the other without shocking ear or sense.[2] Nevertheless, though the verse of both runs in the same measure, I find an essential difference. For the 'Fragments du Narcisse' is definitely composed in a minor key—minor in a melodic sense—and all its harmonies belong to this mode which unifies and prolongs its resonance, and is admirably suited to the reflections and musing of the Self.

> Mais moi, Narcisse aimé, je ne suis curieux
> Que de ma seule essence;
> Tout autre n'a pour moi qu'un cœur mystérieux,
> Tout autre n'est qu'absence.

The melancholy of the moonlit forest is also finely expressed in the same minor key:

> Un grand calme m'écoute, où j'écoute l'espoir.
> J'entends l'herbe des nuits croître dans l'ombre sainte,
> Et la lune perfide élève son miroir
> Jusque dans les secrets de la fontaine éteinte . . .
> Jusque dans les secrets que je crains de savoir,
> Jusque dans le repli de l'amour de soi-même,
> Rien ne peut échapper au silence du soir . . .

---

[1] Cf. Keats, 'Ode to a Nightingale': 'To cease upon the midnight with no pain.'

[2] Henri Mondor, *L'Heureuse Rencontre de Valéry et Mallarmé* (Paris–Lausanne: Clairfontaine, 1947).

Mallarmé said of himself, in a conversation with André Gide, that he had no 'lunar sense'; yet he would certainly have found a formula to express moonlight had he wanted to do so. Valéry succeeds admirably in moonlit effects. The Echo theme in 'Fragments du Narcisse' is in the same mode—are not echoes always in the minor key? Again, in the poignant *adieu* towards the end of the poem the subdued harmonies give an example of minor chords:

Adieu . . . Sens-tu frémir mille flottants adieux?
Bientôt va frissonner le désordre des ombres!
L'arbre aveugle vers l'arbre étend ses membres sombres,
Et cherche affreusement l'arbre qui disparaît . . .
Mon âme ainsi se perd dans sa propre forêt,
Où la puissance échappe à ses formes suprêmes . . .

Compared to this *andante*, the voice of the Faun is like the laughter of Pan:

A l'heure où ce bois d'or et de cendres se teinte
Une fête s'exalte en la feuillée éteinte . . .[1]

He is infinitely more sensual, more 'fay' and even more actual than the ethereal Narcissus. Both attain a spiritual awareness in quite different moods. Nevertheless Mallarmé's masterpiece of summer afternoon has an originality which has not been surpassed.

'La Pythie' is written in octosyllabic verse, and Valéry tells us that it started from the line 'Pâle, profondément mordue,' round which the whole poem was constructed. It runs to no less than 23 stanzas, of which this is the first:

La Pythie exhalant la flamme
De naseaux durcis par l'encens,
Haletante, ivre, hurle! . . . l'âme
Affreuse, et les flancs mugissants!
Pâle, profondément mordue,
Et la prunelle suspendue
Au point le plus haut de l'horreur,
Le regard qui manque à son masque
S'arrache vivant à la vasque
A la fumée, à la fureur!

The use of alliteration and a swift almost panting rhythm give urgency to the formal and somewhat Wagnerian expression. No one seems to

[1] Mallarmé, *L'Après-midi d'un faune, Œuvres complètes*, 50.

have remarked how closely Valéry has followed Racine's *Cantique sur les vaines occupations des gens du siècle*, written in seven-syllabled lines. In Racine's verses the Word also triumphs, though it has a different significance. Here are the sixth and seventh verses from the *Cantique*, which readers may compare with Valéry's poem.

> O Sagesse! ta parole
> Fit éclore l'univers,
> Posa sur un double pôle
> La terre au milieu des mers.
> Tu dis; et les cieux parurent,
> Et tous les astres coururent
> Dans leur ordre se placer.
> Avant les siècles tu règnes;
> Et qui suis-je, que tu daignes
> Jusqu'à moi te rebaisser?

> Le Verbe, image du Père,
> Laissa son trône éternel,
> Et d'une mortelle mère
> Voulut naître homme, et mortel.
> Comme l'orgueil fut le crime
> Dont il naissait la victime,
> Il dépouilla sa splendeur.
> Et vint pauvre et misérable,
> Apprendre à l'homme coupable
> Sa véritable grandeur.

Valéry's Pythie (Pythia), the priestess of Apollo, represents poetry, and is seen here at bay:

> —Ah! maudite! . . . Quels maux je souffre!
> Toute ma nature est un gouffre!
> Hélas! Entr'ouverte aux esprits,
> J'ai perdu mon propre mystère! . . .
> Une Intelligence adultère
> Exerce un corps qu'elle a compris!

How far we are from the religious fervour of Racine! The Pythie's fury is turned against all the abuses of the sacred art, and first of all the neglect of classical form:

> Douce matière de mon sort,
> Quelle alliance nous vécûmes,
> Avant que le don des écumes
> Ait fait de toi ce corps de mort!

She has nothing but scorn for *vers libre*:

> Crois-tu, quand se brisent les cordes
> Que le son jaillisse plus beau?

Surrealism and general obscurity are also denounced, for

> L'eau tranquille est plus transparente
> Que toute tempête parente
> D'une confuse profondeur!

Finally after much eloquent despair a new voice is heard, and a new prophetic utterance foretells the future of poetry:

> Honneur des Hommes, Saint LANGAGE,
> Discours prophétique et paré,
> Belles chaînes en qui s'engage
> Le dieu dans la chair égaré,
> Illumination, largesse!
> Voici parler une Sagesse
> Et sonner cette auguste Voix
> Qui se connaît quand elle sonne
> N'être plus la voix de personne
> Tant que des ondes et des bois!

On the whole this poem is easy to understand, though sometimes the detail is difficult to interpret, unless we recognise certain symbols which appeared in *La Jeune Parque*. The general conclusion is that the poet of the future must return to form and to the expression of what is actual in the world of nature around him.

'Le Sylphe' and 'L'Insinuant,' the two light lyrics that follow, seem to stand side by side to whisper the secrets of the poet's inspiration: the one 'dans le vent venu,' and the other of which he says,

> Je sais où je vais
> Je t'y veux conduire.

Light as winged seeds and as perfect—one feels that any prose commentary would almost blow them away.

In 'La Fausse Morte' there is an erotic and easy symbolism in the idea of the unfinished poem 'en qui revient la vie' to which the poet must return. In it a theory on sleep—better expressed in *La Jeune Parque*—becomes an abstract of sensibility rather than the sensibility of an abstract as its author intended, and the last line is commonplace.

All the lyrical *Charmes* have expressed the intellectual acts of creation which lead to a poem, and signify the different approaches to poetry through chance, a state of grace, or prolonged meditation. What is of special interest here is the insight which reveals the mind of the poet, that inner and abstract life which uses the most intense moments of exterior and actual life to symbolise an intellectual state.

'Ébauche d'un serpent' sums up the knowledge, the result of long and patient meditation, combined with the awareness of the intellectual relationship of the poet with the universe, which he perceives and which he submits to the same drastic analysis as he applied to his own thought. Spiritual and amusing, the poem is also one of the most profound of these *Charmes*. It is a complex and condensed composition, at once theological, dramatic and burlesque. Like the 'Pythie' it is a monologue in octosyllabic verse. The character of the Serpent, half tragic and sinister, half farcical, was suggested by Wagner's Beckmesser in *Die Meistersinger*, and the means used by the musician may have inspired the poet's methods.

Valéry noted that the whole difficulty of the work lay in the changes of tone, and said that he had purposely exaggerated the assonances and the alliterations.[1] Certainly in no poem has he more magically used the possibilities of language, or shown greater virtuosity in the choice of dominant harmonic values. The whole construction is a triumph of formal art.

The poem, for English readers, is in many ways a modern synthesis of Milton's *Paradise Lost*, seen entirely from the point of view of the Serpent, who here (as he might seem in Milton's poem) is the real hero of the drama. The central theme is the temptation of Eve, and the cosmogony is dealt with through Satan's reactions, that is to say the poet's. The Serpent symbolises the poet's thought, as the sun represents his conscious knowledge, which is also his imagination:

> Soleil, soleil! . . .Faute éclatante!
> Toi qui masques la mort, Soleil,
> Sous l'azur et l'or d'une tente
> Où les fleurs tiennent leur conseil;
> Par d'impénétrables délices,
> Toi, le plus fier de mes complices,
> Et de mes pièges le plus haut,
> Tu gardes les cœurs de connaître
> Que l'univers n'est qu'un défaut
> Dans la pureté du Non-être!

[1] Paul Valéry, letter to Alain (1930), *Lettres à quelques-uns*, 184.

This is an aspect of that doctrine of the search for an absolute of consciousness which, be it even for a brief moment, would surpass itself and go beyond its earthly limitations.

The significance of the poem is marvellously conveyed in every verse. The slightly hissing harmony, sometimes almost a whispered rustle in the swift movement of images, compels both ear and eye.

> O Vanité! Cause Première!
> Celui qui règne dans les Cieux,
> D'une voix qui fut la lumière
> Ouvrit l'univers spacieux.
> Comme las de son pur spectacle,
> Dieu lui-même a rompu l'obstacle
> De sa parfaite éternité;
> Il se fit Celui qui dissipe
> En conséquences, son Principe,
> En étoiles, son Unité.

For the Creator wished to be *himself* and his first word was *Moi*. He wished to come out of his Eternity and to abandon his Absolute Unity, which was blind and inconceivable, comparable only to *le néant*—the abyss. To say 'Moi,' or 'I am,' is already to form a Self in opposition to whatever else exists. Such is the Serpent's representation of the Creator's original fall.

Here the act of consciousness which created the drama of *La Jeune Parque* is considered metaphysically as a disaster. The Creator, in dissipating his being, in wishing to become a Self, has sown the principle of individuality, and so pledged his creation to wish *to be*; and from the first '*I am*' arose the opposite Self, the Serpent.

> Cieux, son erreur! Temps, sa ruine!
> Et l'abîme animal, béant! . . .
> Quelle chute dans l'origine
> Étincelle au lieu de néant! . . .
> Mais, le premier mot de son Verbe,
> MOI! . . . Des astres le plus superbe
> Qu'ait parlés le fou créateur,
> Je suis! . . . Je serai! . . . J'illumine
> La diminution divine
> De tous les feux du Séducteur!

And thus face to face with the Satanic hatred

> Si profond fut votre malaise
> Que votre souffle sur la glaise
> Fut un soupir de désespoir!

So man, born of a sigh of despair, in the image of his maker, became at once an instrument of Satanic vengeance:

> A la ressemblance exécrée,
> Vous fûtes faits, et je vous hais!
> Comme je hais le Nom qui crée
> Tant de prodiges imparfaits!

Characteristically this last line gives significance to the Serpent's attitude, as into the ear of the titanic Eve he pours his venom, beneath the tree of Knowledge whose branches fill the universe. In an instant of extreme tension—'Quel silence battu d'un cil'—through which the tempter whispers, *la soif de métamorphoses* is suggested as one of the emotional delights implied in Eve's acceptance of the fruit he offers her:

> Génie! O longue impatience!
> A la fin, les temps sont venus,
> Qu'un pas vers la neuve Science
> Va donc jaillir de ces pieds nus!

A pæan of praise follows for the tree of Knowledge, which is the centre of the poet's universe:

> Tu peux repousser l'infini
> Qui n'est fait que de ta croissance,
> Et de la tombe jusqu'au nid
> Te sentir toute Connaissance!

But the Serpent comes as a blight on its precious fruits:

> Mais ce vieil amateur d'échecs,
> Dans l'or oisif des soleils secs,
> Sur ton branchage vient se tordre;
> Ses yeux font frémir ton trésor.
> Il en cherra[1] des fruits de mort,
> De désespoir et de désordre!

The final verse sums up this admirable sketch for Satan in which the creation is considered as a sinister farce.

> Beau serpent, bercé dans le bleu,
> Je siffle, avec délicatesse,
> Offrant à la gloire de Dieu
> Le triomphe de ma tristesse . . .
> Il me suffit que dans les airs,

---

[1] 'Cherra' ancient future of verb *choir* = to fall.

L'immense espoir de fruits amers
Affole les fils de la fange . . .
—Cette soif qui te fit géant,
Jusqu'à l'Être exalte l'étrange
Toute-Puissance du Néant!

Thus in his ironic acceptance of the myth, Valéry perceives that intuition becomes knowledge and that beyond knowledge there reigns an absence which is absolute.

After the sustained effort of 'Ébauche d'un serpent,' there are several short lyrics. In the first 'Les Grenades' the secret architecture of the poet's mind is compared to a pomegranate:

Dures grenades entr'ouvertes
Cédant à l'excès de vos grains,
Je crois voir des fronts souverains
Éclatés de leurs découvertes!

In the next poem, 'Le Vin perdu,' the offering is that which the poet makes in giving his poems:

Perdu ce vin, ivres les ondes! . . .
J'ai vu bondir dans l'air amer
Les figures les plus profondes . . .

In 'Intérieur,' of only twelve lines, the charm of subdued light fills the room; that 'la femme' symbolises the poet's imagination matters little, for the images of his thought are perfectly united:

Comme passe le verre au travers du soleil,
Et de la raison pure épargne l'appareil.

This image has also been used in an early provençal poem where the Virgin is compared to a glass through which the sunlight passes.[1]

The 'Ode secret,' Valéry tells us, was written after the Armistice of 1918. This gives us the key to the symbol, the solar myth of Hercules who, overthrown by Apollo, was promised a place in the evening sky, when the sun

. . . touché par le Crépuscule,
Ce grand corps qui fit tant de choses,
Qui dansait, qui rompit Hercule,
N'est plus qu'une masse de roses!

---

[1] 'Domna, rosa sine spina,' quoted by F. Raynouard, 'Choix de poésies,' *Lexique romain* (Paris, 1836), I.

The two last verses which speak of the night sky remind us of Valéry's thoughts on reading *Le Coup de dés*, which he calls poetry raised to the power of a starlit sky. The inner sense is both personal and universal.

'Le Rameur' is saved from being merely occasional verse by its symbolic expression of the poet's effort. The slow beat of its regular movement enhances this effect:

> Je veux à larges coups rompre l'illustre monde
> De feuilles et de feu que je chante tout bas.

For his aim is sure: 'Je remonte à la source où cesse même un nom.' We should compare this poem with 'Valvins' of *Album de vers anciens*.

The volume of *Charmes* ends with 'Palme,' which completes the unity of the whole work. It is also to some extent the answer to the questions raised in 'Ébauche d'un serpent,' and 'Le Cimetière Marin,' which is included in this collection. The calm of an *andante* movement pervades this musical poem in which the poet's attitude and the fulfilment of poetry are affirmed; and the Self whose progress has been followed throughout *Charmes* finds here its ultimate expression. For that state of perfection, which may be reached only through infinite patience and transcendent calm, is the real triumph of the Universal Self.

> De sa grâce redoutable
> Voilant à peine l'éclat,
> Un ange met sur ma table
> Le pain tendre, le lait plat;
> Il me fait de la paupière
> Le signe d'une prière
> Qui parle à ma vision:
> —Calme, calme, reste calme!
> Connais le poids d'une palme
> Portant sa profusion!

The vision of the palm tree with its burning bush of flaming flower— 'sa profusion'—is an apt symbol for poetry, and the simplicity of the language partakes of that profound consciousness from which poetry is born:

> Patience, patience,
> Patience dans l'azur!
> Chaque atome de silence
> Est la chance d'un fruit mur!

The whole poem is a 'charm' which in moments of agitation and despair can bring us back to that inner peace which life too often tends to destroy. It shows us too that Valéry's intellectual vision led him by various paths to the conclusion that thoughtful effort is man's chief justification.

4. THE MELODRAMAS

C'était une débauche de discipline et de construction formelle. (P. V. SUR AMPHION)

Ever since his first enthusiasm for the formal and dramatic art of the high mass in the cathedral of Montpellier, Valéry had kept his idea of a liturgic drama. As early as 1900, he had discussed, while lunching with Pierre Louÿs and Claude Debussy, the project for a ballet. Some days later, in a letter in *vers libre*, Valéry sketched his conception of a ballet in which the scenery, voices, action and music would all be perfectly homogeneous—that is to say, equally removed from all the usual incongruities of the theatre—expressing a complex value; and he adds:

J'avais songé incidemment au/Mythe d'Orphée, c'est-à-dire/l'animation de toute chose par/un esprit, la fable même de/la mobilité et de l'arrangement./Voyez-vous quelque chose dans/cette direction? . . .
I had incidentally thought of/the myth of Orpheus, that is to say/the animation of all things/by a mind, the very fable of/mobility and of arrangement./Do you see something in this direction? . . .[1]

At the time, nothing came of this scheme. It was not until 1932, in collaboration with Arthur Honegger, that he was able to realise in his *Amphion* his dream of the birth of architecture from the inspiration of music. As this work did not correspond exactly to opera, ballet or oratorio, Valéry called it a melodrama; and he wanted it to have the character of a religious ceremony, in which the action should be restrained, subordinated to the significant and poetic substance of each of its movements.[2] This idea of formal unity is very close to a liturgic conception of drama. The bringing together of precise conditions, the unity of rhythm in the different parts throughout the performance,

[1] Paul Valéry, letter to Claude Debussy (1900), *Lettres à quelques-uns*, 62.
[2] Paul Valéry, 'Histoire d'Amphion,' *Variété*, III, 95.

excluded all forms of naturalism in so far as they might lessen or inter-fere with the profound sense of the work.

The legend of *Amphion*, who constructed temples to the music of his lyre, lent itself admirably to Valéry's ideal of formal art. Yet though the verse is musical enough, it adds nothing essentially new to his reputation beyond the principle it serves to illustrate. 'You have read a libretto with eyes that were looking for a poem,' he wrote, in reply to criticism. He had, he said, published the text in order to establish what his intention had been, for unfortunately he had not been able to impose his ideas on the actual production, in which he had hoped to renew a liturgic convention, but had been forced to see it turned into a sort of ballet in which indiscipline and incoherence or fantasy had reigned.[1]

Evidently a systematic co-ordination between all the different elements of the piece: music, voices, actions and lighting, had been difficult to obtain. Valéry had long meditated on this problem. Starting from the idea of poetry with a fixed form, he had imagined a theatrical performance, controlled by equally measured, limited and rhythmic rites, maintained at a sufficient distance from any actual imitation of daily life. The action should take place in a separate harmonious world of art in which speech necessarily would become song. It was in fact the mixture of song and realistic actions which he disliked in con-temporary opera, and which led to his attempt to oppose this dis-ordered realism by a thoroughly stylised performance which was intended to evoke an almost religious emotion in the audience.

Two years later in 1934, again in collaboration with Arthur Honeg-ger, Valéry's *Sémiramis*, in three acts and two interludes, was in its turn presented at the Opéra de Paris. Pride, the pride of being unique, one of Valéry's favourite themes, is the motif of this piece, and Sémi-ramis of *Les Vers anciens* appears again as the personification of pride. The simple story of the captive, who becomes the queen's lover and in consequence must be put to death, is told in a series of mimed episodes, and the words only begin in the third act. The text, which is necessarily overshadowed by the music, has little of linguistic interest.

The *Cantate du Narcisse* was written in 1938 as a libretto com-missioned by Madame Germaine Tailleferre for a cantata. As poetry it is definitely inferior to the other Narcissus poems. Though always harmonious, the verse is too often facile, but it has the merit of per-fectly fitting its musical setting. Yet Valéry seems to have been dis-

[1] Paul Valéry, letter to S. A. Peyre (1933), *Lettres à quelques-uns*, 209.

appointed in the result obtained through the required simplifications to fit his art to music. The part assumed by the human voice in reading poetry had always deeply interested him; but his collaboration with musicians remained little more than an interesting experiment. Added to this he was tired he said, 'comme fatigué de moi-même et du reste.'

'Je suis seul. Je suis moi. Je suis vrai. . . Je vous hais,' cried Narcissus, and the cry seems to come from the poet's deepest consciousness. May we not see in this final act of the Narcissus drama—in which the nymphs, after corrupting his solitude, slay their hero—the symbol of the world that demands everything from the poet, whom it finally destroys, leaving only the echo of a voice, a flower?

Yet although these melodramas add little that is new to Valéry's poetic achievement, they nevertheless are of considerable interest as an attempt to purify opera. In this endeavour Valéry was not alone. Already Jacques Copeau, in his studio in the Rue du Cherche-midi, had initiated students of drama into the idea of stylisation and effective purity in the essentially impure art of the theatre. This idea had probably originated from the Japanese conception of drama.

In 1924 Copeau had left the Vieux Colombier, where he had produced some fifty plays, and retired with his chosen pupils to create 'a monastery of Comedians', a sort of convent where 'one entered into Comedy as one enters into Religion,'[1] at Pernand Vergelesses in Burgundy. Here Copeau proposed a drastic reform of the theatre. Chief among his pupils was Michel Saint-Denis who later took charge of the Compagnie des Quinze, which during the thirties had a brilliant artistic success in both Paris and London, with the formal plays of Obey.[2]

However, the idea of theatrical stylisation was not accepted by everyone. Gide, who had been present at one of Copeau's lectures on the subject, considered the whole conception to be chimerical and thought that the mirage of sanctity had led Copeau astray. On Valéry's melodramas Gide does not appear to have made any comment.[3]

It might be possible to deduce from Valéry's melodramas some conclusion as to the results of combining poetry and music in a single movement. On the one hand poetry has its own integral music, just

[1] Henri Massis, in *La Parisienne* (avril 1954), 407.
[2] Michel Saint-Denis stayed in London for many years as producer at the Old Vic.
[3] André Gide, *Journal* (1931).

as music has its own intrinsic poetry. On the other hand music may enhance poetical effects, and poetry may add substance to music. When it was first suggested that Debussy should set *L'Après-midi d'un faune* to music, Mallarmé was reported to have said that he thought that he himself had already done so. The problem was solved when Debussy wrote his famous *Prelude* to the poem. But the fact remains that the human voice is the link between the two arts. Either music may accompany poetry, using all its powers to illustrate the poem; or the words may be so simple that they fall like solitary echoes of the music through that silence which is a lateral effect in musical composition.

VI

The Prose Works

I. A LITERARY CAREER

Ce qui soi-même se nomme le 'Monde' n'est com-
posé que de personnages symboliques. (P. v.)

AFTER THE PUBLICATION of *Charmes,* Valéry turned more and more
to writing prose. Apart from the later works—*L'Idée fixe,* the *Dia-*
logues, Mon Faust and *L'Ange,* which, excepting the first, may be considered as poems in prose—the greater part of his literary output consisted of essays, lectures, introductions and criticisms which illustrate
the wide range of his knowledge. In 1920 the 'Avant-propos' for the
Connaissance de la déesse of Lucien Fabre was published, and a year
later 'Au sujet d'Adonis' appeared as a preface to a new edition of La
Fontaine's *Adonis,* works to which I shall return. These together with
other essays were collected under the title of *Variété,* of which the first
volume appeared in 1923, to be followed later by four more volumes in
the same series. The two first Socratic dialogues were published in 1923,
and were reprinted with the third dialogue, 'L'Arbre,' in 1944. In
addition to these publications, lectures and readings were constantly
demanded.

In notes given to a friend many years later,[1] Valéry said that after
1917 his life became 'Un vacarme', a complete scrimmage. From this
time he undertook an arduous and brilliant career. This activity had
not been sought by him, he always insisted that his essays were never
written for his pleasure. 'I never wrote anything, and I write nothing,

---

[1] Valery Larbaud, in 1928.

except when constrained and forced to do so,' he confided to Gide in 1929. This is borne out by the fact that almost all his prose work was commissioned, often as introductions to other peoples' work.

With the loss of his secretarial post, through the death of Edouard Lebey in 1922, Valéry was doubtless obliged to devote himself to literature. The fact that he consented in 1926 to publish extracts from his notes—his morning meditations—seems to show that economic conditions had made it necessary for him to overcome his aversion to publicity.

By 1927 he was perhaps the most celebrated poet and critic in France, and that year he was elected to the Academy. Henceforth he gave himself *âme et corps* to Parisian society, where his wit and charm made him extremely popular. Very soon he became a public figure as Director of the Centre Universitaire Méditerranéen de Nice, and also as Professor of Poetry at the Collège de France, where a fashionable audience listened in coughless silence to his psychology of poetry,[1] while he spoke.

> D'une voix douce et faible disant de grandes choses:
> D'importantes, étonnantes, de profondes et justes choses,
> D'une voix douce et faible.
>
> Et d'une sorte de murmure
> En français infiniment pur.
>
> Cette puissance chuchotée,
> Ces perspectives, ces découvertes,
> Ces abîmes et ces manœuvres devinés,
> Ce sourire congédiant l'univers . . .[2]

This smile dismissing the universe, directed as it was on *le beau monde*, was unfortunately obliged to include in its dismissal much of poetic significance. That silence from which poetry is born was now much curtailed, and Valéry virtually stopped writing poems about 1922. After that date we catch glimpses of him lecturing abroad: in London, surrounded by anxiously devoted ladies, with his fair head rising from his fur collar, rather suggesting a tired golden eagle who finds itself amiably received *dans la basse cour*, somewhat astonished to be there; or in Paris, the welcome guest of learned societies; or making the regulation calls of the academic candidate; or as the central figure at after-

---

[1] Unfortunately only the inaugural lecture was officially recorded.
[2] Paul Valéry, 'Psaume sur une voix,' *Autres Rhumbs*, in *Tel Quel*, II, 164.

noon or evening gatherings of intellectual and aristocratic friends. The abstract Laure had perhaps just cause to be jealous.

He, who had so categorically scorned all the outward attributes of 'greatness,' who had condemned great men precisely for their acceptance of this fictitious adjective to which they conformed, now discreetly played the part that he had formerly denounced. Naturally enough, his enemies[1] were to say that all his life had been a preparation, through a system of denials and acceptances and careful refusals, for this final worldly triumph. But reality is never as simple as any *engagé* point of view would have it seem to be. The truth is much less easy to grasp and far more difficult to express. For it was in fact a series of circumstances that ensnared, without essentially changing, the poet.

First there was the necessity of continuing to earn sufficient to maintain the habitual family budget, and this made it imperative for Valéry to accept literary work. Hence the need of academic suffrage and the social obligations it involved. Secondly there was the point of view of society to consider. For Valéry was made to please. His graceful manners and his wit made him at home in the *beau monde*. And more, his acceptance and approval of the best in traditional and classical arts was at once appreciated by the most exclusive circles of Parisian society. Nor could it have been otherwise. Here was a phenomenon rare indeed; a poet, the most accomplished; a gentleman, the most gracious; a witty companion sensitive to beauty and learning; an intelligent and amusing dialectician: in short, a distinguished Parisian. Was it surprising that society, with its slowly dying tradition of literary salons, should claim, and insist on absorbing, such a treasure?

Alas for Monsieur Teste. Was it possible that the ascetic who had so carefully ruled and regulated his life, should so completely accept all that he had condemned? In vain might he declare that his friends had thrust greatness upon him, that society served as his club or café. It is true that in no café would he have found such an intelligent and sympathetic audience as that of the receptions which he now attended.

Perhaps the only regrettable aspect of this change was the great quantity of work that it involved. Now there was little time for serious poetry: it was either a cantata for a friend's music, or those tenuous melodramas, which could now be staged easily enough. For a time at least, it seemed that Narcissus had been betrayed, that the Nymphs of the poem had triumphed.

[1] Enemies is perhaps rather too harsh, the envious would suit better.

N'as-tu pas de ton rêve épuisé le malheur?
Sens-tu frémir des bois l'horreur voluptueuse?
Viens . . . Abandonne-moi ta grâce infructueuse,
Songe qu'il n'est plus temps pour toi de me haïr,
Narcisse, et laisse-toi séduire à te trahir . . .[1]

Henceforth Valéry's finest works, with the exception of a few rare lyrics, were written in prose: prose sculptured from the very rock of his thought, as perfect as he could make it. Such are the *Dialogues*, *Mon Faust*, *L'Ange*. The lyrical period which began about 1911, ended in reality about 1922. So when Valéry told Gide that his epitaph should be: 'Here lies Valéry killed by the others,' it would have been more exact to say: 'Here lies the poet. . . .'

2. A NOTE ON VALÉRY'S PROSE

Il était fait pour comprendre, et il comprenait
toujours là où il se trouvait.

(L. P. FARGUE SUR VALÉRY)

The series of prose essays which appeared at different dates in five volumes under the title of *Variété* contain almost all the critical works among which the famous attack on Pascal (1923) deserves a separate study, and will not be dealt with here. Poets, men of letters and theories of poetry and æsthetics were all considered. Since most of his subjects were imposed by circumstances, having been commissioned by different publishers, Valéry tells us that each time he had to establish his own point of view, so that whatever the apparent theme, he could develop his own line of thought. As a result there is an underlying unity in these otherwise heterogeneous studies. Indeed it is remarkable how inevitably everything is referred to an analytical process which rests on 'the unshaken themes of his thought,'[2] so that his mind is always admirably reflected and becomes the central interest in all he writes. 'No matter what I am considering,' he confessed, 'I feel compelled to begin at the beginning, that is to say my own

---

[1] Paul Valéry, 'Cantate du Narcisse,' *Poésies* (1942), 210.
[2] 'Thèmes inébranlables.' Valéry, letter to Gide in *Correspondance André Gide–Paul Valéry*, ed. Robert Mallet (Paris: Gallimard, 1955).

beginning, in fact to approach the subject as if no one had ever done so before.'[1]

Precision in both thought and expression characterises all the prose works. Neither dogmatic nor scholastic, Valéry avoids preaching. He touches on profound thought with an easy grace that disarms prejudice on the part of his readers. And he has the Italian gift of combining depth and animation, lightness and learning; he liked to think that he saw aspects which no one else had noticed in those things which everyone sees.

Nor was he afraid of appearing difficult to his readers, but obliged them to make a certain mental effort, counting on the courtesy of their complete attention. Indeed patience is often needed while he meticulously develops each part of his argument. Nevertheless, an attentive reader is rewarded, captivated by the combined qualities of fluent persuasion and logical use of syntax. *Poète malgré lui*, Valéry compels a change of mood by a change of rhythm: now the movement is leisurely and sinuous, now precise and trenchant, and then leaps forward to excite our emotional interest in the most abstract conceptions. This power of expressing his sensibility through intellectual arguments is one of the essential aspects of his genius. There is nothing arid in his arguments, yet everything is dominated by and submitted to the flame of discriminating intelligence.

Rarely has any writer been so thoroughly conscious of the working of his own mind in its creative moments. Hitherto this quality had been attributed rather to mathematicians than to men of letters. Although he always differentiates between the direct communication of prose and the language of poetry, the intensity of his intellectual vision and the sensitiveness of his ear to prose rhythms show Valéry to be primarily a poet. His thought also reveals resources of poetry; while the spiritual liberty of a mind long trained to honest lucidity gives value to all it expresses.

The whole tradition of French literature seems to have contributed to the quality of Valéry's prose style. If Descartes is here his principal master, there are also echoes throughout his work of Bossuet, La Rochefoucauld, Montesquieu and Voltaire.

I have shown in speaking of his *poétique* how by using words in their original or classical sense Valéry gave freshness to language; and how he considered that literature should utilise the phonetic

[1] Paul Valéry, 'Poésie et pensée abstraite,' *Variété*, V, (Paris: Gallimard, 1945), 297.

properties as well as the rhythmic possibilities of speech, which ordinary conversation neglects. These properties, he considered, should be classified and organised, and, after being strictly defined, should be used systematically in prose as well as in poetry.[1] He considered the formation of 'figures of speech' to be indivisible from the formation of language itself, since all 'abstract' words were abstracts obtained 'by some abuse or some transformation of their original significance, followed by the forgetting of their primitive sense.'[2]

3. VALÉRY AS CRITIC

The less poetical the critic, the less just the critique,
and the converse.   (POE)

Throughout the five volumes of the *Variété* series we may trace a system of criticism, opposed to contemporary methods, in which a new point of view is suggested as a surer basis on which to build critical studies. Thus Valéry's attitude is in direct opposition to that of Sainte-Beuve—attacked later by Proust. Here Valéry evokes and defines his Intellectual Comedy, that is to say, the drama of the human mind. It was the intellectual activity that went to the creation of works of art, the creative *act*, rather than the objective work resulting from it, which held his attention. This is what he meant, when in his course of Enseignement Poétique at the Collège de France, he began by proposing to his audience 'the analysis of the positive phenomena of the production and the accomplishment of works of the intellect.' Here he considered that only conclusions arising from personal experiences were valid for each poet. He had indeed no desire to make general and all-embracing statements such as scholastic philosophers insist on.[3]

At the risk of over-simplifying Valéry's approach to criticism, we may say that its first rule is, put yourself in the poet's place, and this illustrates passages on Mallarmé, Poe and Rimbaud which might well serve as autobiography for Valéry himself. His intention was to perceive and note the workings of the thought of the poet he was dis-

---

[1] See Quintilian, *Institutes of Oratory*. This work is mentioned by Gustave Fourment, *Correspondance Fourment–Valéry* (Paris: Gallimard, 1957).
[2] Paul Valéry, 'Enseignement de la poétique,' *Variété*, V, 291.
[3] Cf. Paul Valéry, 'Leçon inaugurale du Cours de Poétique,' *Variété*, V, 297.

cussing, to grasp the substitutions and transformations that took place in the intellectual life of his subject, and thus understand the acts of observation and imagination in the creative mind; he considered that the outer circumstances of life are of no great consequence. This psychological view of literary criticism was first proposed by Poe, who said that works of art could be best explained by understanding the actions of the mind which created them. Poe's method was triumphantly demonstrated in Valéry's various essays on such writers as Descartes and Mallarmé.[1]

Valéry summed up his idea of the critic's function in saying that it should be 'to analyse the particular intellectual intention of the author under consideration,' and that to do so the critic must examine the expressive inventions—such as sound, sense, forms of syntax, concepts and images—which the poet uses to increase his power and penetration.

This attitude towards criticism is demonstrated in a series of intellectual portraits. The essay on La Fontaine, 'Au sujet d'Adonis'[2] (1920) is one of the most remarkable for its insight and for the delicate precision of its outlines. We are shown that this dreamer whom we may have supposed 'Lazy as the clouds in which his gaze is lost, this man who loses his time as he loses his socks,' was in reality a poet of intellectual vigour; for the 'veritable condition of a veritable poet,' as internal evidence shows the author of *Adonis* to be, is all that is most distinct from the state of dreams.

> I see there [says Valéry] voluntary research, flexibility of thought and the mind's consentment to consummate difficulties and the perpetual triumph of sacrifice. . . . Even he who wishes to write about his dreams must be thoroughly awake.

This essay helped to re-establish La Fontaine as a major poet.[3] It is also a piece of eloquent pleading for form and music in poetry.

Another significant study is that on Baudelaire,[4] which reveals the part played by both Poe and his translator in the development of modern poetry. Valéry starts his essay by observing that, both as poet

---

[1] Cf. Paul Valéry, 'Je disais à Stéphane Mallarmé,' *Variété*, III (Paris: Gallimard, 1936), 7. 'Lettre sur Mallarmé,' *Variété*, II (Paris: Gallimard, 1929), 211. 'Fragment d'un Descartes,' *Variété*, II, 7, etc.

[2] *Variété*, I (Paris: Gallimard, 1924), 51.

[3] Cf. Taine, Sainte-Beuve, Gide, etc., on La Fontaine.

[4] Paul Valéry, 'Situation de Baudelaire,' *Variété*, II, 141–74, from which quotations in text are taken.

and as critic, Baudelaire had the force of genius which enabled him to choose his own masters, and so turn from the founders of the Parnassian group to discover for himself a new intellectual world in the work of Edgar Allan Poe.

In this sense Baudelaire was the direct forerunner of Valéry. In Poe, Baudelaire had discovered the inventor of an association between logic and imagination, a combination of principles which Valéry developed for his own needs. Certainly Baudelaire had been the first to discover in Poe 'an architect of literature' who understood and used all the resources of his art. Charmed by the extraordinary promise and the many original opinions revealed by Poe, Baudelaire's destiny was henceforth changed.

At the time of Baudelaire's coming of age, Romanticism was at its apogee; a brilliant generation was in possession of the world of letters. Hugo, Lamartine, Musset and Vigny were the masters of the moment. Valéry invites his readers to put themselves in the place of a young man beginning to write in 1840 'nourished by those poets whom his instinct imperiously commanded him to destroy,' for on all sides they seemed to block his way and to fill the space which was vital to his own development. At all costs he must isolate himself from such an exceptional group of great poets, all in full vigour at the same epoch.

Baudelaire's problem is amusingly stated by Valéry thus: how to be a great poet without being any of 'the others.' This question was Baudelaire's *raison d'état*, since 'in the domain of creation, which is also the domain of pride, the need to be different from the others is inseparable from existence itself.' In his project for a preface to the *Fleurs du mal*, Baudelaire had written, 'Famous poets having divided among themselves the most flowering provinces of poetry . . . I will do something else.' It was thus that Hugo's faults became the virtues of Baudelaire who, reacting against the romantic conception of poetry, cultivated a more solid substance and a more learned and purer form, rare qualities which the romantic giant had overlooked. Against Hugo's long experience of a constantly practised art, Valéry places Baudelaire's instinctive sense of criticism.

This sense, which is classical rather than romantic, was allied in Baudelaire with the power of analysis and also with the spontaneous qualities of discrimination and scepticism, precious qualities which show intellectual vitality. Valéry claims Baudelaire as a classic on the assumption that a classical poet is one who possesses the faculty of criticism and who applies it intimately to his own work. 'There was in

Racine a Boileau—or an image of Boileau.'[1] I need not dwell on Valéry's arguments in favour of a classical art, for I have considered them in discussing his poetics. What one should notice here is that he constantly returns to the same problem, and defines his subject each time according to the angle from which he approaches it. All his critical works plead for his ideal of pure poetry.

After commenting on the occasional lapses into prosaic statements, which Valéry sees as a major fault, he sums up Baudelaire's art as a combination of spirit and flesh, mind and body, a blending of solemnity, warmth and bitterness, of eternity and intimacy and also a rare alliance of will-power and harmony which distinguish him clearly from the Romantics and the Parnassians.

It was Valéry who first stated that the French owed to Baudelaire 'the return of poetry to its own essence.' He concludes by saying that one of Baudelaire's greatest glories was his decisive influence in the formation of future great poets. Neither Verlaine nor Mallarmé would have been what they were, had they not read *Les Fleurs du mal* at a receptive age. And while Verlaine and Rimbaud continued from Baudelaire in the order of sentiment and sensation, Mallarmé extended his achievements in the domain of pure poetry. And we might add that Valéry, in the realm of intellectual analysis and that combination of creative intuition and ecstasy which belongs to this realm, has been Baudelaire's greatest successor. I have stressed the importance of his appreciation of Baudelaire, because it throws light on Valéry's own works; and also because what he said has been the basis of much modern criticism.

The essays on Descartes which occur in *Variété* and elsewhere deserve a more detailed study than is possible here. In 'Une Vue de Descartes,' Valéry argues that the famous *Cogito ergo sum* is, for the philosopher's theme of the lucid self, 'the waking addressed to his pride and to the resources of his being.' It is the effective expression of the Self which travels from uncertainty to certainty, and which we follow until we too become sure of this Pure Self, the least personal, which should be the same in all and universal in each.[2]

Another interesting point in this essay is the importance given to the expression of a thought in the workings of a philosophical mind. Valéry comments on the perfection of Descartes' style, which is a model of adaptation of speech to thought, and in which the level and

---

[1] Paul Valéry, 'Situation de Baudelaire,' *Variété*, II, 155.
[2] Paul Valéry, 'Une Vue de Descartes,' *Variété*, V, 209.

detached manner of a geometrical statement composes admirably with a certain discreetly poetic grace. The *Méthode* of Descartes is said to be 'the development of consciousness for the purpose of knowledge.'

The same theme, presented somewhat differently to show that the structure of expression has in itself a sort of reality, is returned to in the essay on Bossuet.[1] Valéry maintains that the love of form, which is a Mediterranean characteristic, is the stamp of classical art. All classical poets proceed by construction, but modern poets proceed by accidents, speculating on an effect of surprise. Form has the rigour and eloquence of acts, but ideas have something of the instability of events. This is well observed in the case of Bossuet, in whose eloquence we may admire those compositions in the grand style, as we admire the architecture of a temple whose shrine is deserted, but whose arch remains.[1] Here again Valéry returns to the central theme of the Self in concluding that Bossuet was able to become a master of language because he was master of himself: 'Nul plus maître de langage c'est-à-dire de soi-même.'

To one who knows the perfidy of language and who consequently challenges the possibility of precise expression, while making every effort to fortify it and make it more exact, there is the absolute necessity of returning to the constant factor of the Self. This point of view is admirably demonstrated in an essay on Stendhal[2] in which Valéry boldly declares that the truth is inconceivable in literature. How could it be otherwise, he asks, when consideration of the reader, who has become the public, together with the idea of success and fame, lurks behind the author's chair? This is surely a valid criticism of Stendhal's position and ambitions.

In all these critical studies, whatever the point of departure, the problem of the mind and its language is developed and becomes the central theme, while the entirely subjective method leads to the construction of a theory of the intellect which includes the consideration of all artistic creation. So too we may say that in this search for an absolute of consciousness an absolute of imagination has also been evolved, in the process of giving life and significance to the working of the mind, through that power which transforms disorder into order; and this, as Valéry so often says, is part of the artist's function.

This point of view is sustained in 'La Crise de l'esprit,'[3] read as a

---

[1] Paul Valéry, 'Sur Bossuet,' *Variété*, II, 43.

[2] Paul Valéry, 'Stendhal,' *Variété*, II, 75.

[3] Paul Valéry, 'La Crise de l'esprit,' *Variété*, I, 9. First appeared as 'Une Conquête méthodique' (1895).

lecture in 1932. Here the mind's consciousness of itself is opposed to the wild confusion and lack of foresight in all political life. This essay begins with the famous phrase 'Nous autres, civilisations, nous savons maintenant que nous sommes mortelles.'

Apart from works on literary subjects, Valéry wrote a considerable number of essays, which he himself classified as *quasi-politiques*. In these he shows remarkable insight, concerning contemporary social and political problems, and his judgements have been frequently quoted by eminent men. In *Regards sur le monde actuel*, and in numerous other essays, many of which were published in the *Variété* series, he repeatedly suggests and discusses the adoption of a positive method to be applied to political and social questions and insists on the necessity of intellectual guidance in the chaos of modern affairs.

The idea of a method, the ideal of a new basis for political life, which would prepare *le réel à l'état pure*, as opposed to the accepted historical method, is constantly referred to in considering the actual problems with which these essays deal; and this application of a method, which Valéry saw as universal, carries the poet's ideas into other spheres than that of poetry.

To reconstruct the intellectual drama which lies behind all real works of art, the critic has to consider all the different personages who play their part in it. The dramatic action is that of the author's mind and his personal conception and use of language, for these alone express his validity.

> I call a book great when it gives a nobler and more profound idea of language. For in good writing the phrase takes form, the intention is grasped and things remain spiritual . . . therefore new ideas should be unhurried and ripened . . . as if they had not just been discovered but forgotten and refound.[1]

This axiom sums up his own achievement in his critical studies.

Valéry did not deny the existence of inspiration: he merely wanted it to be kept in its right place, and refused to give it the whole credit of creating a poem, which, however, it might suggest. He accepted what he described as 'given,' that is to say, thoughts or phrases that rise spontaneously in the poet's mind; he considered them as flashes of light, illuminating what was to be worked on and rightly belonging to the period of preparation. He accepted emotion and creative intuition

---

[1] Paul Valéry, *Tel Quel*, I, (Paris: Gallimard, 1941), 180.

as the sources of that intellectual sensibility which is the origin of all poetic creation. Such forces were however to be disciplined to a lucid and extreme attention which was for him a better state of mind for creative art than a state of fine frenzy. And he even declared; 'I find it outrageous to write in a state of enthusiasm. . . . I should infinitely prefer to write something mediocre in full consciousness and in a state of complete lucidity, rather than a masterpiece in a state of trance.'

Valéry had noted that the rules of classic art teach us by their arbitrary nature that the thoughts arising from our daily needs, sentiments and experiences are only a small part of the thoughts of which we are capable. Thus intellect must be present in every poem; either apparent or hidden 'it swims holding poetry out of the water.'[1]

Always careful to keep intact his own independence, he wisely declared that all theories on art can have no universal application. They are theories made by the poet for himself. The critic who attacks them does not realise this important fact. So one might criticise a tool 'not knowing that it was made for a man with only three or perhaps six fingers.[2] Here there can be no right or wrong; no professorial authority should presume to be a universal law-giver. Valéry considered that the poet was one to whom the problems inherent in his art were a secret and almost sacred obligation, and those very difficulties had in themselves the virtue of a creative force, and were often the source of fresh ideas.[3]

Of course there are many different approaches to poetry. For some poets, such as Apollinaire and many others, ideas often entirely insignificant in themselves not only suggest spontaneous expression but may even constitute the whole fabric of the poem, which, being the direct impression of the moment, is as simple as speech, but is nevertheless capable of proposing its own idiom, suggesting its own image. Such poems are generally short.

For other poets, such as Wordsworth for instance, poetry is the expression of an idea of life directly inspired by a sensitive reaction to aspects of romantic nature, sometimes rising to the universal note of pure poetry. If, as Matthew Arnold said, Wordsworth 'was admired for the wrong things, insight into human nature and moral ideas which

[1] Paul Valéry, 'Rhumbs,' *Tel Quel*, II, 73.

[2] *Ibid.*, 8.

[3] In this connection we may compare Valéry, 'Rhumbs,' *Tel Quel*, II, 77: 'Le grand intérêt de l'art classique est peut-être dans les suites de transformations qu'il demande pour exprimer les choses en respectant les conditions *sine qua non* imposées. Problèmes de la mise en vers. Ceci oblige de considérer de très haut ce que l'on doit dire.'

are distinct from poetry,'[1] it is evident that those things had *intruded* into the poetic universe. That is also what Baudelaire inferred when he said that had Hugo been a 'pure poet' he would not have been so much admired by the public. This is true of the public attitude to both Hugo and Wordsworth. How often one sees examples of this in religious or sentimental verses. It is the religion or the sentiment that pleases their public, and the pure poetry of Wordsworth's highest moments, as also that of the Hugo of the *Contemplations*, is too often overlooked.

4. MORNING MEDITATIONS

All theories are really fragments, meticulously
prepared, of an autobiography.   (P. V.)

In 1926 Valéry published for the first time certain extracts from the morning meditations contained in his note-books. This was a concession to the public and may be partly explained by the fact that he had solved the problem of 'comment plaire et se plaire' by imposing his own point of view and thus establishing his spiritual independence. He had arrived at that mature state in which, without any fear of betraying his disciplined manner of thought, he could publish extracts from his meditations, whose spontaneity was in part the result of patient concentration.

In these selections from the note-books there is no particular attempt at unity. The ideas are not linked by any special line of thought, but are merely grouped under different headings. They convey, as Valéry says, 'instantaneous ideas independent of each other'; they are 'successive throws of dice.' Yet their autobiographical value is indisputable. In them we see Valéry's thought in action, and nothing can better help us to understand the subtlety of his mind than these fragmentary texts, to which I have often referred.

The first of the selections he called *Analecta*. Here he comes fairly close to the ideas of his system though he does not actually refer to it. The purity of his style confers a poetic charm on the psychological and artistic themes. The various Notes published between 1926 and 1940

[1] Matthew Arnold, 'Wordsworth,' *Essays on Criticism*, 2nd Series (London: Macmillan, 1921), 122–62. Cf. A. E. Housman, *The Name and Nature of Poetry* (London: Grant Richards, 1933).

were collected in 1941 in *Tel Quel* (vol. I) which contains *Choses tues* (1930), 'Moralités,' 'Ébauches de pensées,' 'Littérature' and *Cahier B 1910*. *Mauvaises Pensées et autres* appeared in 1942; and in 1943 *Tel Quel* (vol. II) which was made up of *Rhumbs*, 'Note,' *Autres Rhumbs*, *Analecta et suite*.

Throughout these works we may trace a rigorous self-questioning which is always Valéry's manner of approach, whatever his theme may be. He starts from what is self-evident and proceeds to examine his reactions to all that his mind accepts, and by this means he progresses towards a personal statement. We find in the Notes many of his ideas which he developed in the *Variété* series; and many of the themes are noted here such as the origin of myths, 'au commencement était la fable'; poetry, dreams, waking, consciousness, knowledge—and here as elsewhere his insistence on form is categoric. Here too the problem of language is treated as a problem of the real consciousness of thought, sometimes at length, sometimes briefly in an aphorism, as: 'A poetic idea is one which, if expressed in prose, calls for poetry.'[1]

The aphorisms alone deserve a special study; they have the insight of the French school of La Bruyère, La Rochefoucauld, Voltaire, Vauvenargues and others. The aphorism is a spiritual exercise which French men of letters have made particularly their own. It allows for no half-truths or any vague *à peu prés*. French aphorisms at their best shine with the lustre of single jewels. The special characteristic of Valéry's contribution to this form of expression is that he generally applies it to poetry or language, rather than to humanity, though he does sometimes speak of authors rather than their work thus:

> The notion of 'great poet' has engendered more little poets than it was reasonable to expect from the combinations of Fate.[2]

And again:

> Most men have such a vague idea of poetry that this very vagueness is for them a definition of poetry.[3]

And here is a definition to dispel such vagueness:

> Poetry is literature reduced to the essential of its active principle.[4]

[1] Paul Valéry, *Choses tues*, in *Tel Quel*, I, 38: 'Idée poétique est celle qui, mise en prose, réclame encore des vers.'
[2] *Ibid.*, 35.
[3] Paul Valéry, 'Littérature,' *Tel Quel*, I, 143.
[4] *Ibid.*, 144.

Amusingly he says that

> The subject of a poem is as foreign to it and as important as his name is to a man.[1]

When he speaks directly of men there is sometimes an ethical judgement:

> In the long run we judge our friends by the delicacy of their tact.[2]
> Most people stop at the first stages of the development of their thought.[3]
> The absence of a thing is often the force which makes us imagine it.[4]
> As there are men of the world so too there are men of the Universe.[5]

In several passages he infers that as the expression of a true sentiment is always banal, perfection of expression becomes a defence, putting good manners between ourselves and others, and also between our different interior selves.

Returning to literature Valéry says that the most perishable part of a work is its newness, for we never know in advance what works will live or endure since all have the need of circumstances and these indeed often favour the less authentic; classical works are perhaps those which lose nothing after having been laid aside for years.

Again and again throughout the Notes Valéry returns to consider poetry under different aspects. He is sometimes disdainful, and generally clear and forcible. The part played by the human voice and the necessity of the rôle in poetry of 'that voice which the poet expects and waits for' is one of his constant themes. The place of inspiration, construction and form, verses given and verses calculated, are all returned to. Here is a theorem which echoes Poe: 'When poems are very short, the effect of the slightest detail is of the order of importance of the effect of the whole.'[6]

Dreams are a favourite subject of reflection, and in *Autres Rhumbs*,[7] Valéry confesses that he finds it difficult to make an exact study of them. According to his habit of watching himself think he even tried

[1] Paul Valéry, 'Littérature,' *Tel Quel*, I, 145.
[2] Paul Valéry, *Autres Rhumbs*, in *Tel Quel*, II, 171.
[3] Valéry, *Choses tues*, in *Tel Quel*, I, 55.
[4] *Ibid.*   [5] *Ibid.*, 51.
[6] Paul Valéry, 'Théorème littéraire,' *Tel Quel*, I, 156.
[7] *Rhumbs* = same word in English: a naval term for the intervals between the 32 points of the compass. Valéry's *Rhumbs* are the divergencies from a certain constant element in the profound and essential intention of his mind—'asides.' *Tel Quel*, II, 9.

to imitate the state of dreaming while awake, but without much result, for dreams are phenomena which we can examine only during their absence: we must be asleep to truly dream, and we must be awake to reconstruct and examine an act which belongs to a very minor state of semi-consciousness. Dreams are essentially insignificant and incoherent. They are beyond our will, and the mind of the dreamer 'resembles a system on which exterior forces have no power, and which the interior forces cannot bring about either by displacement or rotation.'[1]

The 'Moralités' (*Tel Quel*, I) characteristically evoke a climate of clear thinking and good-natured tolerance in questions concerning the outer world of politics, tendencies and beliefs. Valéry will not accept a soul without a body, remarking that all such suppositions lead us to 'see without eyes, touch without fingers, act without acts, and finally die without dying, such is the principle of this strange preoccupation with immortality. . . .' In another Note he says that 'man cannot sincerely sell himself to the devil or give himself to God.'[2]

'Man thinks therefore I am—says the Universe'[3]: thus Valéry expresses the idea of that cosmic consciousness which is reflected in the part we play in what we understand as the Universe. . . .

As the great Romantics discovered their communion and their relationship with nature, and thus extended their poetic consciousness to new fields of vision, so now the most sensitive minds are aware, or becoming aware, of man's relationship to the cosmos.

So we may consider the Romantic Movement, in its widest conception of universal nature, as a sort of polite introduction to those fierce and untamed forces by which we are surrounded and which eventually we are obliged to acknowledge. Humanity stands facing this future as a pilgrim whose mind has the faculty of conscious awareness, a capacity for knowledge and an intuitive intelligence; with the staff of thought in his hand, a sack of dreams on his back . . . alone.

Therefore the poetry which is to be the expression of the intellectual attitude of our age, should express a cosmic or universal consciousness.

[1] It should comfort bad spellers to know that 'it is a gross stupidity to consider spelling as a sign of culture, it is the manœuvring of language which shows and exacts culture' (*Tel Quel*, I, 25). Yet how often we see books damned because the critic has found a fault in spelling, while the general style passes unremarked.
[2] Paul Valéry, *Choses tues*, in *Tel Quel*, I, 78.
[3] Valéry, 'Moralités,' *Tel Quel*, I, 88.

This conception was, as I have shown, expressed in all its freshness by Mallarmé in *Un Coup de dés*, and it is also approached in *La Jeune Parque* where it is a lateral but fundamental effect throughout the poem, a universal background to human destiny.

Although Valéry did not accept orthodox religious beliefs he cannot be dismissed as nihilist or sophist. He held a definitely creative doctrine in his belief that by cultivating the Self, man might rise to a higher level of intellectual life, through the act of spiritual concentration which changes him in giving him greater understanding. Thus man becomes more than himself and enters as fully as possible into an intellectual experience of universal attributes. In 1927, in a letter to the R. P. Gillet, Valéry stated his views on the subject of religion simply and clearly. He said that 'agnosticism was not for him an *a priori* principle,' but that it was 'the general attitude assumed by a man who cannot prevent himself from examining to the best of his ability what other people propose that he should think and believe.' And he considers, 'his first intellectual duty is to use all his mental activity on all the propositions which come from himself as well as from others.'[1]

All such questions, he adds, resulted in a quantity of Notes, 'fixed fragments' as he calls them, of those morning meditations which were essential to his spiritual welfare: those hours of Monsieur Teste, in which the only constant that he refers to is the Pure Self.

5. THE DIALOGUES

i. 'EUPALINOS OU L'ARCHITECTE.'

Le gouvernement d'un royaume demande une certaine harmonie comme la musique, et de justes proportions comme l'architecture. (FÉNELON)

The *Dialogues* bring us to the centre of Valéry's doctrine of formal art. The Socratic dialogue, in the form of question and answer, which first establishes its premises through definition and analysis, is a mode of expression admirably suited to Valéry's theories, and allows

[1] Paul Valéry, letter to R. P. Gillet (janvier 1927), *Lettres à quelques-uns*, 163.

the reader to follow him in the act of thinking and in the intimate life of his thought.

'Eupalinos ou l'architecte,' a meditation on formal art, gives us Valéry's mature judgement on the themes discussed in many of his essays. Here the drama of the Intellectual Comedy turns on the conflict between the desire to know and the desire to construct. Socrates who looked for universal knowledge and Eupalinos the architect who designed temples symbolise different aspects of Valéry's mind, different 'selves,' which were capable of being reconciled in the creation of a work of art.

The key to the symbolism is the constant allusion to poetry, represented by the formal art of architecture, and this theme is extended to the consideration of general conditions of artistic creation. Like Phaedrus, who is here conversing with Socrates, Valéry never separates the idea of a poem from its construction. A poem for him is an act 'more glorious than a victory,' and this conception leads to a sort of universal application of his system of poetics.

The scene opens at the frontiers of the transparent Empire of the Dead, in the land of shades on the bank of the river of Time, the philosophers' Styx which bears all things away. Here Socrates and Phaedrus seem to continue the conversation of Plato's *Phaedrus*. Both comment regretfully on their function as shades, which Socrates sees as that of a dreamer for whom figures and thoughts are strangely altered by their flight. The truth is before us, but we do not understand it, he argues, foreseeing the conclusion of Valéry's ultimate Angel, who during an eternity continued 'to know and not to understand.'[1]

Whence, asks Phaedrus, comes the desire for eternity which one sometimes notices in the living? Even the wisest and the most inspired of men wish to give rhythm and harmony to their works in order to defend them from oblivion. Socrates (who marvellously resembles the shade of Monsieur Teste) replies that this is mere vanity, for even the wisest men have absurd ambitions. But ambition, insists Phaedrus, may result in producing harmony from chaos.

From this starting point, they continue to discuss, not without ironic regrets, the enduring qualities which only extreme care produces in a work of art. This most Valérian theme leads Phaedrus to speak of his friend Eupalinos the architect, who seems to him to have the power of Orpheus to move stones to ordered beauty, and who, having solved the difficult problems of his art, directed his workmen by simple

[1] Cf. below p. 245, 'The Last Phase.'

orders and numbers. Such art had led Phaedrus to consider that the idea of a temple was inseparable from the idea of its construction. This theory, so often repeated throughout Valéry's works, is followed by similar analogies to his poetic doctrine. For everything that he says of architecture, music or dancing, is applicable to his idea of poetry as a possible formal art.

Thus, like the poet, Eupalinos gives the greatest importance to the joining up of different parts of his work by imperceptible modulations, so that 'the spectator is led unaware to a state of bliss by imperceptible curves and by minute yet all-powerful inflections, and also by those happy combinations of the regular and the irregular which the architect has introduced and concealed, making them as powerful as they were indefinable.' This refers to those passages, the joining up of recitatives and periods, to which Valéry gave great attention.

Socrates almost pities Phaedrus' enthusiasm for art which by force of circumstances has become merely a memory; while as a philosopher he himself may continue to 'search among the shades for a shadow of truth.' Alas, muses Phaedrus, nothing of beauty can be separated from life, and life is that which dies. He attacks the Platonic doctrine of æsthetics of which the essential weakness is that it explains beauty by its conformity to an abstract and ideal model, and quotes Mallarmé, *le très admirable Stephanos*: 'Gloire du long désir, Idées!' But the conception of these ideas, of which Plato is the father, seems too simple to explain all the diversity of beauty: the changing of mens' preferences, the new impressions and the disappearance of works once greatly admired. Nor will Socrates accept the idea of a supernatural beauty, for in natural beauties to which he is not insensible, he sees everywhere 'l'homme et l'esprit de l'homme.'

Valéry speaks for himself when he says that all natural beauty is for him only as 'the ornament of his meditations,' the delightful surroundings of his doubts and the favourable site for his own interior constructions. The things of beauty take him far from themselves and lead him to see 'man and the mind of man.'

The poet's second nature is equally well represented through the reported ideas of Eupalinos. The more he thought of his art the more he became aware, with a surer delight and greater clarity, of his own being. As he said:

> I lose myself during long spells of waiting; and find myself again through the surprises I give myself; and by means of these successive degrees of my silence I advance in my own edification; and I draw near to such an

exact correspondence between my aims and my powers that I seem to myself to have made of the existence which was given me, a sort of human handiwork. . . . By dint of construction, I really believe that I have constructed myself.

This is a precious note in Valéry's intellectual autobiography, and he continues to give us authentic information in explaining the long and indirect preparation for his poems: telling how he has looked for accuracy in his thoughts so that, originating clearly from an ordered meditation on things, they might be changed, as of their own accord, into the acts of his art:

I have distributed my attention; I have reorganised problems; I begin where I had ended, so as to go a little further. . . . I am sparing of reveries, I plan as if I were constructing. Nevermore, in the shapeless spaces of my mind, do I contemplate those imaginary structures, which are to real constructions what chimera and gargoyle are to real animals. But what I think is feasible, and what I do is intelligible. . . .

In an eloquent passage, architecture is endowed with musical qualities, for some buildings seem to be mute, others to speak, while the most rare, which are analogous to poetry, seem to sing.

But what is beautiful is most difficult, and perfection in any work of art is as rare as the man who is capable of making an effort against himself, that is to say, capable of choosing a certain Self, and of imposing it on himself. So a poet with the ability to meditate to the extreme of his being, and therefore to extreme reality, would undoubtedly advance to a perfect adjustment between visible forms and the ephemeral union of successive sounds. Such a man would partake of the creative powers of a god. Undoubtedly his most precious power would be that of linking analysis and ecstasy.

Such a state is indeed rare, and Valéry says that when he approaches it he is already different from his ordinary self, as a taut string is different from a slack one. Then everything is clear and seems easy to him. He feels that his need for beauty, equal to his unknown resources, creates by itself the figures that satisfy it. He desires with all his being and the powers come flocking, charged with light and error, and must be controlled, marshalled, composed. 'I temporise with these ideas,' he says, 'and hold them at a distance for the flash of a moment,' an instant of liberty during which the poem is born. This is the very substance of the poems 'L'Aurore' and 'Les Pas' (Charmes).

At this point the fine myth of the casting of a rose in bronze is introduced to explain the birth of a poem. The roses are life, fragile and fleeting; the wax symbolises the artist's work; the fire is a symbol of time; and the liquid metal represents a state of exceptional power in the poet's mind.

This dialogue is very close to the poetry of *Charmes*. When Socrates says that he wishes to hear the song of the pillars and to imagine in the clear sky the monument of a melody, we are irresistibly reminded of the 'Cantique des colonnes.'

> Nous chantons à la fois
> Que nous portons les cieux!
> O seule et sage voix
> Qui chantes pour les yeux!
>
> Vois quels hymnes candides!
> Quelle sonorité
> Nos éléments limpides
> Tirent de la clarté!

Again, when he compares words to bees which sting us to attention, we think of 'L'Abeille.' In speaking of music he compares the state of being enchanted with 'une Pythie dans sa chambre de fumée.'

In a thoughtful analysis of the qualities of music and architecture, the classical attributes inherent in both are shown to be also necessary to poetry. As I have dealt with this question in discussing the poetics, I need not dwell on it here but it is interesting to note that what Valéry says of listening to music may be profitably applied to the reading of his own poems, where the actual words fade into a pattern expressing a state of spiritual awareness. As in music, the phrase becomes a poetic statement in which the image is so thoroughly imbued with the thought, as to become thought itself and no longer merely an image.

Though poetry is the only art not directly discussed here, the whole discourse is full of critical significance. The admirable statement on Geometry which follows is also relevant to Valéry's poetics. For in this characteristically psychological theory of geometry Socrates proves that it is nothing else than an application and supreme effect of language.[1]

At the centre of a studious silence, says Socrates, words, even the most complex, become simple. Ideas which were identical, but distinct,

[1] Cf. Valéry's definition of mathematics in 'Discours en l'honneur de Goethe,' *Variété*, IV, 93. Also, above, Chapter III, 'The Intellectual Comedy,' 3: 'Valéry and the Philosophers,' p. 102 and note.

become united. Intellectual forms which resemble each other combine and simplify themselves. Notions, common to different propositions, serve as a link between these propositions and then disappear allowing other things, to which they were separately attached, to unite. But if language can construct, it may also corrupt. Therefore an altar to it would have two [*sic*] faces differently decorated: one would be almost unformed, signifying common speech in which words are lost through usage; the second face 'would eject from its mouth a clear fountain of everlasting water' . . . and yet a third [*sic*] would have 'that rigour and subtlety which they say the Egyptians knew how to express on the face of their gods. . . .'

'For us Greeks,' says Socrates, 'everything is in the form.' And the Greeks have one word which designates three things: form, reason and calculation. For what is reason if not a discourse, when the meanings of the terms are well defined and permanently established, and adjusted to each other and clearly composed? This argument applies also to calculation, numbers being clear and simple signs of thought.

Again through the mouth of Socrates, Valéry speaks of his passion for constructing which so troubled his mind that he hesitated between philosophy and art. In a long and careful analysis of this theme he explains how everyone has the capacity of developing himself in several different ways. Thus an object picked up on the shore first awakened in him the idea of construction, and how it operates, first in nature, and secondly, and differently, in man.[1] This leads him to define the difference between the philosopher and the artist or poet: for the philosopher forms a wider conception than the poet—he wishes to utilise everything; but in the poet's work nothing figures except what is useful and necessary to the effect, for words may be admirable tools which wait for acts and forces to use them. Here the various forms, and the extensions and developments possible in art are all considered.

Then Phaedrus recalls another of his friends, the Phœnician, Tridon the Sidonian, a real sea-dog, a type of Mediterranean pirate and boatbuilder, whom Valéry may have seen at Sète or Marseilles. This man from Sidon never ceased to study the question of navigation. He grappled with the problems of his art, identifying himself with the ocean that 'origin of all that lives, but an impenetrable tomb with the movements of a cradle.'

[1] Paul Valéry, 'L'Homme et la coquille,' *Variété*, V, 12. 'Ce coquillage que je tiens et retourne entre mes doigts. . . .' Cf. Valéry, 'Mon Faust: Fragments unédits' in *Paul Valéry vivant* (Paris: Cahiers du Sud, 1946), 239, for the same idea.

Is it fantastic to find in this Tridon a portrait of Huysmans? As far as I know, this question has not hitherto been raised, but it seems probable that Valéry was thinking of his old friend, who, like Tridon, was not content to follow classical models but constructed according to his personal ideas: a boat should be, as it were, modelled by the sea itself, thought the Sidonian; and language, thought Huysmans, should be as agitated and palpitating as life.

After a picturesque account of this man who made something actual after his own fashion, Socrates regrets the arid abstraction of his own past life: for what is more vain than the shade of a sage, he asks, unless it be the sage himself, who leaves behind him only various sayings immortally abandoned? He laments:

> I made use of a truth and a sincerity more false than myths and inspired words. . . . I taught what I invented. What an artist I destroyed in myself! I could have built, sung—O thoughful loss of my days. . . . What things I have disdained, I feel myself to be my own judge in my spiritual hell. While the facility of my famous sayings pursues and afflicts me . . . my actions which have not taken place, my works which have not been born. Vague and enormous crimes are those crying absences and murders of which the victims are things everlasting. . . .

Phaedrus, while trying to console the philosopher, agrees that nothing is so bitter as lost opportunities, but concludes that evidently, if we have left things undone, it is because we could not have done them without troubling the whole course of the world. Socrates retorts with delight that to trouble, and even to overthrow, the universe is precisely what everyone would like to do: 'For we should all like to consider that all things and the opulence of Time are only a mouthful for *our* mouth, and we could not think otherwise.'

With ironical humour Socrates imagines a corrective existence in limbo which should defend his former existence with illusions as to his past, as the living defend themselves. Yet doubts continue to assail him and he fears that his search for God, through the medium of thought alone, has served no useful purpose. Of what use had it been to question the deity unceasingly on the most variable and even ignoble questions of the 'just and the unjust,' for the God that one finds thus is 'but a word, born of words and returns in a word.'

So the answer which we make for ourselves is never anything other than the question itself; and every question the mind puts to itself is, and cannot be anything other than, naïvety. On the contrary it is in

acts and the combination of acts, that we ought to find the most immediate sentiment of a divine presence; and the best use we could make of
our forces which are not used up in living, would be to reserve them
for the pursuit of some undefined object that infinitely transcends us. . . .
If the universe is the effect of some act, it is in the act of constructing
that we may approach the gods: construction being the most complete
act. A work of art demands love and meditation, obedience to the
finest thought, and the mind's invention of laws.

When the Demiurgus set about making the world, says Socrates,
he grappled with the confusion of chaos. Everything that lay before
him was formless. In the whole of the abyss there was not a single
handful of nature that was not infinitely impure and made up of different substances. . . . The creation is described in a fine passage of poetic
prose, ending with the statement that man the constructor begins
where God the creator stopped. Carried away by the grandeur of his
theme, Valéry's Socrates describes how he would work were he creating the world: setting out all the problems, developing a flawless
method, while exercising an even stricter control on his own mind.

But, asks Phaedrus, are you going to revoke in eternity all the sayings which made you immortal? To which Socrates replies:

> Immortal yonder—relatively to mortals! But here! . . . But there is no
> 'here,' and all that we have been saying is as much a natural sport of the
> silence of these infernal regions as the fantasy of some rhetorician of the
> other-world who uses us as puppets!

And Phaedrus concludes: 'It is in this that immortality strictly consists.'

ii. 'L'AME ET LA DANSE'

'O mes amis qu'est ce véritablement que la danse?'

The dance is a poem: 'this world of exact forces and studied illusions'
represents the mind in movement. It is, says Socrates, the mysterious
movement of life itself transformed into a dancing girl, who would
divinely cease to be a girl if the bound she makes would take her to the
skies. But we cannot go so far as infinity, either dreaming or waking,
so she, likewise, always returns to being herself, and ceases to be a
flake, a bird, an idea. Thus through a thousand transformations life
always returns to itself.

What moment could be happier for the consideration of such questions than the end of a banquet, since philosophy is an after-dinner thought, and the guests are none other than Socrates, Phaedrus and the doctor Eryximacius? Already, as if called up by the words of Socrates, the winged choir of dancers advance into the hall while the air resounds and hums with orchestral prophecies.

Here certitude is a game, declares Socrates, and one might say that knowledge had found its action and that intelligence had already consented to combine with spontaneous graces. For as the dancer 'becomes all that the flute wishes her to be,' so poetic thought follows the rhythm and form imposed by the metrical movement; and Valéry compares the 'clear dancers' to his own thought since 'their hands speak and their feet seem to write,' while he sees in this universal art a lively and gracious introduction to perfect meditation. Here the general poetry of action of the whole human being, which dancing reveals, is symbolic of that pure poetry whose action transports us into a space-time of its own, where, as in dancing, the æsthetic qualities of rhythm and intensity create perfection.

To the raptures of Phaedrus who sees in the dance the delicate qualities of dreams, Socrates replies with the Valérian theory that art is the contrary of dreaming and that hazard is assuredly absent. But 'what is the opposite to a dream if not another dream? But a dream of vigilance and intensity such as Reason herself might have.' Reason while dreaming is alert, armed with closed lips, and is mistress of her utterances. Her dream would be penetrated with symmetry, entirely given up to ordered acts and their consequences. And 'who knows what august laws dream here that they agree together in the design of showing how the real, the unreal and the intelligible are able to melt and mingle together' according to the genius of the poet? For dancers like poems seem to obey invisible laws. And how could the poet's state of mind at the moment of writing a poem be better expressed than in these words: 'a dream of vigilance and of extreme attention'? Those who have passed by there will recognise the authentic moment of creative art. . . .

How pure and gracious, cries Phaedrus, is that little temple, rose and round, that the dancers now compose and which turns slowly like the night. . . . It resolves itself into young girls whose tunics are wings, and the gods seem to change their minds.

Now the chief dancer Athiktè appears and seems to assume a majesty which was confusedly inherent in the spectators, while the grace of her movements teaches them to know better their own hearts. She begins with a simple walk, which has no object but itself, from which all need-less movements have been banished, and which becomes a universal model. Beauty and full security of mind result from her perfect move-ment in which 'the length of her steps is exactly matched with their number which proceeds directly from the music.' Number and length are in secret harmony with her stature.

This image represents a synthesis of all that a poem should be. It is an excellent example of Valéry's use of symbolism to explain the result he wishes to obtain. The dancer is wholly one with her own movement, as is a perfect poem; and we follow the progress of such a poem in the image of her movements.

> Now her eyes are closed; she is alone with her soul, in the heart of her extreme attention.

A moment of silence follows:

> an instant absolutely virgin . . . and then an instant when something is about to break in the soul, in the expectation, of the whole assembly.

There is a 'delicious suspense' in the hearts of the spectators, till the delicate moment arrives when the dancer starts another figure, as 'a bird arrives at the very edge of the roof, breaks away from the stately marble and falls into flight.' This is a moment as flexible and sensitive as those transitions from one passage to another in a poem. All the de-lights of expectation are aroused, as when a poem leads the reader into an exceptional world and 'penetrates the impossible.'

'How alike are our souls in the presence of this marvel—equal and complete for each of us,' cries Socrates, reminding us of the theatre scene in 'La Soirée avec Monsieur Teste,' where the audience assumes a single entity before the stage. Phaedrus, who longs to kiss the dan-cer's feet, is justified by Eryximacius; for are we not made up of organised fantasy? And is not our living constitution an incoherence that functions, and a disorder that works? Do not events, desires, ideas interchange themselves in us in the most necessary and incompre-hensible way? 'What a cacophony of causes and effects.' But the artist's rôle is to put order into the disorder of our sensations.

With all this enthusiasm, Socrates hastens to agree, finding in Athiktè 'Hercules transformed into a swallow'; and he marvels that a head so small, compact as a young fir cone, is able to produce so in-fallibly these myriads of questions and answers that pass from limb to limb, and those attempts that she makes and remakes and as constantly rejects, receiving them from the music and returning them instantaneously to the light.

Not content to stop there, Valéry develops his theme in a truly Socratic manner, leading to the abstract definition in which he delights. For Phaedrus, the dancer Athiktè is an image of the triumph and grace of love: not the fiction or miming of love, or some miserable adventure, or the person of some lover, but the very being of love itself. . . . What is this soul of love? How shall we define it? This universal creature has neither body nor face, but has gifts and days and destinies, life and death, and is indeed nothing but life and death. Desire when once born knows neither sleep nor truce. 'That is why,' concludes Phaedrus, 'only the dancer by her lovely actions can make the soul visible for us.'

On the other hand, for the doctor Eryximacius, who knows the dancers intimately behind the scenes, the dance is simply a manifestation of the dance itself, and nothing more; and the dancer is merely a perfect mistress of the art of dancing acquired through a long apprenticeship, as indeed from one aspect, a poet sees himself simply as a good technician.

Socrates expresses a characteristic point of view when he suggests that the dance is a pure act of metamorphosis. Words are as bees that fly from flower to flower, and such words would be necessary if he were to explain all the thoughts and ideas that throng his mind.

However, Socrates has never been in a hurry to express a final verdict. He always starts by a significant question and now he asks:

Is there any remedy or exact antidote for that ill of all ills, that poison of poisons, that venom which is opposed to all nature; the boredom of living? Not the passing spleen, nor the tedium caused by fatigue, or that of which one knows the limits, but that perfect ennui which is caused neither by misfortunes or infirmities; . . . that state of murderous lucidity which is the result of the cold exact and reasonable view of life as it is. . . .

As La Jeune Parque told her philosopher:

> Que tout fût clair, tout vous sembleraient vain!
> Votre ennui peuplerait un univers sans levain.[1]

Such a state is the Accidia of the ancients which has accumulated its forces in a machine-ridden world.

To Socrates' question the learned doctor Eryximacius replies, in an

---

[1] Paul Valéry, 'Le Philosophe et la Jeune Parque,' *Poésies* (Paris: Gallimard, 1942), 180.

essentially Valérian passage of ironic truth, that there is nothing more inimical to nature than to see things in the cold and perfect light of reason. Indeed the universe cannot endure for a single instant to remain what it is. What are mortals for? he asks. Their business is to know, and to know is assuredly not to be what one is; for the idea introduces into what *is* the leaven of what is not. Truth however sometimes declares itself and sounds a painful discord which clashes with the harmonious system of phantasmagoria and errors. There is no evidence of any cure for this horrible state of pure disgust.

But, insists Socrates, if there is no cure for this rational malady of *ennui* what state of mind is most contrary to it? Evidently the chances of living and drinking deeply are linked with all the other hazards of life. Yet surely, he argues, the enthusiasm which would be the most efficacious remedy for this state of *ennui* is the enthusiasm of action— that state of mental activity, which is that of the Salamander who lives in flame: a state of exaltation and vibration which has the power of flame; the state of the dancer, and of the poet. 'For all that passes from the state of heaviness to the state of subtlety passes by the moment of flame and light'; and the poet, as the dancer, may attain complete possession of his Self and reach a pitch of perfection which can only be momentarily captured.

The dancer therefore symbolises the *chef d'œuvre* dreamed of by poets. She makes us see the moment which engenders the form, as the form creates the moment for us: 'It flies from its shadow through the air, and in this sonorous instant we hear the clashing of all life's shining arms.' This is the endeavour in which the spirit rises triumphant above the everyday world. Thus poetry gives us the power to penetrate into its own unique and different world. And the last word of the dancer, as of the poet, is: 'I was in you, O whirlwind, outside and beyond all things.'

A masterpiece of measure and clarity, this dialogue is enriched by the thought with which the poet informs his theme: that transient state which cannot be indefinitely prolonged, which exists in the poet's act, symbolised by the dance; through which we dream of an existence capable of fixing these rare moments of ultimate consciousness at the furthest limit of our faculties. The dialogue should in fact be considered as a synthesis of Valéry's doctrine in which the spontaneous self, through the action of thought, is transposed to the principle of the pure Self. The dancer becomes the instrument of the dance, and this dance is the action of the mind, wholly dissolved in its act which is the

poem. The personages in Valéry's Intellectual Comedy always represent states of mind—of his own mind. Thus the dancer, one with the
dance, is the pure Self expressed in pure poetry.

iii. 'DIALOGUE DE L'ARBRE'

> . . . *Cette auguste voix*
> *Qui se connaît quand elle sonne*
> *N'être plus la voix de personne*
> *Tant que des ondes et des bois.*   ('LA PYTHIE')

In this dialogue the two speakers appear as essential aspects of Valéry:
his thinking self represented by Lucretius, who sees the whole life of
thought symbolised in the tree; and his poet self by the shepherd-poet
Tityrus for whom the tree proposes different images—a flower, a
woman, a god, a temple, life and love. Together the two voices reveal
a reclassification of spirit and nature, in which Valéry associates himself with the world of plants that partake of universal life. Thus a conception of all life which includes nature and all possible aspects of the
Self is implied. The poet explains how he has modelled the system of
his thought on the double growth in earth and in air of the tree, whose
roots spread from its central being to be nourished by the earth, while
its leaves strive towards the conquest of space. So mind and body are
intrinsically one, as are the sense and form of a poem. There is no
division, for if we would reach out towards spiritual reality, the more
deeply must we search, in the obscure substance of ourselves, that
memory and that tenderness which lies at the source of tears. This is a
significant aspect of Valéry's thought, and throughout the dialogue he
shows us that to meditate should be to advance in symmetry, as does
his thinking tree, which represents his own active meditation, scru-
pulously consistent in its design.

In the opening lines the shepherd Tityrus tells how a poet should
approach his poem:

> I live. I wait. . . . My flute is ready between my fingers, and I attune my-
> self to this admirable hour. I wish to be the instrument of the general
> grace of things. I abandon the whole weight of my body to the earth: my
> eyes live in the quivering mass of light above. See, how the tree above
> seems to enjoy the divine ardour from which it shelters me: in the full

desire of its being, which is certainly of feminine essence, it asks me to
sing its name and to give musical form to the breeze which penetrates and
gently torments it. I wait for my soul. There is a great virtue in waiting.
I shall feel the pure act coming from my lips and all that I do not yet
know about myself in love with the Beech tree is going to come to life.
O Lucretius, is it not a miracle that a shepherd, forgetful of his flock, may
pour out to the skies the fugitive form and as it were the naked idea of a
tree and an instant.

To this Lucretius replies that there is no miracle or marvel which the
mind if it wishes cannot reduce to its own naïve enigma. Yet the poet
feels the very life of the tree, while the thinker would endow it with his
own thought. 'Today my spirit has become a tree, yesterday I felt it to
be a spring,' cries the poet. 'Tomorrow, shall I rise in the smoke of an
altar, or shall I soar high above the plains, feeling the power of a vulture
on his slow wings. How can I tell?' One is reminded here of a passage
in Keats's letters, where he expresses the same idea of the poet's metamorphosis, as he lovingly watches a sparrow bathing.

So the poet stops and gathers the instant, singing the praise of the
tree that arouses his tenderness, in a passage almost as lyrical as that in
which Valéry had so finely sung of his 'Palme':

> Admire comme elle vibre,
> Et comme une lente fibre
> Qui divise le moment,
> Départage sans mystère
> L'attirance de la terre
> Et le poids du firmament! [1]

So Tityrus feels *his* tree to be one with himself as it murmurs through
multitudinous leaves what the dreamer murmurs to the powers of
dream. And the poet responds with his own confidences and even
prayers, so that the tree becomes for him a sort of temple to whose
sublime simplicity he dedicates all his sorrows and joys.

Ironically, Lucretius admires the shepherd's eloquence, and Tityrus
replies in a passage which almost falls into alexandrines:

> Oui, je sais ce que vaut ce que m'enseigne l'arbre,
> Il me dit ce qu'il veut que je veuille sentir.

> Yes, I know the riches of what the tree teaches
> It tells me what it thinks that I should wish to feel.

[1] Paul Valéry, *Charmes*, in *Poésies* (Paris: Gallimard, 1933), 198.

The poet uses nature to embellish his songs: 'Au Hêtre solennel, tu prends de quoi chanter,' insists Lucretius, who then expounds what the thinker finds in the tree—a sort of Hydra whose multiple and voracious roots blindly thrust their way through the earth in the search for water to nourish the force of its outstretched limbs; strong enough to withstand tempest, implacable as time and slowly certain of its progress.

Here Tityrus interrupts, to compare his friend's idea of the tree to love; and after a short discussion on the various aspects of the happy state of loving, he breaks into irresistible song, modestly described as the first state of a future poem, intimately associating the beech tree with love, and ending thus:

> Mais cependant qu'au soleil du bonheur
> Dans l'or du jour s'épanouit ta joie,
> Ta même soif, qui gagne en profondeur,
> Puise dans l'ombre, à la source des pleurs . . .

Like the tree, love yearns towards the sky, and also descends into the obscure substance of being, from which comes our formless sentiment that we have not always been and will cease to be; and that this is indeed the source of tears; the ineffable. Tears are the expression of our incapacity to explain, that is to say, to rid ourselves through speech of the oppression of what we are. . . .[1] There being no thought that, when pursued as near as possible to the soul, does not lead us to those silent boundaries where only pity and tenderness subsist, and the sort of bitterness inspired by that mixture of the eternal, the fortuitous and the ephemeral which is our lot.

It is on this theme that the shepherd-poet meditates during the summer nights, when he watches over his sleeping flock, while

> a whole herd of stars, harried here and there on the horizon by the silent lightning or crossed by the unexpected flight of meteors, seem to browse on time, and as a flock crops its way step by step, they crop the future without respite.

The wide simplicity of this impressive figure moves us by its intuitive poetry and proves that those eyes, which appeared to be always contemplating some inner abstraction, could also notice and delight in the characteristic movements of sheep as well as stars.

---

[1] Cf. passage on tears in *La Jeune Parque*, which helps to elucidate this idea.

At this nocturnal hour the tree seems to be deep in thought. It is a being of shadow. Now the birds are asleep it is the only living thing. It trembles inwardly. One would say that it spoke to itself. It is haunted by fear, as we are at night when quite alone with ourselves, and at the mercy of our own truth.

We have only ourselves to fear in our capacity for suffering,[1] muses the philosopher Lucretius. Gods and destinies have no power over us except through the treason of our own sensibility. Yet they impose shamefully on inferior minds; their power is not all an act of wisdom; but divinity finds in our feeble bodies, for supreme argument, the torture of the wise.[2]

Like man the tree must die. However, it is not on death that the thoughtful Lucretius wishes to ponder but on the idea that everything born of man's spiritual life is part of nature; and the meditating tree in its symmetrical growth becomes a model for mens' thought. Here Valéry touches on a theory of the different interior movements of the poet's mind, and, through consideration of cause and effect, arrives at the point where the mind regards itself as one with the nature that animates all things.

Nor is the poet distinct from his work: his poetry forms his whole being and substance, as he in turn creates his poem. So Lucretius would emulate the unity of all things by not separating matter from spirit, or the poet from his poem. In human substance there is to be found at no great depth, the same power which produces in the same way all life: all that is born in the spirit is nature itself. In all creation there exists a secret link, a similitude which may engender hate as well as love. This constitutes one of those reclassifications, in which Valéry restated for himself the unity of all spirit with life, as opposed to the arbitrary idea of a soul and a separate physical nature.

It is therefore not *what* happens which is essential, but the *happening* itself. So the poet intimately associates himself with the world of plants, and with universal life in a cosmic conception of all being, and all possible selves. The real, always infinitely richer than the true, includes, on every subject and in every matter, the great quantity of myths, tales and childish beliefs that the mind of man inevitably produces. Once men have found the truth they should return armed with it to measure all things. Truth can be known only through the use of many

---

[1] Cf. Paul Valéry, *L'Ange* (Paris: Gallimard, 1946).
[2] Cf. two different conclusions on this theme in Shakespeare's *King Lear*: 'The Gods are just . . .' and 'They kill us for their sport. . . .'

artifices; yet nothing is more natural. With this thought we have returned to Valéry's aphorism: in the beginning was the myth.[1]

This leads Tityrus to consider the myth of the tree of everlasting life and the tree of knowledge, and he tells the story of the infinite tree. Before the birth of animals or man, the plant represented the sovereign and unique form of life, and having a kind of thought and the wish to develop, grew from grass into a great tree whose branches covered all Asia. Thus it became the Tree God.[2]

Wholly in sympathy with this legend, Lucretius declares man to be nothing else than a thinking plant, living the same enterprise of growth and conquest as the tree that strives to change everything into itself. If anyone meditates, he argues, it is certainly the plant, for to meditate is to advance further in symmetry; and the blind tree with its spreading limbs grows around itself according to the laws of symmetry. Thus it represents to our spiritual sight, not at all a simple object of humble and passing life, but a strange desire for universal growth. So a plant is a song whose rhythm unfolds a sure form, and discloses in space a mystery of time.

Thus the tree, following the form of its structure and the laws of its nature, is the model of living thought, and of that sequence in thought which Valéry had so finely developed. It is the perfect symbol, and a clear revelation of his ordered meditation. 'Yes,' concludes Lucretius, 'I am elated with meditation, and I feel all the words vibrating in my soul.'

Curiously enough, in this contemplation on the thinking tree, we seem irresistibly drawn into the sympathetic radius of the great English lyrical poets to find a parallel conception and that intimate awareness, which in Shelley's phrase creates 'a being within our being' in a universe of spiritual significance. The *Dialogues* are to be counted among Valéry's masterpieces. They reveal the poetic originality of his thought, showing us aspects of the universal Self fundamental to all great poetry.

[1] Paul Valéry, 'Au sujet d'*Eureka*,' *Variété*, I, 136: 'Au commencement était la Fable, elle y sera toujours.'

[2] Cf. James Fraser, on tree worship in *The Golden Bough* (London: Macmillan, 1922), 109.

VII

The Last Phase

1. 'MON FAUST'

J'ai de mon rêve épars connu la nudité.

(MALLARMÉ)

'ON A CERTAIN DAY in 1940, I was surprised to find myself speaking with two voices and I let myself go and wrote what came.' Thus Valéry introduces his readers to the sketches, the unfinished 'Lust' and the fragments of 'le Solitaire,' which were published together as *Mon Faust: Ébauches*, posthumously in 1946 (N.R.F.)

These two works are incomplete only in so far as their dramatic form is concerned. They are in fact dialogues rather than dramas, and like Valéry's other dialogues they are really intimate conversations between different phases of the poet's mind, or in Valérian phraseology, of different 'selves.' Together they form a whole, a sort of introspection of the mind's progression to the final intellectual and abstract Self, pushed beyond human limits, in whose ultimate drama no dream is allowed to intrude:

> J'en sais trop pour aimer, j'en sais trop pour haïr,
> Et je suis excédé d'être une créature.[1]

If we compare Goethe's idea of duality, as shown in his Faust, with Valéry's conception that each man has the capacity of developing a series of selves within his own consciousness, we find, in the mind of

[1] Valéry, *Mon Faust: Ébauches* (Paris: Gallimard, 1946). Quotations are from *Mon Faust* unless otherwise stated.

the former, a sort of natural disorder which is quite in keeping with the romantic age to which Goethe belongs. Thus his Faust declares: 'Unfortunately two souls live in me; and one incessantly tends to separate himself from the other. The one, lively and passionate, is attached to this world, and clings to it with all the organs of the body; the other shakes off the night that surrounds him and opens for himself a path to the Heavenly Abode.'

The genius of Goethe, noted Edmund Jaloux, was a chaotic mixture of divergent instincts, multiform temptations, contradictory aspirations.[1] On the contrary, throughout Valéry's *Faust*, a disciplined inner life, the life of the imagination, is shown to be of greater significance than the life which is governed by the flux and reflux of material circumstances, for it depends as much as possible on its own acts, and may finally triumph over material considerations because the purified Self—which may replace the more primitive 'Soul'—dares to give up everything, including its individuality, to attain a reality which is absolutely incommunicable. When it reaches the end to which all life comes, if it goes nowhere else, it at least enters into its own negation, which follows a universal law, and thus its exit from life is spiritual rather than material. This is the ultimate conception of 'Le Solitaire.'

Valéry takes from Goethe the traditional figures of Faust and Mephistopheles and the disciple. He places them in his own world together with the characters of his own invention: Lust (Joy) la Demoiselle de Cristal, the servant, the demons and le Solitaire. Both Faust and his sinister accomplice are for Valéry types of universal mind, and therefore lend themselves to be used in a new interpretation to express certain extremes of the human and the inhuman.

The difference between the intellectual outlook of Goethe and Valéry was finely stressed by the latter in his 'Discours en l'honneur de Goethe' (1932).[2] Both followed quite different methods to arrive at the heart of their special problems. Goethe was a Romantic in the widest sense of that wide term: he refused nothing that added to the fullness of life, nor was he baffled by contradictions and opposites, which he delighted to bring together. His passionate lyrical power alternated in his mind with the calm patience of a botanist. Yet he was entirely unanalytical. Thus the spiritual alchemy of his *Faust*, Part II, is strangely

---

[1] Edmond Jaloux, *Vie de Goethe*, quoted by Mme. Edmée de la Rochefoucauld, *Pluralité de l'être* (Paris: Gallimard, 1957), 78 note.

[2] Paul Valéry, 'Discours en l'honneur de Goethe,' *Variété*, IV, (Paris: Gallimard, 1938).

exterior. 'He was,' said Valéry, 'a mystic entirely devoted to the contemplation of exteriority for whom the aspect of things was a tremendous inspiration and reality.'

Every artist has to create his own formulae and choose his own sphere of action. Such a choice is a fundamental necessity, and Goethe like Valéry founded his work on his own conception of art. Goethe's poetry is the expression of an exuberant and sensual reaction to life and a passionate interest in the passion of love. He deals with the aspect of things and searches actively for beauty. He had the power of creating through lyrical and exalted language his own spiritual world; his ideas of the dignity of man and his conception of that spiritual life which is found throughout nature reflect the most profound aspects of the thought of his time.

Valéry's approach to his art is infinitely more subtle; poetry is for him an imaginative construction based on thought. He had compelled his consciousness to observe its own intellectual acts, passing from phase to phase until by a series of transformations analogous to mathematical operations, he had surmounted and eliminated, or absorbed, everything so as to reach the lucid impersonality of pure intelligence. We may symbolise this intelligence in saying that it has been raised to the power of light: penetrating all things without partaking of them, and without changing itself. And this light radiates through all Valéry's experience and art from a mind to which only the transparence of abstraction is acceptable. Thus *his* Faust considers that the substance of his tenderness, which is an abstraction of love, is like a great light.

Yet in spite of this contrast between Goethe's objective preoccupation with what is presented to his consciousness and Valéry's subjective analytical pursuit of consciousness in its purest forms, both poets meet in the traditional characteristic of Faust's intense curiosity and desire for knowledge; and each uses this symbolic figure in his own way. Valéry's nineteenth-century positivism is in sharp contrast to Goethe's eighteenth-century romanticism. Thus the same ideas may occur to both poets under different aspects. In Goethe's *Faust*, Part II, for example, Mephistopheles concludes:

> The past, stupid word! . . . That which is past and the pure void are they not the same? What is this eternal creation worth to us if all that was created is swallowed up in the void. . . . I would much prefer simply the eternal nothingness of the abyss.

When putting this idea in the mouth of Mephistopheles, Goethe considered it nihilist and destructive in relation to the idea of immortality on which his *Faust*, Part II, turns. Yet it is precisely to this arid conclusion that modern thought tends when pushed too far in one direction; for all human knowledge then appears as a relative movement within movement, an eye which perceives light where otherwise blind forces reign. The final action of Valéry's *Faust* leads to this conclusion.

In letting himself go 'to write what comes,' Valéry makes a statement of extreme clarity on that mature knowledge which he had always looked for through mastery of his thought, so as to discover the furthest possibilities of the intellectual and sensitive spirit of man. 'Que peut un homme?' This recurring question so long and carefully studied, had been answered through his art. The power of Self-knowledge had been developed to its highest degree, to be expressed through transcendental poetry. 'I am what I am,' cries Faust. 'It needed so much hope and so much despair, so many triumphs and disasters to reach this point. . . . I am at the summit of my art, at the classical period of the art of living.' It is Valéry who speaks here, knowing that he has reached this harmony of which he has 'instantaneously seen the root, the formula and the significance.'

'A long and difficult game,' says Faust dictating to La Demoiselle de Cristal, 'a game played against the infinity of thought . . . with the gracious aid of chance,' a triumph of mind. At this point Faust discovers a truth which perhaps Monsieur Teste would not have admitted, that 'to separate thought, even the most abstract, from life is a falsification.' And more, Faust has discovered the need of tenderness and affection, which redeem laughter from the 'convulsion grossière' of Mephistopheles.

The two episodes 'Lust, La Demoiselle de Cristal' and 'Le Solitaire ou les Malédictions d'univers' relate different experiences, the first concrete, the second abstract. In the first scene of 'Lust' Faust appears as a man of letters dictating his memoirs. Typically Valérian, the conversation contains many aphorisms, in the course of a sophisticated flirtation. Mephistopheles is announced in the second scene, and it is at once evident that the rôles have changed. Now Faust takes the upper hand, suggesting that the Tempter has lost credit, has in fact become quite old-fashioned, especially in his belief that there is nothing in the world but good and evil, which shows him to be incapable of clear thought.

And Faust adds severely that there is no question here of a revival of the 'banale affaire Marguerite.'

Nevertheless, Mephistopheles has other temptations to offer, which arise from Faust's desire to write a book—The Book, which would be 'the loving body of him who speaks, the waking thought that all of a sudden is astonished to have been able for a time to unite itself with some object, although such unity was precisely its essence and its rôle.' This great work on which Faust meditates should finally detach its author from himself, so that he may free himself from 'everything which resembles something': an echo of that Self which finally refuses to be anything whatsoever. There is a delicate irony in this paradoxical situation of which Valéry makes full use.

Men have changed, Faust explains; after fearing the abyss they have realised that they may learn only from experiment, and this experience has taught them that the old beliefs and fables are virtually dead. Even the fate of Evil is questioned, and the Soul is in danger of extinction, its value greatly diminished, the individual being threatened with annihilation, 'drowned in numbers.' This mass of human material sees very little difference between vice and virtue. Death itself has become one of the statistical properties of this fearful living matter, and has lost its classic dignity and significance. The immortality of the Soul necessarily 'follows the same fate as death which defined it and gave it an infinite price.'

In all this Mephistopheles has quite lost cast; even 'up there'—*là-haut*—in heaven, his efficacity is questioned, for the whole system of which he was one of the essential pieces is now only ruin and desolation. Abashed by all the ironic mockery of this clear thinking, the horrified Devil retires before Faust's arguments, to try his strength against Lust.

In the conversation between Faust and Mephistopheles, Valéry continues to show us his views on the problem of human development, not only since the romanticism of Goethe but indeed from the age of the earlier beliefs which the Faust legend has incorporated since the formation of the tradition which dates from about 1540. Marlowe's post-Renaissance tragedy, with the great poetry of its first and last scenes, dealing as it does with the final phases of the individual—

> O soul, be changed into little water-drops
> And fall into the ocean, ne'er be found!—

seems, through the lurid light of its own age, and its sensitiveness to mental suffering, to approach nearer to Valéry's conception than to

Goethe's scheme of poetic idealism and final vision of 'a paradise on earth,' for 'free people in a land of liberty.' Valéry returns to the problem of the individual, which is also a universal problem, and admits of no vast and wordy scheme as in the German-pastor aspect which sometimes Goethe conveys.

In the second act, Faust, conversing with the Disciple, insists on the vanity of all human endeavour. He argues that genius is merely a constant habit of thought, that all works are unsatisfactory to their author for one or other reason, and that glory signifies little since it is the product of beings who live only for a day. Man is a sort of ephemera, and the light of his presence never shines twice. For himself, Faust admits that he has made 'the veritable tour of the veritable world beyond his own time and space.' 'I live, I see, I know,' he says, 'if it is to live, to see and to know, to live again and to recognise or know again.' Alas, no idea, however striking, appears to him as a new idea, but as something that he has thought many times before.

This is not at all what the enthusiastic Disciple had expected. He had hoped for some profound advice from the Master. But Faust insists that nothing good can come from the experience of others: 'have not all politicians read history; yet one would say that they had done so only to learn the art of reconstructing catastrophies!' Pressed for some word of wisdom, Faust makes the Disciple a present of four words: 'Prenez garde à l'amour.'

In a short scene by himself the young man expresses his disgust with the naturalness of the supernatural. He had hoped for something more spectacular. Then Mephistopheles, whom he takes for the Master's secretary, treats him more seriously, consenting to explain the significance of Faust's words, while Lust (Scene 4) laments that after all the Soul is an empty word, and goes to look for Faust.

In the fifth scene of Act II, the theme of the universality of the Self is developed. The opening lines show that there is to be no romantic development but an intellectual reverie. 'J'arrive, Mademoiselle,' says Faust, offering Lust a rose. 'Mais prenez vite de quoi écrire . . . les idées viennent en foule.' However, the beauty of the garden and the evening light make him feel that he only wishes to exist in the present moment. 'Me voici le présent même. Ma personne épouse exactement ma présence,' and he feels in perfect relationship with whatever happens. 'Faust,' he muses, speaking to himself, 'is knowledge—*Connaissance pleine et pure.*' In an ardent soliloquy, he comments on the state of living in which everything is contained in the same instant and all things have equal importance: 'C'est un état suprême, où tout se résume en vivre.' To live! 'I live, I breathe, I am, is not that extraordinary,' he cries. Everything around him, the garden, the warm earth, demand that he should simply be content to breathe, and to see what is already there—no matter what it is.

This implies a sort of 'self-time', when time and the self seem to form a single entity, a pure and universal Self which dares to be undivided and one with the universe. This consciousness of self-time may be compared to space-time. In this significant scene, consciousness is more fully developed than was possible in Goethe's romanticism.

Wakened from his reverie by Lust touching his arm, the sense of touch brings Faust back to the material world; and Mephistopheles, having taken the form of the traditional serpent—here a green grass-snake of the Midi—laughs when Lust picks a ripe peach, which she bites, and asks Faust to share.

This scene ends the second act of 'Lust'; and the general conclusion is that of Valéry's poems: 'il faut tenter de vivre.' To live, and to know how to live, is the greatest possible *chef d'œuvre*. Here Valéry transposes his idea that to know how to create a work of art is of greater importance than the work itself.

Throughout the drama, we are shown three different aspects of love: Mephistopheles' Rabelaisian conception of it as a gross convulsion (a description also applied to laughter) is opposed to Faust's mysterious tenderness whose substance 'is like a great light,' a tenderness which springs from an admirable intelligence 'of which it is the perfume,' while for the Disciple love exalts his being to the power of a song.

The first scene in Act III recounts the temptations offered to the Disciple by Mephisto and his Demons. More Goethean than the other scenes, it is in fact rather dull. In the second scene the Disciple falls in love with Lust, whose entry marks the third scene. She pities the sleeping youth who looks so young and helpless. To Mephistopheles, Lust remains a mystery; and her attitude towards Faust is well described when she replies to the question whether she loves him or not, 'How do I know. His absence is presence, and his presence appears to me as something impossible, almost no longer him, since to see him is no longer to think of him. It is as if I were less with him.'

At this point the entry of the serving-man gives comic relief. In the following scene the Disciple and Mephistopheles discuss the difficulties of modern developments in which there are neither souls nor devils, and the youth regrets the past. He would like to be capable of knowing, doing and wishing, and in a long conversation they seem to be reconstructing the ancient *Faust* drama—while perfectly aware that they are doing so. Finally, the Disciple finds himself thoroughly disabused and alone. When in the last scene Lust enters with her lamp, she appears to the young man to be the one real person in the place. Faust has disappointed him, and made him feel himself to be nothing, and 'the other' has belittled all his reasons for wanting to live. It is not surprising that he feels that Lust alone can dispel his humiliation. But Lust inhabits a world of her own, and gently abandons him to his fate.

The fourth act is replaced by 'Le Solitaire.' In this Second Fragment we follow Faust—or the Self—to the arid heights, beyond the flowering slopes of imagination, to contemplate a different aspect of things, where Le Solitaire inhabits a bare peak on the naked edge of thought where life can scarcely endure. Here Faust arrives accompanied by Mephistopheles whom he has encouraged to make this painful ascension, but who refuses to stay there as he does not like heights. But Valéry's Faust, unlike Pascal, unlike Nietzsche, looks into the void with interest—or indifference. From this barren height, where there is only stone, snow, a little air, the Self and the stars, short of which life stops, he reflects on the chaos, below and above the thin strip of life between the enormous nothingness of the All.

The strangest thing about this life which swarms and burrows on the thin crust of the earth, and 'which sometimes thinks,' is 'that the effort of its thought is all directed and applied to mask or to deny the most evident condition of its existence'; and Faust asks whether life can only exist in the ignorance of what life is.

Perhaps like the unicellular specimen under the microscope, life itself cannot escape from the drop of water which contains it. Like Virginia Woolf's moth on the window we cannot get out: and in fact most of us do not even wish to do so. Men do not like to face what is unpalatable. They accept their presence in the world. Their lives are instinctive.

Different philosophers and poets have given different answers to the questions which a fully developed consciousness puts to itself. Aristotle has said that the end of human activity is right action; and Goethe declared that the secret of life is living and that this has always been known. Neither of these conclusions are very different from each other, or from Valéry's central theme of Self-realisation, though in its

239

intellectual developments Valéry's inner life is something other than Goethe's grosser egoism.

The conclusion that everything ends in annihilation is so unpleasantly evident, that if we do not hide our heads in the mist of some mystical belief, all we can do is accept it with courage, lucidity and grace, and like 'the Spartans on the sea-wet rock'[1]—sit down and comb our hair. Such acceptance gives a special intensity to the artist's creative joy—his desire to re-incarnate the beauty that must die, after which

> Men must endure
> Their going hence, even as their coming hither
> Ripeness is all,

and finally, as Valéry's Faust says,

> le langage s'embrouille et la philosophie prend la parole. . . .

Following those undeniably barren conclusions, Faust desperately looks for a further significance; for something beyond what he already knows. In this essential solitude dwells Le Solitaire the most extreme personification of the completely abstract Self—starting from a series of abstractions constructed from the elements of thought and incarnating an Absolute of Sensibility. 'I am at the highest point of my art,' Faust had said, and beyond this there remained the rarification of all being: Le Solitaire. 'He is much worse than the Devil,' says Faust, 'for he denies everything either spiritual or material.' All human activities are questioned; thought and even intelligence, the pretended marvels of science, language—all are damned by this strange phantom of Teste, who has passed beyond the limits of human destiny in a desperate effort to enlarge the bounds of experience, and the means of greater knowledge.

This figure of solitary obsession is not to be lightly dismissed. He symbolises Valéry's effort to surpass the conditions of man's fragmentary perceptions. The Self has now attained an Absolute: everything is purified to the state of light in which all grosser material elements appear as flaws and in which individuality and being have no place:

> . . . l'univers n'est qu'un défaut
> Dans la pureté du Non-être![2]

[1] A. E. Housman, *Last Poems* (London: Grant Richards, 1922), 51.
[2] Paul Valéry, 'Le Serpent,' *Charmes*, in *Poésies* (Paris: Gallimard, 1933), 165.

To Le Solitaire words can communicate but little: nothing pure, nothing substantial, precious or real is transmitted by them. Reality is in fact incommunicable. Even the order of the heavens is a convention of what men desire it should be:

> Le firmament chante ce que l'on veut
> A l'un parle de Dieu
> A l'autre oppose un froid silence . . .

In this purity of non-being, this conceptual Calm beyond all sensual knowledge, man creates his own miracle. But with such miracles Le Solitaire will have nothing to do.

'A Species beyond insanity,' comments Faust, while the *alter ego* looks for something at the level of abstractions but abstracted from nothing but its abstract Self: a world of ultimate, instantaneous and untenable non-becoming evoked in the sheer nudity of his song:

> A moi Splendeurs du pur, à moi, peuple superbe,
> Puissances de l'instant, Sainte diversité!
> Venez! Hautes Vertus, sourires sans visages;
> Sonnez, Voix sans parole et Parole sans voix,
> Riez, Rires du rien, ce rire est le total du compte,
> Riez, la nuit n'est rien, le jour n'est rien,
> > Mais VOUS!
> Troupe sans nombre et non pas innombrable,
> Vol d'une jouissance et voluptés sans chair,
> Forces sans formes, puissances sans prodiges,
> Exterminez mystère, énigmes et miracles,
> Vous qui m'avez guéri du nombre des soleils,
> Des stupeurs devant l'ombre et devant les abeilles,
> De l'éblouissement du mirage Infini. . . .

So the final abstraction of the Self must pass like a great wind clearing the mind of everything, including the desire to live, since there is no knowledge beyond:

> Oh . . . Passez en moi, Vents superbes!
> Couchez en moi toutes les herbes,
> Rompez les ronces du savoir,
> Foulez les fleurs de ma pensée,
> Broyez les roses de mon cœur,
> Et tout ce qui n'est pas digne de ne pas être!

'I should like to see what becomes of this madman,' cries Faust, and the only answer he receives is to be precipitated into the void.

An immense intellectual curiosity had led Valéry to attempt not only to answer the question have we any ideas beyond our experience, but to pose for himself a new problem: having purified our experience to an absolute abstraction, how far and how truly may we create a new dimension of consciousness?

In the 'Intermède: Les Fées,' which concludes the piece, Faust wakes surrounded by Fairies of Memory expressing different ideals and urging his return to life. But he has gone too far to turn back, 'Ame ivre de néant sur les rives du rien.' If all his search has been fruitless, it has at least taught him the vanity of all desires, and in verses hewn from the absolute of his thought he concludes:

> Je ne hais pas en moi cette immense amertume
> De n'avoir pu trouver le feu qui me consume,
> Et de tous les espoirs je me sens délié . . .
>
> Si grands soient les pouvoirs que l'on m'a découverts,
> Ils ne me rendront pas le goût de l'Univers.
> Le souci ne m'est point de quelque autre aventure,
> Moi qui sus l'ange vaincre et le démon trahir,
> J'en sais trop pour aimer, j'en sais trop pour haïr,
> Et je suis excédé d'être une créature.

Yet if life cannot affirm any certain truth it may at least deny the false:

> Ton premier mot fut NON . . .
> Qui sera le dernier.

This negation of all that is impure has become in the Valérian sense a denial, and also a challenge, in which the pure Self asserts itself in defiance of all limitations, to propose and impose the ideal of an Absolute which dares to sacrifice everything to the light of intellectual consciousness.

Besides the two sketches for 'Mon Faust' which we have been considering, there exist other fragments which were intended for future works. These were written at Cassis where Valéry stayed with friends.[1] Here he liked to write or walk in the *pinède*, one of those characteristic groups of pine trees on the Mediterranean where even the winged shadows seem filled with light from the sea and the sky; such as Dante knew on the Italian coast.

In one of these Faust Fragments Valéry returns to his fable of the

[1] Paul Valéry, 'Mon Faust: Fragments inédits,' *Paul Valéry vivant* (Paris: Cahiers du Sud, 1946), 239. Quoted by permission of M. Jean Ballard.

object picked up on the shore, 'which resembles nothing and serves no purpose,' a symbol of life, which he used in 'Eupalinos.'[1]

But the most remarkable passage is that in which he reveals a new aspect of himself in explaining how much he longs to share his thought with the woman he loves. After so much abstract questioning we are at last given the respite of a human response.

> O Lust, I should have so much liked you to be very close to my work. Work is not the word, it is more the effort to construct oneself. Yes, the idea in the state of being born, and tenderness which is love always in the state of being born. It makes me frantic to think of this alliance of ideas and tenderness, and all the other values instituted by men appear to me only as miserable frauds, since we must always come back from glory and all its riches to the heart and the mind, these two responses to life itself.[2]

Thus love finds its place in the Universal Self, and partakes of that intellectual life which is Valéry's real world. This harmonious communion for which he longs is more than a mutual participation of thought. It is that poetry of existence which communicates all its life and joy.

The whole passage, which is too long to quote, is one of the rare instances in which Valéry speaks directly and not symbolically of love. He shows us the anxious wisdom of his own life, expressing a desire to which there could be no adequate response. Laure or Lust: it matters little who their human prototypes were. What is significant is that through his poetry the poet cries for a vital participation in his thought, which is something different from a simple understanding of what he says; and despairing of ever realising this ideal, he creates from the figures and shadows of figures around him a dream mistress of his own perfection; and dies regretting some or other unfulfilled desire of love.

[1] Cf. Valéry, 'L'Homme et la coquille,' *Variété*, V, (Paris: Gallimard, 1945), 12.
[2] Valéry, 'Mon Faust: Fragments,' *Valéry vivant*, 239. Quoted by permission of M. Jean Ballard.

2. THE WAR

Sub signo doloris

Perhaps only those who were in France during the years 1940–45 can fully understand the horror of that time. Over and above the general misery, one recalls the mental anxiety of all those who were even in the smallest degree artist or poet. It seemed to be the end of everything one had lived for.

Valéry had foreseen and foretold the disaster more clearly than most people. Now all that he stood for was threatened; as he said in a speech on the radio in 1939, the enemies of France were the veritable enemies of thought. To uphold intellectual liberty became more than ever the object of his life. He was in Paris when war was declared, and at the time of the general exodus he took his family to Dinard, where he heard of the armistice. He returned to Rue Villejust in the autumn of 1940.[1]

During all this tragic period he worked continually on his *Faust* which was never finished. Through the winter months when food and fuel were lacking, he continued to cross Paris in the over-crowded Métro to give his lectures at the Collège de France. In spite of the extreme cold he kept his habit of working in the early morning.[2] *Mélange* and *Mauvaises Pensées*, collections of aphorisms from his notes, appeared on 1941, and the first edition of *Mon Faust: Ébauches* was published in the same year. In 1943 *Tel Quel*, II, appeared and in 1944, *Hommage à Voltaire*.

Dismissed from his function as administrator of the Centre Méditerranéen at Nice, he continued to uphold its ideals, answering his own anxiety of doubt as to the use of his intellectual powers with a steadfast conception of the high function of the artist. A characteristic incident is recorded in *Paul Valéry Vivant* (Cahiers du Sud): after one of his lectures Valéry was met on the threshold of the Collège de France by a German officer who demanded, 'What is taught in this college?' Valéry replied, 'This college is a place where speech is free.'

In December 1944 he gave a lecture on Voltaire at the Sorbonne. This was the first time since 1940 that he had spoken in an official cere-

---

[1] A. R.-V. [Agathe Rouart-Valéry], 'Vie de Paul Valéry,' *Paul Valéry vivant* (Paris: Cahiers du Sud, 1946), 11–20.

[2] I am indebted to Mme. Julien-Cain for these details.

mony. His last lecture at the Collège de France was given in March 1945. He was already ill and exhausted by a racking cough.[1] In the last months of his life Valéry completed his prose poem *L'Ange*, and there are many moving passages in the Note-Books of this time referring to his state of mind.

He died on July 20, 1945, in his house in Paris. A national funeral was accorded to this pure poet, as it had been to Victor Hugo. Valéry was buried in the Cimetière marin at Sète, high on the headland beyond the quays, in the lap of blue space, a meeting place of spiritual and temporal silence, folded in the immense light.

3. 'L'ANGE'

J'ai fait ce que j'ai pu . . .

(P. V.)

L'Ange, the angel of intellect, is Valéry's last word, his farewell to life. Written for the most part in 1921–2,[2] it was revised by the poet towards the end of his life and the finished version is dated May 1945. A year later it was published in a limited edition. In this intimate monologue the last poignant question is posed; the ultimate problem is stated in the final drama of the Self.

The essence of all tragedy is that it is the last act in a man's life, from which there is no return. Its grandeur lies in the expression of this fatal moment, when the doomed spirit remains steadfastly true to itself, face to face with the inevitable, when at the last, 'man has only himself to fear in his capacity for suffering.'[3] This is the instant when the mind questions its own spiritual substance. The expression of this absolute is the very embodiment of the classical spirit. As Greek tragedy recounts the states of intellectual suffering common to all humanity, whose reactions, called forth by spiritual conflict, are universally applicable, so too Valéry's theme is the same universal tragedy. In this dramatic monologue a further height in self-expression is attained.

But this work is more than a triumph of expression, it is above all a triumph of the spirit, of that absolute Self, so long sought, that can now

[1] A. R.-V. 'Vie de Paul Valéry,' *Valéry vivant*.
[2] I am indebted to M. J. P. Monod, who showed me a document to this effect.
[3] Quotations from Paul Valéry, *L'Ange* (Paris: Gallimard, 1946).

rise above circumstances to question 'Il y a donc autre chose que la lumière?' light which symbolises intellectual wisdom.

The poem in prose is composed in rhythmic periods or phrases of extreme severity and simplicity; yet like all Valéry's poetic conceptions it has the emotional quality of music, reminding us of the great second movement in Beethoven's Seventh Symphony. Perhaps never before has any poem come closer to the passionate humanity of such music.

L'Ange might also be considered as the final word in the Narcissus sequence, more so than the repetitive melodramas; it is a concentrated effort to state a pure abstraction of a universal experience. 'Une manière d'Ange était assis sur le bord d'une fontaine.' Thus we are shown this celestial Narcissus, 'this sorrow in a human form' who questions the spiritual substance of his pure mind. The Angel, the perfect intelligence, sees the face of man—his own face—a prey to infinite sorrow, and he asks, 'Who is he who loves himself so much that he torments himself?' This typical question had always been one of Valéry's defences against that anguish which he described so bitterly as his real vocation. Now surpassing Monsieur Teste, beyond the poetic Parque, and more human than the negations of Le Solitaire, the Self, fully armed with angelic powers of perception, continues to consider a destiny which is no longer personal but universal, no longer a progress but a final phase.

'This face is certainly my face, these tears my tears,' and yet 'am I not that transparent power of which this face and those tears and their cause and that which would dispel this cause, are only the imperceptible durable seeds?' Thus the Angel questions, but in vain his thoughts

arise and spread in all the completeness of the sphere of thought; in vain similitudes correspond to each other, and contrasts declare themselves and are resolved. . . . The intelligence which consumes without effort all created things without being changed or altered by them, cannot recognise itself in this tear-stained face in those eyes whose light has become full of tenderness through the imminence of tears.

In numerous passages throughout his works Valéry has spoken of tears, but nowhere with more conviction and simplicity.

Thus the pure Self is revealed in whose mind 'all the ideas live at equal distance from each other, and from himself'; and such is the 'perfection of their harmony and promptness of their correspondences' that one might have said that had he vanished, 'the system of their simultaneous necessity, shining like a diadem, would have subsisted by itself in its sublime plenitude.'

The poem ends on the simple sincerity of its final phrase: 'And during an eternity, he continued to know, and not to understand.' This is the poet's last offering to that perfection of spirit and intensely intellectual life achieved after so many transmutations, such complete harmonies, of which his whole being partook, so that he could say 'I have attempted to create poetry from the human being.'

Analysing the scattered differences of things, optimist without hope, idealist with one unlimited ideal, Valéry raised the human mind to the highest possible consciousness and unity; and in doing so re-established poetry in the classical status of a formal art, an art of thought, a spiritual construction. By this means he proposed for humanity a new intellectual and universal Self, of whom the Angel remains the symbol for future generations.

Bibliography

I. WORKS BY PAUL VALÉRY

'A.B.C.,' *Commerce*, V (automne 1925).

Agathe ou la Sainte du sommeil (unfinished poem). Paris: Gallimard, 1956.

'Amateur de poèmes,' *Anthologie des poètes français*, III. Paris, 1904. *Album de vers anciens*. Paris: Monnier, 1920.

Analecta. La Haye: Stols, 1926.

Ange, L'. Paris: Gallimard, 1946.

'Aphorismes,' *Nouvelle Revue Française* (septembre 1930).

'Aphorismes,' *Hommes et Mondes* (octobre 1946).

'Au Concert Lamoureux en 1893,' *Commerce*, XXVI (hiver 1930).

'Au sujet d'Adonis,' *Revue de Paris* (février 1921).

'Au sujet de Berthe Morisot,' *Catalogue de l'Exposition, Musée de l'Orangerie*. 1941.

'Au sujet du Cimetière marin,' *Nouvelle Revue Française* (avril, 1933).

'Au sujet d'*Eureka*,' Preface to *Eureka*, by Edgar Allan Poe. Paris: Helleu et Sergent, 1921.

'Au sujet de Nerval,' *Textes et prétextes*. Paris, 1944.

'Autour de Corot,' *Vingt Estampes de Corot*. Paris: Editions des Bibliothèques de France, 1932.

Autres rhumbs. Paris: Editions de France, 1927.

'Avant-propos,' *Connaissance de la déesse*, by Lucien Fabre. Paris: Société Littéraire de France, 1920.

'Bilan de l'intelligence,' *Conferencia* (1 novembre, 1935).

Bucoliques de Virgile: Traduction en vers. Paris: Scripta et Picta, 1944.

Cahiers, 23 vols. Facsimile. Paris: Centre nationale de la Recherche scientifique, 1956–60.

Cahier B 1910. Paris: Gallimard, 1930.

Calepin d'un poète: Essais sur la poétique et le poète. Paris: Gallimard, 1933.

'Cantiques spirituels,' *Revue des deux mondes* (mai 15, 1941).

'Cas Servien, Le.' *Postface* to *Orient* by Pius Servien. Paris: Gallimard, 1942.

Choses tues. Paris: Gallimard, 1932.

'Commentaires de Charmes.' Preface to *Charmes: Poèmes de Paul Valéry* commentés par Alain. Paris: Gallimard, 1929.

Commerce. Cahiers trimestriels publiés par les soins de Paul Valéry, Léon-Paul Fargue, Valery Larbaud et Dunoyer de Segonzac. Paris: Société générale d'imprimerie, 1924.

Conférences. Paris: Gallimard, 1939.

'Conquête méthodique, Une,' *New Review*, XCII (Jan. 1897) (under title 'The German Conquest').

Correspondance André Gide—Paul Valéry, 1890-1942, ed. by Robert Mallet. Paris: Gallimard, 1955.

Correspondance Paul Valéry—Gustave Fourment, 1887-1933, ed. by Octave Nadal. Paris: Gallimard, 1957.

'Coup de dés, Le,' *Les Marges* (février 1920).

'Cours de poétique du Collège de France,' *Annuaire du Collège de France* (1938-1944).

'Cours de poétique: Notes sur dix-huit leçons,' *Yggdrasill Bulletin mensuel de la poésie en France et à l'étranger* (25 décembre 1937-25 février 1939).

'Crise de l'esprit, La,' *New Athenaeum* (April–May 1919).

Degas, Danse, Dessin. Paris: Gallimard, 1938.

De la diction des vers. Paris: Le Livre, 1926.

'Descartes,' *Revue de métaphysique et de morale* (octobre 1937).

'Descartes, Une Vue de.' Preface to *Les Pages immortelles de Descartes.* Paris: Corréa, 1941.

Discours aux chirurgiens. Paris: Gallimard, 1938.

Discours de l'Histoire. Paris: Les Presses modernes, 1932.

'Discours en l'honneur de Goethe,' *Nouvelle Revue Française* (1 juin 1932).

Discours prononcé à la Maison d'Education de la Légion d'Honneur. Melun: Imprimerie administrative, 1933.

Discours prononcé au Deuxième Congrès international d'Esthétique. Paris: Alcan, 1937.

'Discours sur Bergson,' *Revue philosophique* (mars–août 1941).

Divers essais sur Léonard de Vinci. Paris: Le Sagittaire, 1931.

Eupalinos ou l'architecte, L'Ame et la danse, Dialogue de l'arbre. Paris: Gallimard, 1944.

Existence du Symbolisme. Maestricht: Stols, 1939.

'Fontaines de mémoire.' Preface to *Fontaines de mémoire* by Yvonne Weyher. Paris: Le Divan, 1935.

'Fragments des mémoires d'un poème.' *Revue de Paris* (15 décembre 1937).

Fragments sur Mallarmé. Paris: R. Davis, 1924.

'Goethe,' *Conferencia* (1 novembre 1933).

'Histoire d'Amphion,' *Conferencia* (5 août 1932).

Histoires brisées. Paris: Gallimard, 1950.

Hommage à Albert Thibaudet. Paris: Gallimard, 1936.

'Hommage à Marcel Proust,' *Nouvelle Revue Française* (1 janvier 1923).

'Hommage à Voltaire,' *Bulletin officiel de l'education nationale* (1945).

'Homme à la coquille, L',' *Nouvelle Revue Française* (11 février 1937).

Idée Fixe, L'. Paris: Gallimard, 1934.

'Images de la France.' *La France: Architecture et Paysages*. Paris: Librairie des Arts décoratifs, 1927.

'Infini esthétique, L',' *Art et Médecine* (février 1934).

'Inspirations méditerranéennes.' 'Prélude' to *Recherche de Paul Valéry* by Yves Andouard. Albi: Editions du Languedoc, 1945.

Introduction à la méthode de Léonard de Vinci. Paris: Gallimard, 1919.

Introduction à la poétique. Paris: Gallimard, 1938.

'Je disais quelquefois à Stéphane Mallarmé,' *Nouvelle Revue Française* (1 mai 1932).

Jeune Parque, La. Paris: Gallimard, 1917.

'Léonard et les philosophes,' *Commerce*, XVIII (hiver 1928).

'Lettre à Albert Coste,' *Cahiers du Sud* (mai 1932).

'Lettres à Albert Coste,' *Paul Valéry vivant*. Paris: Cahiers du Sud, 1946.

'Lettres à André Fontainas,' *Réponses: Lettres de 1917–1928*. Paris: Le Pigeonnier, 1928.

'Lettre à Albert Thibaudet sur Mallarmé,' *Fontaine*, XLIV, (été 1945).

'Lettre d'un ami,' see *Monsieur Teste*.

'Lettre à Jean de Latour,' in *Examen de Valéry* by Jean de Latour. Paris: Gallimard, 1935.

'Lettre à Jules Valéry,' *Paul Valéry vivant*. Paris: Les Cahiers du Sud, 1946.

'Lettre de Madame Teste,' see *Monsieur Teste*.

Lettres à Pierre Louÿs, see *Quinze lettres à Pierre Louÿs*.

'Lettre-préface au R. P. Rideau,' in *Introduction à la poésie de Paul Valéry* by Émile Rideau. Paris: Desclée de Brouwer, 1944.

Lettres à quelques-uns. Paris: Gallimard, 1952.

'Lettres à Stéphane Mallarmé,' in *Vie de Mallarmé* by Henri Mondor. Paris: Gallimard, 1942. Also in *L'Heureuse Rencontre de Valéry et Mallarmé* by Henri Mondor. Paris–Lausanne: Clairefontaine, 1947.

'Littérature,' *Commerce*, XX (été 1929).

Log-Book, see *Cahiers*.

Mauvaises pensées et autres. Paris: Gallimard, 1942.

Mélange. Paris: Gallimard, 1941.

'Mémoires d'un poème,' *see* 'Fragments des mémoires d'un poème.'

'Méthodes: Education et instruction des troupes,' *Mercure de France*, XXIV (octobre 1897).

'Méthodes: La Sémantique,' *Mercure de France*, XXV (janvier 1898).

'Méthodes: Le Temps,' *Mercure de France*, XXX (mai 1899). (Article on *The Time Machine* by H. G. Wells.)

'Méthodes: "Durtal",' *Mercure de France*, XXV (mars 1898). (Article on *Durtal* by J. K. Huysmans.)

Mon Faust: Ébauches. Paris: Gallimard, 1946.

'Mon Faust: Fragments inédits,' in Jean Ballard, 'Celui que j'ai connu,' *Paul Valéry vivant*. Paris: Cahiers du Sud, 1946.

Monsieur Teste. Paris: Gallimard, 1929. Augmented ed., 1946.

'Moralités,' *Commerce* XXIV (été 1930).

'Note et Digression,' *Introduction à la méthode de Léonard de Vinci*. Paris: Gallimard, 1919.

Œuvres complètes. ('Bibliothèque de la Pléiade.') Paris: Gallimard.
'Oraison funèbre d'une fable.' Preface to *Daphnis et Alcimadure* by Jean de la Fontaine. Paris: Havermans, 1926.
'Passage de Verlaine,' *Le Gaulois*, 27 janvier 1921.
'Pensée et art français,' *Conferencia* (15 décembre 1939).
'Peur des Morts, La.' Preface to *La Peur des Morts* by Sir James Frazer.
Pièces sur l'art. Paris: Gallimard, 1936.
Poésie et pensée abstraite. Zaharoff Lecture, 1939. Oxford: At the Clarendon Press, 1939.
Poésie: Essais sur la poétique et le poète. Paris: Guégan, 1928.
'Poésie de La Fontaine, La,' *Dictionnaire des Lettres Françaises*, 1944.
Poésies. Includes *Album de vers anciens, La Jeune Parque, Charmes*. Paris: Gallimard, 1933. A new edition, 1942, to which is added 'Pièces diverses,' 'Cantate du Narcisse,' 'Amphion,' *Sémiramis*.
'Politique de l'esprit, La,' *Conferencia* (15 février 1933).
Préface to *Carnets de Léonard de Vinci*, tr. by Louise Servicen. Paris: Gallimard, 1942.
Préface to *Lettres persanes* by Montesquieu. Paris: Terquem, 1926.
'Préface pour la deuxième traduction en anglais de *La Soirée avec Monsieur Teste*,' *Commerce*, IV (printemps 1925).
'Prince et la Jeune Parque, Le,' *Les Annales* (avril 1927).
'Propos de Valéry,' see 'Works on Valéry,' below p. 252.
'Propos me concernant,' in A. Berne-Joffroy, 'Valéry Présent,' *Présence de Valéry*. Paris: Plon, 1944.
'Propos sur l'intelligence,' *Revue de France* (15 juin 1925).
Propos sur la poésie. Saint-Félicien-en-Vivarais and Paris: Au Pigeonnier, 1930.
'Propos sur le progrès,' *Lumière et radio* (10 décembre 1929).
Quatre Lettres de Paul Valéry sur Nietzsche. Paris: L'Artisan du Livre, 1927.
'Questions de Poésie,' Préface to *Anthologie des poètes de la N.R.F.* Paris: Gallimard, 1936.
Quinze lettres à Pierre Louÿs, 1916–1917. Paris: Monod, 1926.
'Reflexions sur l'art,' *Bulletin de la Société française de philosophie* (avril–mai 1935).
Regards sur le monde actuel et autres essais. Paris: Gallimard, 1945.
Retour de Hollande, Le. Maestricht: Stols, 1926.
Rhumbs, Notes et autres. Paris: Gallimard, 1933.
Sémiramis, Mélodrame. Paris: Gallimard, 1933.
'Situation de Baudelaire,' *Revue de France* (15 septembre 1924).
Souvenir de J. K. Huysmans. Paris: A la Jeune Parque, 1927.
'Stéphane Mallarmé,' *Conferencia* (15 avril 1933).
'Stendhal.' Préface to Stendhal, *Œuvres complètes*, 4 vols. Paris: Champion, 1927.
'Style,' *Style et art* (février 1945).
Suite. Paris: Gallimard, 1934.
'Sur Bossuet,' *Commerce*, XIII (automne 1927).
'Sur les "Narcisse",' *Paul Valéry vivant*. Paris: Cahiers du Sud, 1946.
'Sur la technique littéraire,' *Dossiers*, I (juillet 1946).
'Svedenborg,' *Nouvelle Revue Française* (1 juin 1936).

Techniques au service de la pensée, Les. Paris: Alcan, 1938.
Tel Quel. 2 vols. Paris: Gallimard, 1941–43.
'Tentation de (saint) Flaubert,' *Figaro*, 22 septembre 1942.
'Triomphe de Manet,' *Les Nouvelles Littéraires*, 11 juin 1932.
'Variations sur une pensée,' *Revue Hebdomadaire*, 14 juillet 1932.
'Variations sur la céramique illustrée,' *Catalogue de l'exposition des céramiques à Sèvres.*
Variété, 5 vols. Paris: Gallimard, 1924, 1929, 1936, 1938, 1945.
Vues. Paris: La Table Ronde, 1948.

II. WORKS ON PAUL VALÉRY, OR RELEVANT TO HIS THOUGHT

Aguettant, Louis. *Les Dialogues de Paul Valéry.* ('Variétés du Pigeonnier.') Paris: Au Pigeonnier, 1926.
Alain. *Charmes de Paul Valéry*, commentés par Alain. Paris: Gallimard, 1929.
——— *Idées.* Paris: Gallimard.
——— *La Jeune Parque de Paul Valéry*, commenté par Alain. Paris: Gallimard, 1936.
———*Propos de Littérature.* Paris: Hartman, 1934.
Alembert, Jean le Rond d'. *Discours préliminaire de l'Encyclopédie.*
Arland, Marcel. *Anthologie de la poésie française.* Paris: Stock, 1926.
Aron, J. K. 'L'Œuvre de Paul Valéry,' *L'Arche* (octobre 1945).
Austin, L. J. 'Mallarmé et le rêve,' *Mercure de France*, LXXIII (1 janvier 1953).
——— 'Paul Valéry compose le Cimetière marin,' *Mercure de France*, MLXXVI–MLXXVII (avril–mai 1953).
Bachelard, Gaston. *Le Nouvel Esprit scientifique.* Paris: Presses universitaires de France, 1947.
Ballard, Jean. 'Celui que j'ai connu,' *Paul Valéry vivant.* Paris: Cahiers du Sud, 1946.
Baudelaire, Charles. *Œuvres complètes.* ('Bibliothèque de la Pléiade.') Paris: Gallimard, 1928.
Béguin, Albert. *L'Ame romantique et le rêve: Essai sur le romantisme allemand et la poésie française.* 2 vols. Paris, Corti: Cahiers du Sud, 1937.
Bémol, Maurice. *Paul Valéry.* Paris: Les Belles Lettres, 1949.
Benda, Julien. *La France byzantine, ou le triomphe de la littérature pure.* Paris: Gallimard, 1945.
——— *La Trahison des clercs.* Paris: Grasset, 1927.
Bendy, Ernest. *Paul Valéry et l'art de la prose.* Goteborg: Gument, 1936.
Bergson, Henri. *Durée et simultanéité: à-propos de la théorie d'Einstein.* Paris: Alcan, 1922.
——— *L'énergie spirituelle.* Paris: Alcan, 1920.
——— *Essai sur les données immédiates de la conscience.* Paris: Alcan, 1889.
——— *Matière et mémoire.* Paris: Alcan, 1897.
Berne-Joffroy, A. *Présence de Valéry.* Paris: Plon, 1944.
Bolle, L. *Paul Valéry, ou conscience et poésie.* Paris, 1944.
Bosanquet, Theodora. *Paul Valéry.* London: Hogarth Press, 1933.

Brémond, Henri. *La Poésie pure*. Paris: Grasset, 1926.

———— *Racine et Valéry*. Paris: Grasset, 1930.

Brillant, Maurice. 'Valéry poète et la danse classique,' *Muse de France* (1931).

Brisson, Adolphe. 'Sur Rachel,' *Le Temps*, 1 décembre 1913.

Broglie, Louis de. *Continu et discontinu en physique moderne*. Paris: Albin Michel, 1941.

Bussy, Dorothy. 'Some Recollections of Paul Valéry,' *Horizon* (May 1946).

Cantor, Georges. *Sur les fondements de la théorie des ensembles transfinis*, tr. by F. Marotte. Paris: Hermann, 1899.

Catalogue de l'exposition Paul Valéry à la Bibliothèque nationale. Paris: Bibliothèque nationale, 1956.

Choux, Jean. *Michel-Ange et Valéry*. Paris: Rasmussen, 1932.

Cohen, Gustave. 'Essai d'explication du Cimetière marin,' *Nouvelle Revue Française* (février 1920).

Cousin, Victor. *Œuvres complètes*. Bruxelles, 1840–1.

Curtius, E. R. 'Valéry poète de la métamorphose,' *Hommage des écrivains étrangers à Paul Valéry*. Bossum: Stools, 1927.

———— *Essais sur la littérature européenne*. Paris: Grasset, 1954.

Delacroix, H. *Les Grandes Formes de la vie mentale*. Paris: Alcan, 1934.

———— *Psychologie de l'art: Essai sur l'activité artistique*. ('Bibliothèque de philosophie contemporaine.') Paris: Alcan, 1927.

Descartes, René. *Discours de la méthode, suivi des méditations métaphysiques*. Paris: Flammarion, n.d.

Du Bos, Charles. *Approximations*. Paris: Plon, 1920.

———— 'Pages de journal,' *Revue de Paris* (octobre 1946).

Dresden, S. 'L'Artiste et l'absolu,' *Paul Valéry et Proust*. Paris, 1941.

Eigeldinger, Marc. *Poésie et tendances*. Paris: Zeluck, 1945.

Einstein, Albert. *La Théorie de la rélativité restreinte et généralisée mise à la portée de tout le monde*, tr. by Mlle Rouvière. Paris: Gauthier-Villars, 1921.

———— *Relativity: The Special and the General Theory*. London: Methuen, 1920.

Eliot, T. S. *From Poe to Valéry*. Washington, 1949.

Fabre, Lucien. *Les Théories d'Einstein*. Paris: Payot, 1921.

Fargue, Léon-Paul. 'Physique de Valéry,' *Portraits de famille*. Paris: J. B. Janin, 1922.

Féline, Pierre. 'Souvenirs de Paul Valéry,' *Mercure de France* (juillet 1954).

Ferran, André. *L'Esthétique de Baudelaire*. Paris: Hachette, 1933.

Ferro, Leo. *Léonard de Vinci, ou l'oeuvre d'art*. Précédé d'une étude de Paul Valéry. Paris: Kra, 1929.

Ferrero, G. *Lois psychologiques du symbolisme*. Paris: Alcan, 1930.

Fontainas, André. *De Mallarmé à Valéry*. Paris: Bernard, 1928.

Ghil, Réné. *Symbolisme et poésie scientifique: Les Dates et les œuvres*. Paris: Messidor, 1923.

Gide, André. *Journal, 1889–1939, 1939–42*. Paris: Gallimard, 1946.

———— 'Paul Valéry,' *L'Arche*, X (octobre 1945).

———— *Poétique*. Frontispiece de Dunoyer de Segonzac. Neuchâtel and Paris: Ides et Calendes, 1948.

Goethe, Wolfgang. *Faust et le Second Faust*, tr. by Gerard de Nerval. Paris: Garnier Frères, 1950.

Gillet, le R. P. *Paul Valéry et la métaphysique*. Paris: A la Tour d'Ivoire, 1927.

Gourmont, Remy de. *Promenades littéraires*. 3 vols. 2ᵐᵉ série. Paris: Mercure de France, 1906.

Grammont, M. *Le Vers français et son harmonie*. Paris: Champion, 1922.

Henriot, Emile. *De Lamartine à Valéry*. Paris, 1946.

Henry, Albert. *Langage et poésie chez Paul Valéry*. Paris: Mercure de France, 1952.

Housman, A. E. *The Name and Nature of Poetry*. Cambridge University Press, 1933.

Hytier, Jean. 'Étude de la Jeune Parque,' *L'Arche*, X (septembre 1945).

———— *La Poétique de Valéry*. Paris: Armand Colin, 1953.

———— *Les Techniques modernes du vers français*. Paris: Presses universitaires de France.

Julien-Cain, Lucienne. 'L'Être vivant selon Valéry,' *La Nef* (mars 1946).

Kahn, Gustave. *Symbolistes et décadents*. Paris: Messein, 1902.

Kant, Immanuel. *Critique of Pure Reason*, tr. by Meiklejohn. London: Bohn, 1860.

Lachelier, Jules. *Psychologie et métaphysique, 1885*. Paris: Presses universitaires de France, 1949.

Lafont, Aimé. *Paul Valéry: L'Homme et l'œuvre*. Marseille: Vigneau, 1943.

Laforgue, Jules. *Poésies*. 2 vols. Paris: Mercure de France, n.d.

Lalo, Charles. *Esthétique*. Paris: Alcan, 1925.

Larbaud, Valery. *Paul Valéry*. Paris: Alcan, 1931.

———— *Paul Valéry et la méditerranée*. Maestricht, Stols and Paris: Claude Aveline, 1926.

La Rochefoucauld, la duchesse E. de. *Images de Paul Valéry*. Paris: Le Roux, 1949.

———— *Pluralité de l' être*. Paris: Gallimard, 1957.

Latour, J. de. *Examen de Valéry*. Paris: Gallimard, 1935.

Lavelle, L. 'L'Intellectualisme de Paul Valéry,' *Le Temps* (février, 1942).

Lefèvre, Frédéric. *Entretiens avec Paul Valéry*. Paris: Flammarion, 1926.

Lot, Fernand. 'Regards sur la prosodie de Paul Valéry,' *Grande Revue* (mars 1930).

Louÿs, Pierre. *Œuvres*. Paris: Mercure de France.

Mackay, A. E. 'The Poetry of Paul Valéry,' *Life and Letters* (Feb. 1935).

Mallarmé, Stéphane. *Œuvres complètes*, ed. by Henri Mondor and G. Jean-Aubry. ('Bibliothèque de la Pléiade.') Paris: Gallimard, 1945.

———— *Propos sur la poésie*, recueillis et annotés par Henri Mondor. Monaco: Editions du Rocher, 1953.

Maritain, Jacques. *Creative Intuition in Art and Poetry*. ('Bollingen Series,' XXXV–XXXVI.) New York: Pantheon Books, 1953.

Mauclair, Camille. *Servitudes et grandeurs littéraires*. Paris, 1922.

Maulnier, Thierry. *Introduction à la poésie française*. Paris: Gallimard, 1939.

———— *Racine*. Paris: Gallimard, 1947.

Maurois, André. 'Conférence sur la méthode de Paul Valéry,' *Les Annales* (décembre 1932).

Mondor, Henri. 'Les Derniers Jours du grand poète,' *Le Littéraire* (juillet 1946).
—— *L'Heureuse Rencontre de Valéry et Mallarmé.* Paris–Lausanne: Clairfontaine, 1947.
—— *Les Premiers Temps d'une amitié: André Gide et Paul Valéry.* Monaco: Editions du Rocher, 1947.
—— *Préciosité de Valéry.* Paris: Gallimard, 1957.
—— *Propos familiers de Paul Valéry.* Paris: Grasset, 1957.
——*Trois Discours pour Paul Valéry.* Paris: Gallimard, 1948.
—— *Vie de Mallarmé.* Paris: Gallimard, 1941.
—— *Mallarmé plus intime.* Paris: Gallimard, 1946.
Monod-Herzen, E. *Principes de morphologie générale.* 2 vols. Paris: Gauthier-Villars, 1927.
Nadal, Octave, ed. *La Jeune Parque: Manuscrit autographe.* Facsimile. Paris: Club du meilleur livre, 1957.
—— 'Valéry et l'événement de 1892,' *Mercure de France* MC (1 avril 1955).
Noulet, E. *Paul Valéry: Études.* Édition définitive. Bruxelles: La Renaissance du livre, 1951.
Paryse, Jean-Henri. *Essai sur l'art et la pensée de Paul Valéry.* Paris, 1946.
Paulhan, Jean. 'Aspects de Paul Valéry,' *Solstice* (été 1946).
Poe, Edgar Allan. *Complete Poetical Works with Three Essays on Poetry.* London: Oxford University Press, 1909.
Poincaré, Henri. *La Science et l'hypothèse.* Paris: Flammarion 1902. Translated into English as *Science and Hypothesis.* London: Walter Scott Publishing Co., 1905.
—— *La Valeur de la science.* Paris: Flammarion, 1906.
—— *Science et méthode.* Paris: Flammarion, 1908.
Porché, François. *Paul Valéry et la poésie pure.* Paris, 1926.
Poulet, Georges. *Études sur le temps humain.* Paris: Plon, 1950.
Raymond, Marcel. *De Baudelaire au surréalisme.* Paris: José Corti, 1940.
—— *Paul Valéry et la tentation de l'esprit.* Paris: Zeluck, 1946.
Rénéville, Roland de. 'Le Faust de Paul Valéry,' *La Nef* (octobre 1946).
Rideau, Émile. *Introduction à la pensée de Paul Valéry.* Paris: Desclée de Brouwer, 1944.
Rivière, Jacques. 'Paul Valéry poète,' *Nouvelle Revue Française* (1 septembre 1922).
Rousseaux, André. *Âmes et visages du XX° siècle.* Paris: Grasset, 1932.
—— 'Paul Valéry et le monde actuel,' *Le Figaro littéraire,* 3 mai 1947.
Scarfe, Francis. *Art of Paul Valéry.* London: Heinemann, 1954.
Sewell, Elizabeth. *Paul Valéry.* Cambridge: Bowes and Bowes, 1952.
Sorensen, Hans. *Étude stylistique sur la Jeune Parque.* Kjøbenhaven, 1944.
Souday, Paul. *Paul Valéry.* (Articles reprinted from *Le Temps.*) Paris: Kra, 1927.
Thibaudet, Albert. *Paul Valéry.* ('Les Cahiers verts,' 25.) Paris: Grasset, 1923.
Turquet-Milnes, G. *Paul Valéry.* London: Cape, 1938.
Vriesland, Victor E. van. 'Le Verbe dans la poésie de Paul Valéry,' *Hommage des écrivains étrangers à P. Valéry.* Bossum: Stools, 1927.
Walzer, Pierre Olivier. *La Poésie de Paul Valéry.* Genève: P. Cailler, 1953.

Index